Malintzin's Choices

DIÁLOGOS

A series of course-adoption books on Latin America

SERIES ADVISORY EDITOR:

Lyman L. Johnson, University of North Carolina at Charlotte

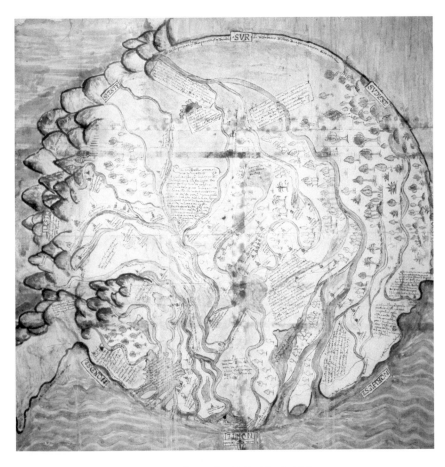

FRONTISPIECE: Map from the *Relación de Tabasco*, 1579.
Although a Spaniard named Melchor de Alfaro Santa Cruz sent
the map to the Crown, its style suggests an indigenous origin.
The original is an impressive fifty-seven by sixty centimeters.
Coatzacoalcos appears on the right. Ministerio de Cultura,
Archivo General de Indias, Mapas y Planos, México 14.

Malintzin's Choices

An Indian Woman in the Conquest of Mexico

Camilla Townsend

University of New Mexico Press

ALBUQUERQUE

LIBRARY OF CONGRESS CATALOGING-IN-PUBLICATION DATA

Townsend, Camilla, 1965–

Malintzin's choices : an Indian woman in the conquest of Mexico /

Camilla Townsend.

p. cm. — (Diálogos Series)

Includes bibliographical references and index.

ISBN-13: 978-0-8263-3405-3 (pbk. : alk. paper)

ISBN-10: 0-8263-3405-9 (pbk. : alk. paper)

1. Marina, ca. 1505–ca. 1530.

2. Mexico—History—Conquest, 1519–1540.

3. Indians of Mexico—First contact with Europeans.

4. Indian women—Mexico—Biography.

I. Title.

II. Series: Diálogos (Albuquerque, N.M.)

F1230.M373T69 2006

972'.02092—dc22

[B]

2006011933

DESIGN AND COMPOSITION: Melissa Tandysh

TO LOREN AND CIAN

Contents

Illustrations

Acknowledgments

I have had this project in mind for many years and have worked on it betwixt and between, accruing many debts along the way. I would like to thank the Colgate University Research Council for funding numerous related research trips as well as two courses in Nahuatl at the Yale Summer Language Institute. Recently, I received grants from the National Endowment for the Humanities and the American Philosophical Society for my research into Nahuatl annals, and as I pursued that project, I gained new insights into this one; the welcome funds indirectly yielded a double harvest. Toward the end, the dean of the faculty of Arts and Sciences at Rutgers, The State University of New Jersey, also helped defray some of the costs of this study.

It is perhaps my language teachers who have been most instrumental in making this work possible. Between them, Jonathan Amith (anthropologist), Michel Launey (linguist), and James Lockhart (historian) taught me what I needed to know to embark on a lifelong study of Nahuatl, passing on their penetrating insights into a fascinating language and putting me eternally in their debt. I have gradually realized that I also owe a great deal to the language teachers of my childhood and adolescence, in that they taught me young to open the linguistic channels of my mind. The most important were probably Jonathan Stapleton, who first inspired me to pursue the Romance languages with all my energy, and Dan Davidson and his staff at Bryn Mawr College, who stretched my abilities in new ways in their efforts to impart Russian to me.

I am profoundly grateful to the patient staffs of archives and libraries in three countries—the Archivo General de Indias (AGI, Spain), the Archivo General de la Nación (Mexico), the American Museum of Natural History (AMNH), Emory University's Special Collections, the Huntington Museum and Library, the Library of Congress Manuscripts Division, the New York Public Library Rare Book Room, Princeton University

Firestone Library, Yale University Library Manuscripts Division, and, finally, Colgate University's Special Collections. At these institutions, staff people who have gone above and beyond include Carl Peterson at Colgate, Barry Landua at the AMNH, and Jesús Camargo, Teresa Jiménez, Estrella Solís, and María del Espíritu Santo Navarro Sánchez at the AGI. In 1998, when I first became fascinated by Malintzin, the staffs of the Museo de la Venta and the Hotel Cencali, both in Villahermosa, bore with me while I used them as a home base in my explorations of Tabasco.

Friends have been of crucial importance in many ways. Karen Sullivan listened to me one summer day a number of years ago. She encouraged me to believe that I could in fact turn myself from an Ecuadorianist into a Mexicanist and that I had the skills to move back in time as well. If a brilliant medievalist believed I could successfully venture into earlier centuries, then, I concluded, I probably could. I hope I have not disappointed her. Certainly, she has been the greatest of help to me, answering my innumerable questions. At Colgate, my colleagues in History and Native American Studies were positively inspiring. Two undergraduate students, Alejandro Delgado and Andrea Suárez-Falken, pushed me in my thinking with their searching questions: I will never forget them. Ray Nardelli in Information Technology kindly digitized the necessary images for me. In the library, Anne Ackerson, Ellie Bolland, Emily Hutton, and Ricki Mueller saved me from myself on more than one occasion. Frederick Luciani and Constance Harsh shared their insights as literary scholars and offered me the warmth of their friendship. At my new home at Rutgers, my delightful colleagues have already begun to share their thoughts with me. I look forward to the years together.

In the wider professional world, other colleagues have been of immense help. I consulted with Piedad Gutiérrez on two documents in 1999 when I was still finding early colonial paleography to be too much for me. David Holtby and Maya Allen-Gallegos of UNM Press were involved and responsive at every step. Lyman Johnson as *Diálogos* editor outdid himself, offering keen insights all along the way. Participants in the "Lost Colonies" conference (March 2004) at the McNeil Center for Early American Studies in Philadelphia and in the Lockmiller Seminar at Emory University in November of 2005 gave me extremely valuable feedback. Others who read parts of the manuscript, answered particular questions, offered me key advice, or challenged my thinking in important ways include Jeremy Baskes, John Kicza, Franklin Knight, Mieko Nishida, Susan Schroeder, Gary Urton, and, most especially, James Lockhart. A number of Lockhart's former students, now well-known scholars in their own right, have welcomed me warmly to the Nahuatl-reading world, among them Sarah Cline, Rebecca Horn, Doris Namala, Caterina Pizzigoni, Matthew Restall, John Sullivan, and Stephanie Wood. History teaches us that it can be quite shocking to find an interloper in one's midst, but they have been the very personification of generosity. I am eternally grateful.

I thank my family with open hands. My parents have learned to accept my chosen work, and even to love me for it. John, the partner of my life, makes me prouder to know him with every year that passes. Our foster daughter, Carmen, long since grown up, has become a woman of remarkable fortitude; she teaches me how to recognize what we cannot change on this earth and to make the best of it. In the last few years, my sons Loren and Cian have demanded my heart and soul, and given theirs in exchange—at least for the time being. Malintzin died when her son and daughter were likewise two and seven. My children, I am grateful for the life and love between us.

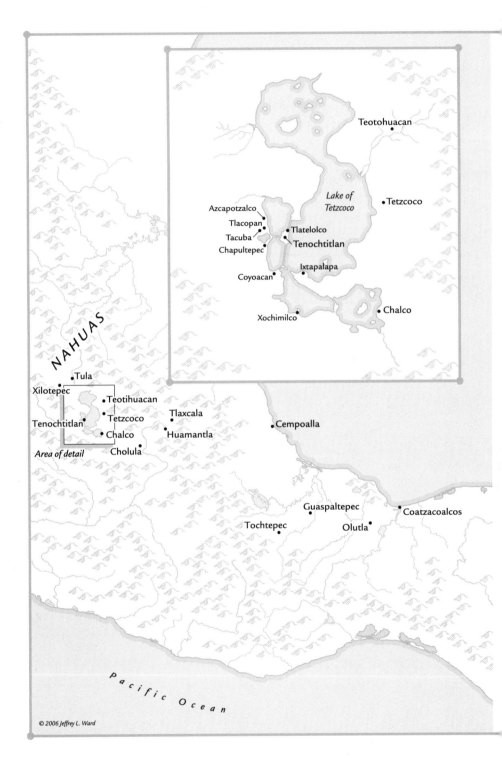

Teotohuacan

Lake of
Tetzcoco

Tetzcoco

Azcapotzalco

Tlacopan

Tacuba

Chapultepec

Tlatelolco

Tenochtitlan

Ixtapalapa

Coyoacan

Xochimilco

Chalco

NAHUAS

Tula

Xilotepec

Teotihuacan

Tenochtitlan

Tetzcoco

Chalco

Tlaxcala

Cempoalla

Huamantla

Area of detail

Cholula

Guaspaltepec

Coatzacoalcos

Tochtepec

Olutla

Pacific Ocean

© 2006 Jeffrey L. Ward

MALINTZIN'S
MEXICO

in the year 1519

Gulf of Mexico

MAYAS

Tulum

Cozumel

Campeche

Champoton

Xicallanco

Chetumal

Cintla
Putunchan

Acalan

Bay of Honduras

Nito

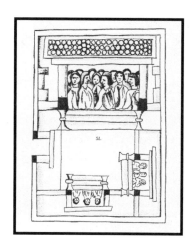

Introduction

IN THE COOL SEASON, WHITE EGRETS GATHER NEAR THE COAST OF THE GULF of Mexico in great raucous flocks, alighting by the hundreds on the trees at dusk, their quivering forms silhouetted against the darkening sky. The twelve-year-old girl who would one day be called Malintzin would have seen them there when she was a slave among the Maya. We cannot know if they were also a lingering childhood memory from the years when she had lived in a fine house in the direction of the setting sun, near Coatzacoalcos, before the men took her away against her will. Perhaps she had lived too far from the water then, or perhaps she was too young when she left to remember clearly. We cannot know much about what she made of the contrast between her past and her present. When she was a child, before she knew what was to be her fate, she had lived among Nahuas, and in that world there was a kind of woman's lament sung in the voice of a captive concubine: "O, mother, I'm dying of sadness here in my life with a man. I can't make the spindle dance. I can't throw my weaver's stick."[1] But though Malintzin in her new life as a slave undoubtedly harbored such feelings as these some of the time, she most likely, in the way of most captives, managed to keep her head bent on her work, tossing her spindle, twisting yarn from raw cotton—until the day her keepers lost their battle with the strangers from the sea and brought her to the newcomers as a peace offering. Nineteen other girls went down to the river with her; none knew what the future held.

The girl who had no choice in the matter but did as she was told would certainly never have guessed that one of her names would soon be inscribed in world history and then endure for over five hundred years, or that she herself would come to signify so many different things to so many different people that the truth about her could no longer be determined. Given the wit and aplomb ascribed to her by those who knew her, it is possible that if she had been told, she would have laughed. For she knew that she was simply surviving—as well as she could—the most ordinary of lives.

By coincidence, she was catapulted to the very center of the drama of two continents colliding: she became translator and mistress to Hernando Cortés during his effort to conquer Mexico, and thus she negotiated with Moctezuma and his successors on behalf of Cortés until—and even after—the Spaniards held the reins of power. The effects of the conquest of the indigenous are still with us today, and so the years in which this woman lived and acted are loaded with multiple meanings that vary widely according to the position of the observer. Europeans and their cultural heirs in the Americas have tended to celebrate the changes that ensued; Native Americans and those who choose to identify with them, on the other hand, have expressed their pain and anger. The feelings of both sides are often passionate, and the young Indian woman is at the eye of the storm. As long ago as 1939, the novelist Haniel Long commented, "She represents more than any one moment of history can hold."[2]

The story of the *image* of Marina, as the Spanish called her, or Malinche, as we call her now, is itself an interesting one, full of sudden plot developments and changes of direction.[3] She was not always the focus of so much attention. In fact, after the people who had actually known Malintzin had all died, almost no one mentioned her for well over two hundred years. In that period, the image of an indigenous helpmeet was altogether too commonplace to merit notice. But in the early nineteenth century, when Mexico broke away from Spain, any friend of the Spaniards came to be seen as a dastardly foe. In the anonymous 1826 novel *Xicoténcatl,* Marina was for the first time suddenly presented as a lustful, conniving traitor. The story had wide appeal in a newly nationalistic setting. A sexy, sneaky

Marina let her people down in story after story for the next two centuries, in Mexico and elsewhere.

In the 1970s, Mexican and Mexican American feminists came to question the paradigm, pointing out that the girl herself had been given into slavery by her own people. Whom was she betraying? What should she have done when she was given into the hands of the armed Spanish men? Would her critics seriously recommend suicide, as an affirmation of herself and her people? Rather than seeing her as a master of Machiavellian politics, said the feminists, we should acknowledge that she was a victim more than once.

In the 1980s and 1990s a number of writers adjusted this notion somewhat, arguing that perhaps she was not *entirely* victimized. After all, she was clearly a resourceful and intelligent young woman, a survivor. She did what she could within her own context to preserve her sense of herself in a complex and shifting terrain, in a world in which it was unclear how to draw lines between groups or what was the best course of action to take. In her time, we must remember, there were as yet no people who saw themselves as "Indians," just varying ethnic groups and some particularly strange new arrivals.

In postmodern North America the new style of thinking has seemed especially apt to some theorists. Malinche can be envisioned as a bridge, a woman who moved successfully between at least three different cultures. Like the Chicano people who are both Mexican and American—and hence, perhaps, neither—she was a hybrid. "She has become the transfigured symbol of fragmented identity and multiculturalism," writes one literary critic.[4]

But in truth, in Mexico, these new versions of Malinche's reality have held little sway. Evolving ethnicities and multicultural identities are clearly more compelling to Mexican Americans (and other North Americans) than to Mexicans. There are exceptions, of course: one Mexican historian asks why, if certain Spanish castaways wanted to stay with the Maya, is it not acceptable for her to have wanted to stay with the Spanish?[5] The majority of the Mexican populace, however, still looks on Malinche with shame and loathing, seeing her not only as representative of conquest by Spain, but of domination by outsiders in general. Many years ago Octavio Paz wrote thoughtfully about the psychological situation in which most Mexicans find themselves in relation to an indigenous ancestor conflated with the *chingada,* the "fucked one," the "duped one":

If the *Chingada* is a representation of the violated Mother, it is appropriate to associate her with the conquest, which was also a violation, not only in the historical sense, but also in the very flesh of Indian women. . . . Doña Marina becomes a figure representing the Indian women who were fascinated, violated or seduced by the Spaniards. And just as a small boy will not forgive his mother if she abandons him to search for his father, the Mexican people have not forgiven La Malinche for her betrayal. She embodies the open, the *chingado*, [in relation] to our closed, stoic, impassive Indians.[6]

"This explains," Paz added, "the success of the contemptuous adjective *malinchista* recently put into circulation [in the 1930s and 1940s] by newspapers to denounce all those who have been corrupted by foreign influences."

The feelings understandably run deep. In 1982 a statue was erected of Malinche, Cortés, and their son, Martín, in Coyoacan, on the outskirts of Mexico City, where the two temporarily took up their abode after the fall of the indigenous capital in 1521. In the midst of the new discussions about Malinche that had emerged in the seventies, the statue was intended to be respectful of her trials and to emphasize the mestizo (or mixed-blood) character of the nation. But the work soon had to be removed due to the strength of feeling evident in student protests that erupted: the young people wanted no monument that presented Malinche in a positive light, for in their minds she was too closely associated with domination by outsiders, and with betrayal.[7]

The impassioned student protestors of 1982 were defending their convictions. As they understood the situation, they were standing up for their nation's sovereignty and speaking up for the downtrodden Indians. But however admirable their feelings and their activism, none of them could have been thinking of the real young girl who walked down a winding path to the river one day in 1519, knowing that she was to be given away to the newcomers as a bedfellow and cook. If the students had been thinking of her, they wouldn't have seen such an obvious enemy, but rather a frightened slave who through a twist of fate found herself in a potentially very bad spot.

There have been many books about the mythical Malinche, but we have long needed a thorough book about the real young woman. We have needed it in order to humanize her and the countless other Indian women like her who were forced to confront the conquest in their own lives. Otherwise they are left to bear the stigma of being considered either provocative or horrifying (or both) and are never seen in all their complexity, as the real people they once were. They survived the most trying of circumstances with as much dignity as they could muster. They deserve better than the stereotypes and accusations that have been flung at them and have too often stuck. And it seems deeply wrong that their cultural heirs should themselves be haunted by crimes that their ancestors—real or symbolic—did not actually commit.

Indeed, there is probably only one compelling reason why a traditional biography of Malinche was not written years ago: that it cannot be done. The evidence simply does not exist to write such a book. The woman left us no diaries or letters, not a single page. We *do,* however, have enough ethnographic evidence about Nahuas and Spaniards for another kind of book, for one that provides full details on every aspect of Malinche's context and places her actions in their proper setting, allowing readers to see what kind of thoughts she might have entertained in such a situation, as well as the extent to which her decisions mattered. Yet such a book is a dangerous one to write: if not executed carefully and with restraint, it could itself become part of the problem, projecting motivations and feelings onto the woman that she in fact never harbored. This is a classic problem in works treating the past of nonliterate or disempowered peoples who did not leave a paper trail for posterity. Operating with hindsight, we may want to explore issues that no literate person at the time ever thought would matter, or that they may even have wanted to hide, and about which we therefore have little or no written evidence. On the other hand, people may have recorded copious details on other subjects. One anthropologist has wryly commented, "While ethnography offers the best data, history offers the best questions, and the two can never be completely brought together."[8] It is a crucial step, then, to disentangle exactly what it is that we are asking and ascertain if there is any meaningful evidence with which to approach that question.

In asking about the woman herself, we are really posing two separate but related categories of questions. First, how did this woman matter in her own time? Did she change the course and nature of the conquest?

Second, what did the turbulent events of her life mean to her? Can we even begin to consider her own interpretations?

Answering the first kind of question, concerning the significance of Malinche's actions, depends upon our knowing exactly what happened, and in this case certainty is elusive. The Spanish chroniclers who mentioned Malinche all wrote with their own agendas, and they were usually distant in time and place when they sat down with their pens in hand. They lied, forgot, and argued with each other. Sometimes writers actually came to believe what they thought would have been fitting to have happened: one chronicler insisted that Malinche actually married Jerónimo de Aguilar, who had been shipwrecked among the Maya and who worked closely with her to form a translation chain between Cortés and Moctezuma; but she married someone entirely different, as everyone else knew.[9] Indigenous men writing historical annals in the second half of the sixteenth century also succumbed to this kind of error, recording what in their innermost hearts they thought should have happened, what made sense to them to have happened. But when all the Spanish chronicles and indigenous annals mentioning Malinche are read together, certain patterns of perception become clear. And when they are read in conjunction with legal documents produced closer to the time by figures who had more concrete and immediate objectives than the characterization of doña Marina, certain facts emerge. When these perceptions and facts are placed in the context of an understanding of Nahua life provided by recent studies of Nahuatl-language sources, a whole picture begins to take shape.

The picture that comes into focus is one in which the young Malinche is indeed of crucial importance in the conquest—but it is also a picture of a world in which there were many potential Malinches. Without her help at certain points, Cortés would almost certainly have died or been forced to turn back. But it seems equally sure that had she not existed, some other Spaniard on some other expedition would have come across another woman much like Malinche, for she was a typical product of the Mesoamerican world as it then was. The many ways in which this is true will become visible throughout the course of this book. Indeed, even without resorting to counterfactuals, we will see that she did not act alone: there were thousands of occasions when indigenous people sided with Spaniards, at least temporarily, for their own excellent reasons.

The second question, touching on Malinche's inner life, is more difficult to approach. Many would argue that out of true respect, we must acknowledge that we can never know her, and let the subject drop. But what does it mean to consign someone to unknowability? In the worst-case scenario, such "blank slates" are vulnerable to the readings and misreadings of whoever chooses to make assumptions about them, however hostile or insulting their preconceptions may be. Such figures are not people but rather symbols and hence can become lightning rods. In the best case, perhaps, they are not reviled but still remain less than fully human in the popular imagination. It is, after all, hard to take seriously characters who never say anything. Our books tend to be full of the profound and witty thoughts of colonizers and others who once held pens in their hands, while slaves, Indians, and other nonliterate figures remain shadowy and relatively uninteresting one-dimensional beings even in the most sympathetic of studies.

It thus becomes important to lay out the full panoply of possibility, to render the context so vibrantly real that the range of Malinche's potential reactions becomes an interesting subject for thought, and her actual decisions and actions resonate more meaningfully. Traditionally, insight into the Aztec world was gained largely through archaeology and texts written by Spaniards. But for many years now, Mexican, North American, and European scholars have also been putting their knowledge of the Nahuatl language to work to aid the cause.[10] The indigenous did not begin to use the Roman alphabet with any frequency until the 1550s, but at that point they began to work actively to create formal texts describing preconquest life as they remembered it, to write down surviving versions of their own historical annals and songs, and to conduct their own mundane affairs in writing—leaving a trail of wills, land transfers, and other documents for posterity to find, many of which unintentionally reveal traditional ways of thinking. All of these sources must be read carefully and without naive acceptance of their assertions, but taken together, they provide a window—albeit a sometimes murky one—into the world in which Malintzin lived and breathed.

In attempting to place the woman's decisions in context, it is of absolute importance not to commit the usual crime of projecting our own concerns onto Malinche but, on the contrary, to remain aware of all the old ideas that have led to motives that miss the complexity of her situation being assigned to her. In the earliest paradigms, for good or ill, whether she is considered to be a heroine or the proverbial "bitch," she is certainly power-ful, manipulating the situation to suit her own ends. In the later construct, she is a victim, raped and abused. In the most recent paradigm of all, she is someone who succeeds in going about her own business following tradi-tional Native American practices, managing to preserve herself intact and even to increase her ability to maneuver for a number of years. The latter is undoubtedly the most realistic portrait, but all three pictures contain kernels of truth. In a life such as hers, there had to have been moments of triumph or glee, moments of agony or self-effacement, and moments of putting one foot in front of the other in a rather prosaic way. We have no right to presume to know exactly when Malintzin had which reaction. On the other hand, we perhaps have a duty to try to understand her life well enough to be able to recognize its rich and painful and complicated possibilities.

What I have tried to write, then, is a book about contexts. In effect, despite the focus on Malintzin, it is more than the story of one woman's life; it is an exploration of indigenous experience in her era. It consists of nine chapters that each treat a different subject even as they proceed chrono-logically through time. In a sense, it offers nine essays, each of which pro-vides an interpretation of a particular aspect of the conquest. The first chapter ("Pelican's Kingdom") attempts to convey the contentiousness of Malintzin's natal world, not only in terms of rivalries between ethnic states, but also in terms of gendered tensions that permeated elite house-holds and left some individuals more vulnerable, and perhaps more alien-ated, than others. The second chapter ("The Men from the Boats") looks at first contact with Europeans from indigenous eyes and quarrels with the traditional notion that the newcomers were envisioned as gods rather than especially well-armed foreigners. I argue that the indigenous had a technological problem, not a spiritual or cultural one, and that they knew it well. Chapter three ("One of Us People Here") explores the compli-cated role that indigenous translators in general and Malintzin in particu-lar played in what was really a process, not a moment, of conquest. In the interactions between natives and newcomers, the newcomers had more power in important regards, but that did not mean that they controlled or even understood what the natives were thinking.

Chapter four ("Tenochtitlan") offers a variety of viewpoints as to what happened in the great Mexica city in the fatal months between November 1519 and July 1520, rejecting the idea that the indigenous were naive in their assessment of the strangers and arguing instead that Malintzin was not the only one to see the technological discrepancy clearly enough and act accordingly. The fifth chapter ("Water-Pouring Song") analyzes both the proximate and ultimate causes of the Spaniards' eventual victory in 1521 and asks the reader to consider its significance from a variety of indigenous perspectives. Chapter six ("Reed Mats") discusses the multiplicity of indigenous experiences in the immediate aftermath of 1521, ranging from cataclysmic loss to triumph over one's enemies to business as usual. Malintzin's own life incorporated all of these. However difficult it was for the Spaniards to understand the complexity of the Indians' reactions, the conquerors certainly did manage to insinuate themselves into the fabric of political authority, which was to have far-reaching implications for all the Native Americans.

In the final chapters, the book shifts gears, moving from an examination of multiple indigenous perspectives back to a focus on Malintzin herself and those dearest to her. Chapter seven ("The Concubine Speaks") argues for the importance of being open to alternative interpretations of actions taken by the indigenous. It is usually assumed that Cortés forced Malintzin to marry an underling when he was done with her, but using the evidence in certain legal cases pursued after Malintzin's death, I argue that if we look at the facts under a different light, then Malintzin, rather than being swept aside, appears to have attempted to exert her will toward the end of her life in the actions she chose to take. In the last chapters ("Doña María" and "Don Martín"), the reader follows the lives of her son and daughter and sees what resulted from the choices Malintzin made. Her children are frequently understood to be emblematic of the experiences of the first generations of mestizos everywhere in Mexico: they are interpreted either as the forgers of a cosmic race, or as *hijos de la chingada*, when in their own eyes they were probably neither the one nor the other. For Malintzin and for her children, the truth was more complicated than many people have wanted to believe; their lives were grounded in harder choices than most of us have recognized.

Tying the chapters with their separate themes together is the story of one woman's life. To my mind, the story is important. It is important for itself, like any tale of old—a good yarn is one of humanity's great accomplishments. The Nahuas, at any rate, certainly thought so. And it is important for another reason. If we are going to have any success in our ongoing efforts to piece together what particular indigenous were probably thinking at any one point, we must know exactly what happened just before the moment under scrutiny, as well as what the Indians were about to do next. The sequence of events can provide crucial evidence.

What I am reaching for is a story told from varying indigenous points of view, with one enslaved woman's perspective located most centrally. I am too far removed in time, place, and culture to be able to convince myself that I have fully attained such a thing. I air possibilities and probabilities, and I am honest when we simply don't know. A parallel book, as it were, runs through the notes, ensuring that my train of thought is as transparent as possible. I entreat readers to look at those notes. After careful consideration, I have decided to protect the story—the narrative—from constant interruptions; it is important that the book be about Malintzin in the last analysis, not about my thinking about Malintzin. An unfortunate result of this, however, is that the detective work and process of drawing conclusions are in some cases consigned to the back pages.

One specific way in which the effort to approach an indigenous perspective affects the narration is that the Spanish play an ever greater role as the indigenous both come to know them better and become more vulnerable to them. The Europeans are gradually transformed from a rather blurry group to a set of specific individuals with defined agendas and known personalities. Readers will thus not find much about, for example, Cortés's early years, but they will gain a stronger sense of his later life. The paramount questions the book seeks to answer are not, after all, about the conquistadors; hence their limited role.

The story is in many ways dramatic—exciting or tragic, or both, depending on your point of view. I hope that readers find it compelling. But we should not deceive ourselves into thinking it is truly surprising. Like most of history, it is just the tale that might be expected, once you have all the preliminary facts. The pragmatic Malintzin, I like to think, would have agreed.

ONE

Pelican's Kingdom

IN FEBRUARY OF THE YEAR 1500, A PRINCE WAS BORN IN GHENT, IN THE Netherlands, whose name would travel round the world before he was twenty. The day he made his appearance, the doctors thanked God, and messengers set off to take the news to his grandparents, Ferdinand of Aragon and Isabella of Castile, for even then it was clear that he was a likely successor to the unified Spanish realm they were in the midst of forging. "Charles," they called him, or "Carlos," in the language of his mother.

His Majesty Prince Charles had not yet graduated from the attire of the nursery to the more manly raiment he would wear from age five onward when another baby was born in what might as well have been the other side of the world, so far was it (as yet) from the politicking of European courts. This one was a girl child, born in a dark room opening onto a brightly lit courtyard in a house near a winding gray river in a place called Coatzacoalcos, near the great sea of the Gulf of Mexico. The midwife offered up a prayer, and it went something like this: "Thou wilt be in the heart of the home, thou wilt go nowhere, thou wilt nowhere become a wanderer, thou becomest the banked fire, the hearthstones." She cut the umbilical cord and tied it off close to the baby's body, paying much greater attention to neatness and cleanliness than had her counterpart in Ghent, though the child was no one important. Most likely, she took the severed cord and buried it efficiently in the hard-packed earthen floor next to the hearth, since the babe was a girl. "Here our lord planteth thee, burieth thee. And thou wilt become fatigued, thou wilt become tired; thou art to provide water, to grind maize, to labor; thou art to sweat by the ashes, by the hearth."[1]

As it turned out, the child would not always stay by the hearth like most girls, but would travel the Mesoamerican world. She would come to know well the name of King Charles I, later called Charles V of the Holy Roman Empire,[2] and for her own reasons would exhort the indigenous to obey him. But none of the soothsayers consulted at her birth would have predicted these things for her, intent as they were on placating the gods and preserving her well-ordered, sunlit world.

Before she was twenty, the girl would be renamed Marina by Spanish newcomers and called Malintzin by other indigenous people. We do not know what name they gave her in the days following her birth. She herself probably would not have insisted on the importance of recording it, had she ever narrated the story of her life. In the indigenous world, people's names changed continuously as their circumstances altered. Someone who loved her may have given her a poetic or a funny name (like "Little Old Woman" or "She's-Not-a-Fish"), but most likely, she was called by one of the names usually given to Nahua girls—Firstborn, Middle Child, Younger, or Youngest—as well as receiving a more formal day sign name. It was most unlucky to be born under the sign Calli (House) or Malinalli (Grass), but these were rather theoretical misfortunes, as almost no one was ever really given an ill-omened name. Instead, a day sign name could be chosen among the more auspicious signs close to the moment of birth—and in a world without clocks, soothsayers advised thinking carefully about announcing whether a birth had occurred before or after the middle of the night. Some historians have loved to surmise that the Spaniards named the girl "Marina" because her name had been the tragic "Malinalli," but this would never have been the case. The name would almost certainly have been avoided by her own people, and even if it hadn't been, the Spanish were not in the habit of interviewing their Indian slaves in order to come up with a European name that seemed particularly fitting. The girl's earliest name is, quite simply, lost to us. In indigenous histories, a king was always referred to by his kingly name from the moment of his birth, though in truth the name was not given to him until later in life. In the same manner, Malintzin must here be Malintzin from the beginning.[3]

As the child learned to smile and laugh, then to sit up and crawl and walk, she found herself in an interconnected world of circles and squares. In the world of the Nahuas—the central Mexicans who spoke the Nahuatl language—people and places were independent entities, like points and lines, but they existed only in relation to each other, like points and lines made into shapes. No one and nothing stood alone. Four walls enfolded the hearth, and four rooms looked in on the courtyard, just as the sky was divided in four directions. Her own family's cornfields lay between other families' cornfields, and all those cornfields blanketed together, with all their many separate names, made up the lands of the kingdom. The lord of the house where she lived was related to the lords of other powerful houses, and the strongest of them all, by mutual consent, was the king. Every year the "great house" (or ward or parish or *calpolli* or *tlaxilacalli*) that she was a part of sent men to fill the labor draft organized by the king's house and paid the requisite taxes; they did so just after another calpolli did and just before yet another, always in the same order, repeated over and over without fail. When war came, they sent their assigned number of men to fight; nearly all their men, whether farmers or craftsmen, were also warriors who were proud to defend the whole.[4]

The king ruled over an *altepetl*—a city-state, or better yet, a small ethnic state—that was composed of these interlocking parts. The one where Malintzin was born lay to the west of the Coatzacoalcos River, which drained into the gulf. "Altepetl" literally means "water-mountain" in the Nahuatl language, as every human settlement needed a water source and a defensible bit of earth to call its own. The region as a whole extended from the small Tuxtla mountain range that looked out over the sea, down through farmlands, and on into the tropical forest and swamplands of the isthmus. Malintzin lived in the middle, in a small state that either paid tribute to or was an organic part of the larger state called Coatzacoalcos, whose king's seat was at the densest settlement in the area, on the very banks of the river. Her children later spoke of Olutla and Tetiquipaque in connection with her birthplace. Again, it is unclear if these were constituent parts of the same altepetl or two distinct altepetls, one subservient to the other. Indeed, the lines between such forms was often rather fuzzy as political arrangements and understandings shifted over time and might even be described somewhat differently by different constituent parts of the realm.[5]

Malintzin had come into a world that existed on the fringes of the political influence exerted by the particular group of Nahuas known today as "Aztecs." Despite the usual epithet, there was no true "empire" in the modern sense, and there was certainly no Pax Romana. There were many kingdoms, some more powerful than others at any one time, ranged in shifting alliances. A world of many kingdoms necessarily yields many wars, and Mesoamerica was no exception. Indeed, decades after the Spanish came, when elderly indigenous were asked about their memories of the conquest, they very often misunderstood the question and launched into a discussion of a particularly disastrous defeat they had once suffered at the hands of some other indigenous group years earlier.[6]

Still, empire or no, the "Aztecs" were the most powerful figures in the political landscape known to the young Malintzin. They never used that word themselves. It was the Tenochca people who had risen to prominence; their ethnic identity was Mexica (me-shee´-ka), and they shared that identity with the people of another neighboring state, the Tlatelolca, who were closely allied to them. The Mexica, then, would have loomed before Malintzin as something of a sinister specter, for in that era they were attempting to bring the lands close to the coast under their control, and Malintzin's family would have felt the pressure. Her later ability to manipulate courtly language—which in Nahuatl has its own grammar—as well as her aplomb in the face of royalty and her clear-sighted understanding of the Mexica political arrangements all indicate that she was raised in a nobleman's household, one that would have been inextricably involved in any political shifts.[7]

The Mexica were relative newcomers to an ancient land whose people had long planted corn, built pyramids, charted stars, and sung poetry. Waves of nomadic barbarians from today's Arizona and New Mexico had come sweeping down into the well-settled and prosperous central valley of Mexico over the course of the preceding centuries; the Mexica were among the most recent of the many Nahuatl-speaking arrivals. They carved out some swampy lands for themselves that no one else had wanted on the fringes of a lake in the very center of the great valley and began to enmesh themselves in local politics, first as mercenaries then as warriors fighting on their own behalf. In about the year 1350, struggles for political dominance in the area became particularly intense, and the altepetl of Azcapotzalco gradually emerged as the strongest power, though with a longstanding rival in the old and beautiful state of Tetzcoco. In the 1420s, however, civil wars between the kings' sons by different women in both Azcapotzalco and Tetzcoco led to a great reshuffling of alliances. The ruling dynasty of the Mexica, who had long paid tribute to Azcapotzalco, united with a dispossessed heir of Tetzcoco and were able to bring down the once dominant city and emerge as a power themselves. Tetzcoco and the Mexica city of Tenochtitlan, together with an altepetl called Tlacopan, formed the "Triple Alliance" that would control the valley until the arrival of the Spanish. There was no question that Tenochtitlan, with the largest population, was the senior partner in the alliance.

The power of the Tenochca people grew with snowball effect. Tenochtitlan would make an offer to another altepetl to join its "league," as it were, most often allowing the others to retain their own governing dynasty if they paid a substantial annual tribute. The city-state being approached could accept the terms peacefully, or face a war with the Triple Alliance and their ever-increasing subject states. If the city-state lost that war, the leaders could expect that many of their people would be taken prisoner and become human sacrifice victims in Tenochtitlan. The Mexica worshipped generous gods who had made all life possible; in return they asked occasionally for the ultimate gift that humans could give them. It did no harm, thought the priests of Tenochtitlan, if the human hearts they offered the gods were usually those of their enemies.

Who became an enemy seems to have been determined largely by economics. Generally the Mexica approached a new region when it held desired resources. They had by no means yet attained a wide enough area of dominance to be able to control access to all the goods they needed, though they were apparently attempting to move in that direction. In the interim, they relied on trade. Aztec merchants claimed that they were brave, in the way of warriors, in that they had to venture forth into areas that did not owe—or at least did not yet owe—allegiance to the Tenochtitlan dynasty and that were sometimes feeling truculent. It was not unheard of for merchant seekers of new goods to be flayed alive.[8]

In Coatzacoalcos, when Malintzin was born, the merchants came to trade for luxury goods. They wanted the feathers of tropical birds, which were not easy to obtain, as the people practiced conservation: one person would catch and hold a bird, while another plucked the desired plumes. Even more, the men from the mountains wanted emblems of the watery world: shells, mother-of-pearl, and treasures washed up on shore or brought back by divers and fishermen, like shark teeth, sea urchins, tortoise shells, crocodile skins, snails, coral, and the sword of the swordfish. Artisans could take mother-of-pearl, for example, and whittle tiny fish so wrigglingly alive with motion that the gods who received them in the great temple in Tenochtitlan might have taken them for real. In that temple, as in Coatzacoalcos, the sea was central to the people's vision of the cosmos; it was the source of life. The people near the coast lived in concert with the ocean, sliding in and out effortlessly in their canoes. They knew the power of the ocean, sometimes even held its power, and the men from the great city wanted what the gods had given them. So far, the Tenochca had come prepared to pay for what they desired, rather than demanding that certain goods be rendered to them in tribute, but the situation could hardly be assumed to be permanent.[9]

It is probable that Malintzin's household itself comprised a lineage of conquerors from an earlier era. Coatzacoalcos was home not only to Nahuatl speakers, who comprised the elites, but also to those who spoke Popoluca (meaning "babble" in Nahuatl). Popoluca is part of the Mixe-Zoquean language grouping and its speakers had probably migrated from the south about a thousand years before Malintzin's time. More than two thousand years before she was born, the high culture of the ancient Olmecs had flourished on the same isthmus, the first to give rise to many of the elements of the great Mesoamerican civilizations, like monumental architecture and writing. By the sixteenth century, however, the Olmecs were long gone, leaving only their giant statuary behind, and the Popoluca speakers had a lower social status than the more recently arrived Nahuas. Indeed, they seem to have been political tributaries of the Nahuatl speakers. Olutla was largely populated by Popoluca and was probably a dependency of the Nahuatl-speaking Tetiquipaque. Two such polities were to some extent mutually tied together in an economic sense—Olutla, for example, did not have ideal terrain for growing beans, though it had no problem growing corn. But we must not imagine a world of theoretical equals tied together by trade: Olutla's ruling lineage would have been Nahuatl speaking, despite its Popoluca population. None of this, however, indicates that

Malintzin's family would have been perceived—or have perceived themselves—as foreigners, or as in any way allied with the Mexica. The migration of their forebears had occurred so long ago as to have receded into legend. For Malintzin, the only concrete result would have been that as a child she learned to move in and out of at least two languages with equal ease; it was a skill that would later stand her in good stead.[10]

Her home would have been like all homes—with cool, dark stone or earthen rooms on three or four sides of a courtyard—yet more elegant than some because the male head of household was almost certainly a nobleman, or *pilli*. We cannot know how powerful or wealthy he was. Malintzin apparently later told Cortés that her father was related to the lord of the area,[11] which makes perfect sense, as that was the defining characteristic of the pilli. In every extended noble family, one man inherited the chiefly line and became the dynastic overlord, or *tecuhtli*—apparently not Malintzin's father. Or perhaps she meant that he in fact was a tecuhtli and was related to the king, or *tlatoani,* of the entire altepetl. Depending on how grand her father was, the basic architectural pattern was repeated once or even several times over within one complex, with one central courtyard and its associated rooms being the finest and most ornately decorated. In the middle of the smoky room in which Malintzin and her mother and full siblings slept stood the hearth, with the requisite grinding stone for corn, griddle for tortillas, and cooking pots for stews. At the sides of the room lay reed mats and blankets for the night and boxes and baskets to hold spinning and weaving supplies, clothes, toys, and the inhabitants' other possessions. Just outside the door that opened onto the courtyard and let in the light, there always stood a broom, used every morning in the sacred act of beating back chaos and disorder.

Malintzin was not destined to be a great warrior and win renown for herself in that way, but she would hardly have rued that fact. Like all girls, she knew that women had their own importance, that the men needed them as much as they needed the men. Complementarity was the unspoken watchword. In protecting the hearth, the home, women protected life itself. Indeed, the four-cornered house was a model of the four-cornered cosmos, and the cosmos was itself a great house, just like the polity; thus women tended their homes just as devotedly as priests and priestesses tended the temples. Nor were their regular and ritualized days devoid of passion and high drama: just as a man became a hero in battle, a woman became a hero in giving birth. After all, they each captured a soul. Men who died in battle went to a special heaven for the brave; so, too, did women who died in childbirth. Women's importance would not have been lost on any child, for it went beyond philosophy and poetry and was part of the everyday. On a most prosaic level, it was a simple fact that men and their households could not eat without the labor of women—as became painfully obvious every time an angry wife delayed a meal.[12]

As a child, Malintzin ran about barefoot with her hair down; when she was older she might possibly be given sandals and would wear her hair in the braids or twisted knobs sported by married women. She already dressed as they did, in a wraparound skirt and simply sewn blouse, or *huipilli*. The costume was universal among her sex; what varied was the quality of fabric and the kind of decorations used. One young girl might have a plain cotton shift and blouse; another might have a blouse woven with feathers or embroidered with gemstones.[13] It all depended on who one's father was, and beyond that, who one's mother was. There, indeed, was the rub: if Malintzin experienced any discontent or particular vulnerability in her early life, it would not have been because she was a girl but, rather, because her mother was most likely a relatively powerless concubine. The role of the Nahua wife and mother of heirs was unquestionably an honorable one and probably no more constraining than that of any man, who had perforce to become a warrior. But some Nahua women became concubines outside their natal communities. Their lives have most often been left in the shadows, unexplored.

That wealthy and powerful men could have more than one wife did not by itself spell trouble for the women. Since women did not approach marriage with the expectation that a husband would be a daily companion or partner in life's trials, it was not necessarily damaging to have an imbalanced relationship. Polygyny actually offered some unquestionable advantages to the wives. A larger proportion of women lived richly in a material sense than would otherwise have been the case, since only men who had the wherewithal to support a large household married multiple times. Furthermore, the extensive work of food and textile production, childrearing, and domestic chores is much less onerous in a compound with many female hands, and as women grow older they can look forward to a less labor-intensive, supervisory role. Polygyny also eliminates the negative repercussions associated with men's choosing to have multiple relationships clandestinely, and pregnant and postpartum women in particular gain in certain respects: in Tenochtitlan, for example, men were proscribed from demanding sex or labor from women nearing or recovering from childbirth.

Yet none of this would do away with the pain and anger sometimes experienced by women living in a household in which they were far more replaceable than the male decision maker or leading wife and mother of the heirs. It is significant that the verb *tequixtia*, which technically means "to put someone out," was defined as "to throw a woman or servant out of the house" in the earliest complete dictionary, for women and servants were the only ones at risk of eviction and had to conduct themselves accordingly.[14] The intersection of the systems of marriage and servitude left many people vulnerable—among them, apparently, Malintzin.

It was a complex situation and deserves to be examined carefully in order to clarify how any one woman and her children might fit within the matrix. In the first place, the vast majority of those deemed "slaves" were women. As is typical in ancient systems of slavery, they were domestic servants, not chattel used to keep the economy alive. The Nahuas' agricultural system was never slave dependent. Even when a conquered altepetl was considered to be working the land for an overlord from another state, the people were more akin to tenant farmers. The term "slave" (*tlacotli*) was used to refer to prisoners of war held for human sacrifice, to merchants' burden bearers, and, most often, to girls and women in households doing domestic work and serving as concubines.[15]

How had these women come to be enslaved? In some cases, their parents had chosen to sell them, or they had entered the state voluntarily, theoretically with the right to buy back their freedom again someday. People entered into such arrangements for themselves or their children only when famine or other hard times drove them to it, but there was still a stigma attached. A young girl who had come to be enslaved in another way cries out in a Nahuatl song that she deserves better treatment than she is receiving, because after all, it was not as if her own family had sold her. "Did you buy me anywhere?! Did my uncles and aunts come to trade?!" storms the singer. And women who sold themselves into slavery were especially liable to be accused of laziness, a terrible insult for anyone of the female sex. "Because of what she did [that is, her sloth] . . . she took to another, she lived by concubinage. In that house, too, she was not diligent, she accomplished nothing." How safe such a woman was from resale and how well she was treated in general clearly depended to some extent on her family's social position before the sale and the tightness of her kin ties to the surrounding community. Some concubines would have been relatively well protected. Many girls and women, however, were living far from home, either because they had been sold and then transported by traveling merchants or because they were in fact war captives.[16]

The traditional assumption about Nahua prisoners of war is that they became sacrifice victims, their beating hearts removed from their bodies so that their life force might be given to the gods. This did happen to some captives. But not to all. It could not. In the wake of war, whole peoples sometimes temporarily lost their freedom; they could not all be marched to the top of a pyramid and bent over the bloody stone. The villages of the losers did often face sacking and destruction. A peace agreement, however, might be reached that left just a few captives tied up and following the caravan of the victors. A defeated altepetl's fate—and that of its women—depended on what kind of point the victors wanted to make, whether they wanted to grind a recalcitrant enemy down or leave an opening for some sort of postwar partnership. Some of the prisoners were in fact taken for sacrificial ceremonies; others became concubines of the victorious warriors or were sold to long-distance slave traders. The leaders of a capitulating polity could sometimes do "damage control" either by offering up slaves to their enemies or by voluntarily making a peace offering of some of their own sisters and daughters, who, it was understood, were to become concubines or even secondary wives, not sacrifice victims.[17]

A virtual slave, then, taken from a defeated enemy, could in some instances and in some regards be considered a wife. There were indeed many gradations of wives and concubines, not simply two categories, as we understand the words. In some cases, marriage ceremonies were conducted, while in other cases they were not: it depended on a woman's particular situation. Different words that would all be translated by us today as "concubine" conveyed whether or not a woman had been freely given by her family or forcefully taken, for example. Of course, the highest-ranking women in the household were always ceremonially married. Indeed, one of these might conceivably be more powerful than the husband, if she came from an altepetl or family to be reckoned with. A man might have married such a woman by choice, considering himself lucky to be able to cement an alliance, or he might have been pressured to do so if he paid tribute to the woman's altepetl or lineage.[18]

The distinctions between the various women in a household were made manifest in the fate of their sons and daughters. All the children were born free, even those of the most menial slave women. And none were "illegitimate" or without any rights in the European sense. But there were distinctions nevertheless. Children of the wives of rank were called *tlazopilli* (precious children); children of other women were *calpanpilli* (household children). One mother's children would stand to inherit land and, in some cases, the chiefly line. Who this was could occasionally shift about, depending on the relative standing or power ranking of the various altepetls or calpolli from which the women hailed, which could change over time. At the other end of the spectrum, some relatively disempowered women's children were particularly vulnerable to being sold in hard times, or to being gifted to enemies who were threatening war or had won a battle, or even to being sacrificed in rare and special ceremonies that called for homegrown children rather than foreign ones.

Nahua women thus occupied a range of social and political positions and often had to jockey for their place. A woman who had been brought to her husband's home in a time of war, yet was from a powerful altepetl and so had been ceremonially married, or one who came as an offering from a weak altepetl in order to prevent bloodshed, might find herself treated no better—and perhaps worse—than a clearly defined tlacotli who came from a well-known local family that had stumbled into hard times or than a girl who had caught the eye of the dynastic overlord in the market and been pressured into entering his household. None of these had much hope of having her children inherit (though anyone could aim high in periods of flux), but each one could regularly maneuver for a better position relative to others and try to raise the value of her children's stock.

On the one hand, the women all worked together in the one well-lit area—the courtyard they shared in common—joking together and helping to care for each other's babies. They lived together for years, sharing good times and bad; this is the stuff that love is made of. On the other hand, they experienced painful and threatening rivalries and had to learn to sublimate their anger. There was a genre of song popular at that time— at least in the central valley—that was sung as if in the voice of a relatively powerless concubine. At one moment the woman would sing joyfully about the pleasures of her life, about sex and children, sharing, spinning, and dancing. "I long for the flowers, I long for the songs. In our spinning place, our customary place, I am intoning the songs of the king. I twirl them together into a strand, like [braided] flowers." At another she would lament, "It is heart-rending, here on earth. Sometimes I fret. I consume myself in rage. In desperation, I suddenly say, 'hey, child, I would as soon die [*manoce nimiqui*].'"[19]

"Manoce nimiqui," someone once sang. "I would as soon die." They are memorable words and would have resonated with more than a few women. Somewhere between about age eight and age twelve, Malintzin herself suddenly faced the abyss: one devastating day, she found herself in the hands of long-distance slave traders. They took her by canoe down the wide, muddy river to the billowing salt sea and then headed east, following the coast. The roots and tendrils connecting her to family, calpolli, and altepetl were severed in an hour.[20]

It is possible that even she did not know exactly what had happened, or precisely who had betrayed her. She would not have been at all uncertain about what had occurred if the Aztec army had attacked her village and she was simply a prisoner of war who had been turned over to traders, along with many others. In fact Cortés and one of his followers, Bernal Díaz, both refer to skirmishes having been fought not long before their arrival between parts of Coatzacoalcos and the easternmost Mexica garrison at Tochtepec.[21] But the prisoner-of-war scenario is highly unlikely. If Malintzin had simply been taken in battle, that fact would almost certainly have come out later in her dealings with the Spanish, as there would have been nothing dishonorable to her about it. Instead, Hernando Cortés and several others who knew Malintzin all believed she had been stolen away by merchants.[22] This could mean kidnapping in the most traditional sense, but young Nahua girls from elite families were not in the habit of wandering alone in deserted areas where they could be grabbed with impunity by passersby, nor were Aztec merchants known for such thefts. Almost certainly, there were those among her own people who had been complicit in her being taken.

They could have had any number of reasons. They may have been trying to stave off a concerted attack from the Tochtepec garrison by giving a typical peace offering. This seems especially likely, as Cortés's secretary in fact wrote that the merchants stole Malintzin away in a time of war, and Bernal Díaz mentioned the anger of the people of Coatzacoalcos because of the incessant demands for women and other gifts by the belligerent Mexica. Or if it was a lean year, the household may simply have needed goods that the passing merchants had. The household may have been punishing her—or her mother—for unmaidenly behavior: certainly recalcitrant dependents had been threatened with sale before. Someone with some power may simply have hated her. More than one of these scenarios could easily have been true at once.[23]

Bernal Díaz, in a separate narrative, offered a story that seems farfetched in the extreme compared to the many plausible scenarios. He said that she was royal on both sides, that her father died, and her mother, having remarried, wanted her out of the way so that her son by her second husband could succeed instead. She smuggled her off to the merchants and gave it out that the girl had died. It is true that if Malintzin's father had died, his primary wife could have sold her if she were the daughter of a powerless concubine. That may have happened. But such a primary wife would not have sold her own daughter. Beyond the unlikelihood in human terms, it makes no sense within the Nahua scheme of things for a wife to have inherited so much political power, or, if for some unusual reason she had, for a daughter to have stood in the way of the succession. In any case, how could the child possibly have known what story was given out after her disappearance? Scholars have long noted that the story parallels that of the virtuous Christian knight Amadís de Gaula, which was one of Díaz's favorite tales and newly published in Spain.[24] So perhaps he made it up all on his own. Or maybe Malintzin encouraged him to believe at least parts of it. Díaz himself remarks on the narrative's uncanny resemblance to the story of Joseph, and Malintzin was busy studying Christianity at the time he knew her. The story of the beloved child, the half brother by another mother, sold into slavery by his own half siblings and later himself attaining power over those who rejected him could easily have moved someone in her situation. Díaz certainly wanted to believe that the Marina whom he admired was a princess cheated of her inheritance; Malintzin herself probably preferred he believe this than know the full truth. Whatever she did or did not understand about Spanish attitudes toward slaves and slavery, she herself came from a world in which it was shameful simply to have been sold by one's family and to have been forced to live as an outsider in the homes of others.

What had happened to Malintzin was not in fact terribly uncommon. The long-distance slave trade was active. When Mexica merchants moved outward from the central valley seeking exotic goods, they brought along trade goods of their own—artisan products, crops from the highlands, and slaves. "The ones whom they used to go to sell there might be women and girls, or might be little boys." Malintzin had been picked up as girls often were, to be traded further east. The slaves were apparently sold where they were needed for time-consuming aspects of domestic cotton production—including ginning, beating, spinning, and perhaps even weaving, though the latter was a high-status job integral to women's identity that may have been consistently claimed by the mistresses of households. Archaeologists have shown that spindle whorl frequencies are higher at early Mexica sites than at sites dating from the period of Mexica dominance; the task of producing yarn was shifted to more distant regions as the Mexica became more powerful. Many of the outlying regions paid their tribute in cotton, and the coastal Maya cultures consisted primarily of urban centers populated by elites and their slaves who lived off textile production and trade.[25]

That was where Malintzin was headed now. The merchants' rowers moved efficiently through the waters they knew so well. After traveling more than 150 miles along the coast, they turned in to what at first appeared to be an inlet but turned out to be a huge inland sea. Looking down from above, a god could see that two great arms of land, like the front claws of a crab, reached out and around the giant lagoon, and between them lay a long, thin strip of an island that almost touched the tips of the two arms. Thus the opening from the sea—between the tip of one arm and one end of the island—was small; newcomers imagined a little bay, until they entered and found they could not even see the farther surrounding shores. But the waves diminished dramatically, proving it to be some sort of lagoon, not a parallel ocean. The crystal blue of the water almost matched the crystal blue of the wide, arching sky. Pelicans flew overhead in that vastness; they were the tlatoani, the kings of the waterfowl, the heart and soul of the aquatic world, and could call the wind to sink a boat that tried to chase them.[26]

The rowers knew exactly which inlet to follow out of the lagoon in order to get where they wanted to go. They entered an intricate swampy maze of creeks and islands lined by mangroves. Looking down into the relatively still, clear water, a person in the canoe could see plants swaying below in that parallel world, with brightly colored fish darting silently in and out of their own jungle. The travelers were in Xicallanco now. The merchants made their way to a familiar place to tie up the canoes.

Xicallanco was renowned in the Mesoamerican world as a great entrepôt of trade. Malintzin could not have grown up in Coatzacoalcos without hearing of it. It was a sprawling port, a crucially important neutral zone in a world divided between Nahuas and Maya. Here they could trade together without needing to do battle. Not only could they each bring their goods by sea, but they could also travel along the four rivers that emptied into the area, bringing large swaths of inland territory into the trade zone as well. Xicallanco was a crowded, practical, businesslike town full of small buildings and stalls, with no monumental architecture meant to withstand the centuries. It had a cosmopolitan energy. At least four languages could regularly be heard along the Venice-like watery streets, but Nahuatl was the lingua franca and the native language of the most powerful merchants and governors.[27]

Malintzin was sold for some cacao beans or bolts of cloth or other common medium of exchange. Her purchasers were Chontal Maya, who lived along the coast of the gulf. At least that is how she would have thought of them in her own mind; the word *chontalli* meant "foreigners" in Nahuatl. The "Phoenicians of Mesoamerica," they have been called by modern historians. They rowed her westward again but only a short distance of about fifty miles, not nearly as far as her homeland. They stopped at the mouth of the river of the lord of Tabasco and turned inward, tying up their craft and making their way up the bank. Mosquitoes would have swarmed them, but they smeared themselves with a special grease made to repel them. This was a darker world than Malintzin had yet known, for along the river the tropical forest made a canopy that cut off the light. She saw huge ceiba and mahogany trees and smaller palms and rubber trees. They left the boats and followed the paths where passing feet had worn away the grass and exposed the gray earth. It was hard packed sometimes but could be muddy in this rain-inundated world, requiring that little wooden footbridges be laid here and there. Birds called piercingly to each other, some familiar to her, some strange. In a patch where the trees broke and an open plain soaked up the sunlight lay the densely populated village where she was to live. The homes were elevated and made of small mud bricks, never of stone, as they sometimes were in the world she had left.[28]

The town of Putunchan and the cluster of nearby villages comprised a world of merchant-nobles and their slaves. Farmers inhabited the lands around the more urban area, growing food staples and immense quantities of cacao, but here the wealthy merchants, who were also the governing families, lived and conducted their business. They were known far and wide for their high culture, their books and jewelry. Golden butterflies glinted in the women's hair, and strings of golden grasshoppers and turtles hung about the men's necks. Colorful painting decorated the walls of the rooms, the themes reflecting the wide-ranging travels of the merchants. Some of the comparable coastal towns were dominated by immigrant Nahuas. Putunchan was not, but Nahuatl speakers did reside there in their own enclave, and most of the local Mayas—the *putuns,* the "merchants"—knew enough of their language to communicate with them. Having the Nahuas there was crucial to the success of the putuns' long-distance trade, for human networks made those businesses possible. Malintzin herself had been purchased by Mayas: we can be certain of this because within a few years she became fluent in Chontal Maya. She also learned Yucatec Maya, a substantially different language, so someone in the household where she lived and worked must have been Yucatecan.[29]

Most of her time was, of course, spent with the women. Here, in this life that must have seemed so different from the one she had thought would be hers forever until just a few weeks before, it was the little girls who ran about with their hair twisted into little horns on their heads and the adults who let their tresses down. The women wore tube skirts with short blouses. In this hot, cosmopolitan town, they were more simply attired than the Maya ladies who still adorn the walls of more ancient classical sites, with their elaborate costumes, high shoes, and flattened foreheads. These women were, however, by no means lacking in respect. Depending on which family they were from, certain women could attain authority within the hierarchy of merchant-governors, and men apparently often tried to "marry up." This would have been good news for wives, who could hope to wield significant power within their homes. It was probably less good, though, for servant girls.[30]

Like Nahua women, Maya wives enjoyed a sense of complementarity if not equality with their men. Their responsibility for childbirth rendered them every bit as important as men. Some women apparently even made pilgrimages to the shrine of Ix Chel, the goddess of childbirth, on the island of Cozumel, though whether any came from as far away as Putunchan is hard to say. It would have been possible, though, as their merchant husbands certainly went that way. They were also creators, literally and figuratively, in their weaving. The art had been invented by the wife of the sun and given to human women as a powerful gift. It was not to be taken lightly; in their books, it was the venerable elderly women who did the weaving.[31]

In the real world, young wives wove, too. Perhaps even the slave girls did, as the Chontal produced textiles in quantity. The slaves were probably needed in other ways, however. If the elite women committed their time to weaving, then someone else must have been grinding the corn, making the tortillas, fetching the water, and chasing the toddlers. And weaving itself requires a host of other activities that the merchants' wives were probably loath to do, and which were not commemorated in their people's books and stone carvings, but which someone was obviously handling. Someone had to plant, care for, harvest, and store the cotton and maguey. Then the fibers needed to be extracted and worked, requiring long, painstaking hours of beating and carding. Yarn had to be spun. Dyes had to be made out of plants or shellfish and then the yarns boiled in them, over and over. Finally the backstrap looms needed to be warped in preparation for the actual weaving of cloth. The basic techniques were the same all over Mesoamerica: Malintzin would have played with a spindle as a young girl of three or four and would have learned how to use it effectively by age five. In Putunchan, she knew what to do.[32]

We will never know how Malintzin was treated or how she came to feel about her captors. In the interest of preserving peace and harmony in the household, the putuns probably extended basic kindness to most of the enslaved women. It remains true, however, that skeletal remains tell us that even in one Maya area where women were in some ways venerated, they did not eat as well as men and did not live as long. This was true even of elite women, and slaves certainly fared worse. Their status affected their lives in very real ways.

It is also likely that Malintzin first came to be used sexually in this period. Whether she felt forced or not was probably a complicated question. The captive woman in the surviving Nahua song alternates between trying at times to establish a warm and erotic relationship with her master and at other moments feeling violated and angry; both reactions would be eminently plausible under the circumstances. It does seem, however, that sexual relations were in general more fraught, more tension ridden among the Maya than among the Nahuas, perhaps because women's sexuality seems to have been considered more of a threat, a more potent force. Women of childbearing years could not enter certain sacred places. Among some groups, elite young girls wore shell pendants in their pubic area, symbolic of the power of the sea, understood to be feminine; the pendants were removed at marriage. Meanwhile, however, enslaved girls who probably never wore such pendants—as they were never married and yet certainly had sexual relations—moved freely about the household, submissive, and yet with the unleashed power of the sea.[33]

Whatever Malintzin felt, it is virtually certain that she hid her emotions well. That is always the safest course for the enslaved, and Nahua peoples in general did not make a habit of letting their suffering show. Women were expert at deflecting. There was an old song about a dying infant speaking to its mother. It ran something like this: "Little mother, when I die, bury me by your hearthside. When you go to make tortillas, weep there for me. And whenever someone asks you, 'Little mother, why do you weep?' you'll tell them, 'Because the firewood is green, and makes me weep with so much smoke.'" Malintzin, perhaps worst of all in her culture's reckoning, did not even have a hearthside of her own.[34]

She could have become a mother. If she had, she would almost certainly have lived out her years on the shores of the Tabasco. For whatever we may think of ancient Mesoamerican slavery, the men did not sell mothers away from the children they had borne for them. She would have stayed there, watching the flocks of egrets in the evenings. But wherever young girls work hard and are undernourished, they attain menarche later than they otherwise might. Malintzin probably was not fertile until at least age fifteen. If she did in fact conceive, and there were reasons why bearing the child would have made her situation worse, she might have chosen to end the pregnancy: abortion-inducing drugs were available to her. In any case, she was still a childless young woman, available to be gambled away or gifted or sold, when strangers came from across the sea.[35]

They came for the first time in 1517, landing at Champoton, another merchant town farther east along the coast.[36] Rumors had been present for years about powerful invaders living on the islands to the east and patrolling the coast that lay around the bend of the Yucatan Peninsula. In Champoton, it was already clear how they would have to deal with these dangerous new arrivals when they made their first appearance. When the time came, the warriors acted without hesitation, and the foreigners were ambushed. At least half of them were killed and the rest were put to flight. Messages buzzed up and down the Chontal coast: the newcomers were extremely well armed and had the largest canoes ever seen, but they were ignorant and easily confused. Hopefully, they had learned their lesson and would not return.

But they did. They came to the same area again the next year. At Campeche, they landed and stayed in tight formation, using another style of weapon that made it almost impossible to attack them. They took all the food and water they wanted. At Champoton, they proceeded differently than they had the year before. They did not land. Instead they leveled hideous weapons from their boats and killed more than a few. Satisfied, the strangers took sail again and continued westward. They stopped in the great lagoon, sure there must be a settlement there but, in their bumbling, never found Xicallanco. Instead, they kidnapped four unwary young men. In the meantime, messengers had been skimming along the coast. By the time the strangers found the mouth of the River Tabasco and stopped just out of sight of Putunchan, they had been expected for days.

TWO

The Men from the Boats

HUNDREDS OF CHONTAL WARRIORS WAITED HIDDEN IN THEIR CANOES IN THE creeks that led down to the mouth of the Tabasco River. A large fleet rowed out to meet the strangers, who were peering over the edges of their four huge boats. The warriors were confident, for they were present in numbers, protected by padded cotton armor, and well armed with bows and arrows. They still proceeded cautiously, however, having heard that the strangers had terrible weapons. Suddenly a large dog jumped from one of the ships and began to swim excitedly toward land. The young Chontal men gave a great shout and showered it with arrows. Then the panicked Spanish aimed their large metal weapons and fired. Metal balls and small, rough bits of shot sprayed outward. The Indians would learn later that these were small cannons, called falconets. At least one warrior fell back, dying. Both sides retreated to safety.[1]

The next day, another fleet of canoes set out and approached the strangers anew. A Yucatec boy whom the strangers had with them stood up and shouted that they had come to trade for gold and had many presents. He spoke a language that plenty of the merchant Chontal understood, both literally and figuratively. One canoe went near enough to collect some proffered gifts and gave other trinkets in exchange. One of the boys

30

the Spanish had taken near Xicallanco called out to the locals, and they exchanged words with him. The scouting party withdrew, saying they would return. The strangers waited.

That evening, the Putunchan war leaders evidently decided to assume that the expedition was truly intended to be a peaceful one. They would send a delegation, which would attempt to gather information and perhaps ransom the Xicallanco boy. The next morning they sent one of their number to parley. He addressed the man in charge, who called himself Juan de Grijalva. The indigenous spokesman first presented the bearded leader of the newcomers with a number of gifts, including some clothing trimmed with gold, and then accepted in exchange various goods, most importantly a doublet and cap made of green velvet, which was an admirable type of cloth the Chontal nobleman had never seen before, despite all his experience trading in textiles. He asked to be allowed to ransom the boy, but the captain refused.

Through their unfortunate Yucatec hostage—whom they persisted in calling "Julian," though that clearly could not be his name—the bearded

PHOTO 1: View from a coastal Maya tower. Tulum, late postclassic.
Photo by John Graham Nolan.

men said they came from a land far away and were governed by a great king, who wished to be their lord as well. He and his god would do them much good, and give them more gifts, if they would only offer provisions. The Chontal spokesman—or perhaps the justifiably frightened interpreter, Julian—answered that they already had a lord, and a powerful one at that. They would be happy to trade and provide foodstuffs, but the men and their boats must depart immediately afterward, without any delay. The strangers called themselves Christians, Castilians, Spaniards, and a confusing array of other names. They made it obvious that they desired more gold as well as food. The Chontal emphasized that the travelers should continue on and seek out the Mexica if they wanted more of the precious metal, but it was not clear if the strangers understood. In the meantime, the Indians brought some goods to barter. Late in the day, the winds were right for departure. The *quistianos* seized the moment and headed for the mouth of the river. The next morning they sailed in the direction of the setting sun. A few weeks later, they passed by again as they made their way back home. They did not stop, but the putuns later learned that they caused more trouble near Campeche and Champoton before disappearing toward the rising sun.

Gone. They were gone. But for how long? It was already clear that these strangers could easily find their way back to the same place as often as they chose, despite their ignorance of the land. They had done only limited damage here, but they had kidnapped four boys when they paused in the lagoon of Xicallanco and now had refused to let them be ransomed. Probably they were being held to be used later as translators, like the unlucky Julian from Yucatan. Dressed in metal and guarded by their crossbowmen, the strangers were relatively invulnerable and could not simply be persuaded to give the boys up with a volley of arrows. The situation was serious. Putunchan's power and prestige in the area, its ability to serve as a major market hub, depended on its ability to remain aloof from other people's wars and battles, to be permanently safe from attack and invulnerable to tribute demands. They would later tell the Spanish that "they considered themselves a mighty people, and valiant as compared to those of the back country, because nobody dared to take their goods and women by force, or their children for sacrifice."[2] They could not afford to traffic and trade with a people who could put them at risk of appearing weak in their neighbors' eyes; their whole economy would suffer. If the strangers returned, they would have to be driven off. The battle would almost certainly be horrendous, but the strangers were few in number and could surely be defeated.

The indigenous had reason to know that the battle would be a difficult one. Besides the evidence they had seen with their own eyes, there were the troubling stories from the Champoton coast. The newcomers in their great boats were indeed becoming a significant presence in the region. Exactly ten years earlier, in 1508, a convoy had sailed along the coast of the gulf, making landfall in several places. No one knew anything about these strangers then, but a few years later, people began to hear occasional stories of their boats wrecking as they came and went from a settlement they had far to the south, on the other side of the great peninsula, beyond Chetumal. Survivors included not only bearded men, but also others who looked like the people here and were the bearded ones' servants. They said the strangers now governed a huge island that lay six days' sail to the east, where especially adventurous Chontal merchants had occasionally gone. That was apparently why the men of Champoton had decided to take no risks, attacking first with the intention of asking questions later. They did not want such men to gain even a toehold in their territory. Best to make their point immediately. The results of the attack, however, had not been good—more men dead and wounded than they had ever expected. The story had been a powerful motivation for caution in Putunchan's case. They could not continue making peaceful overtures indefinitely, however, as the policy would only lead to other problems if the strangers began to come frequently. If the men and their boats returned, they would have to be permanently chased away.

Weeks and then months passed. The pelicans and other waterfowl came back in July, as usual. The people harvested their corn and cacao and celebrated their feast days. But if Malintzin and the other women had long since ceased to gossip and speculate about the great boats, the subject resurfaced with a vengeance less than a year later. A messenger came, announcing that ten ships were sailing westward from Cozumel. They did not even pause at Champoton but, as had been feared, instead made straight for the place where they hoped to meet with a friendlier reception: Putunchan.

The warriors prepared for a major battle, bringing in many hundreds of men from allied areas and building stockades around parts of the city.

As the strangers drew near, the women and children were evacuated into the countryside, slaves carrying away coffers of the most valuable trade goods. They would have to wait in suspense to hear the tales of the day. Looking out from their boats, the Spanish perhaps turned a shade paler than usual: "The river, its banks and the mangrove swamps were crowded with Indian warriors, which greatly surprised us who had been here with Grijalva."[3]

One of the bearded men spoke Yucatec Maya—they would later learn he had been a castaway near the island of Cozumel for eight years. He called out that they came in peace. This time, however, the men of Putunchan gave no quarter. They would, they said, kill anyone who tried to enter their country. Night came, and each side watched the other, bows and crossbows at the ready. In the morning, the Chontal tried one more time to stave off the inevitable: they sent messengers bearing food, telling the new arrivals to take it and go, before anything unpleasant happened. The captain of the newcomers—a man in his early thirties, who called himself Hernando Cortés—declined. He divided his company into two. One group landed at the mouth of the river on the sea coast and then moved overland toward the town, and the other sailed upriver, then drew near the settlement in smaller boats and began to wade ashore. They relied on their armor to protect them, and the strategy was largely effective. One of them later remembered:

With great bravery the [Indians] surrounded us in their canoes, pouring such a shower of arrows on us that they kept us in the water up to our waists. There was so much mud and swamp that we had difficulty getting clear of it; and so many Indians attacked us, hurling their lances and shooting arrows, that it took us a long time to struggle ashore. While Cortés was fighting, he lost a sandal in the mud and could not recover it. So he landed with one bare foot.[4]

Once ashore, the invaders began to use their crossbows and lances against the Indians, who were armored only in cotton, forcing them to retreat toward the town. With their metal weapons they broke through the stockades, and then the other group of Spaniards, who had been making their way overland, arrived. The Indians withdrew, and the foreigners were left in command of the ceremonial heart of the town—a great courtyard surrounded by temples and halls. There they passed the night with sentries standing guard. Julian, the former translator, had died, but they still held hostage an older Yucatec man, a fisherman whom they had named Melchior. Now, as the Spaniards slept, he took advantage of the confusion and the strange surroundings to make his escape.

Melchior told the Putunchan fighting men that they must disarm the strangers by pretending to regret their attack and promising food; the bearded ones were always eager to believe such nonsense. The Chontal should not, of course, deliver it and instead should attack any small foraging parties the Spaniards sent out, thus cutting them off from their fellows and bringing down the total number available to fight. Eventually they should surround the remaining members of the Spanish camp with a force so large that even with the interlopers' superior weapons they could not withstand it. The putuns tried to follow his advice. Over the next few days, they attacked two foraging parties and killed several Spaniards. Then the Chontal met the foreigners in battle on an open plain where they had stopped, near the village of Cintla. Wave after wave attacked the tight group of metal-clad Spanish, perishing before the lethal steel weapons. The battle went on for over an hour. Surely their beleaguered enemy must be tiring, the Indians thought.

Then, from behind, there suddenly came thundering over the plain *how horses were introduced to the Americas* more Spaniards mounted on huge beasts, like deer, but twenty times as strong. During the night, Cortés had managed to unload ten horses from the ships that were still in the mouth of the river. It was a time-consuming and awkward process, requiring pulleys and canvases, but his men were protected by darkness and their armor while they worked, and their enemies had not known how significant these actions would turn out to be. At the time, the Indians were probably only too happy to have some of the Spaniards cut off from the others. Now the horsemen, who had been struggling through the coastal swamps all morning, came charging over the plain, invulnerable, slashing down Chontal foot soldiers on either side with wild abandon. The warriors had no choice: they withdrew.

Late that afternoon, the military commanders of Putunchan counted their missing men, whose bodies, they knew, were strewn over the fields of Cintla. They had lost over 220 in only a few hours. Nothing like that had ever happened before in all the histories recorded in their annals. They could not afford to keep up a fight like that. Even if in the end they could drive the Spaniards away, it would avail them nothing. They would be left weak and defenseless, vulnerable to their enemies, having lost many hundreds of their own. And then, as was now all too clear, more Spaniards would probably arrive the next year. That very day, they sent a messenger to sue for peace. Through the interpreter, Cortés said that if they made amends, he and his distant king would forgive them.[5]

Over the next few days, the Chontal delivered large quantities of food and gold jewelry to the Spaniards. They also gathered together twenty slave women to offer as a gesture of submission. These were not the daughters or sisters of the warriors, whom a former enemy would be expected to marry in a sign of new friendship and alliance. No, these were slaves, with whom the victors might do whatever they pleased. Twenty was a special number among the Maya. Most likely, the quota was distributed among four or five or even twenty ruling houses or clans, with instructions that each come up with a woman or certain number of women. Perhaps it was pure coincidence, or perhaps she had demonstrated herself to be temperamentally unfit for the life of a dutiful female slave; however it was, some head of household chose Malintzin to be turned over to the enemy.[6]

Shortly after the young women were presented at the foreigners' camp, a well-dressed Spaniard to whom the others showed deference conducted an unintelligible ceremony, speaking a few words over each woman and anointing each with some water that he obviously believed held special power. He gave the women new appellations and told them these were their Christian names. He pronounced the words carefully so they would remember who they were, assigning the name "Marina" to the girl from Coatzacoalcos. In her world, there was no r sound. She and the others heard the rolling sound the Spaniard produced with the tip of his tongue as l. "Malina," then, was her name. At least for now.

Cortés then divided the women among his leading men. A modern historian reminds us what this meant, lest we choose not to think of it. "Once in Spanish hands, the women were summarily baptized and distributed to provide the men with sexual services. This juxtaposition of a Christian sacrament with rape is jarring to our sensibilities, but the sixteenth-century Spaniards were quite frank about it."[7] Indeed, it was important to them to have the women baptized before they initiated relations with them. They would have insisted that this was what made what they were doing different from what the Indians had always done after their own battles.

Maly rove most likely didn't protect her from abuse

The man to whom Cortés chose to give Marina was Alonso Hernández Puertocarrero, first cousin to the Count of Medellín, in Extremadura, Spain, which was where Cortés himself was from. Cortés was an hidalgo—that is, from a locally prominent family, but not of the high or titled nobility. As such, he would have seen Puertocarrero as the most important man in the expedition—someone in a position to raise Cortés's status back home. Indeed, before they had set out from the Caribbean, Cortés had given him a sorrel mare as a sort of signing bonus, intended to demonstrate his great pleasure at having the count's cousin along, as it provided Puertocarrero great status as one of the mounted men on the expedition.[8] That Marina was chosen out of a group of twenty to become another gift to this particular man demonstrates that what numerous conquistadors later said about her must have been true: the child who had been taken from Coatzacoalcos against her will and then had lived as a slave for years had managed to grow into a beautiful and self-assured young woman.

What the Spanish could not see immediately was that Marina also had an extraordinary mind. She undoubtedly followed Puertocarrero silently. He would have had no curiosity about her thoughts. A powerful figure typically does not consider what an underling is thinking, for he does not need to, and Puertocarrero had never demonstrated himself to be an exception in this regard. She, however, was noticing everything, remembering everything. Over the next few days, while they were still in Putunchan, and then on shipboard, she began to learn about the Spaniards and to piece together something of their language. There was one man she and several of the other women could talk to—Jerónimo de Aguilar. He had been cast away on the Yucatec peninsula when he was only a little over twenty. He had lived as a slave himself for eight years and had been ransomed by Cortés only a few short weeks before. He did not know Chontal Maya, but some of the women knew enough Yucatec to speak to him. Those who asked questions eventually learned a great deal.[9]

There was, on the other side of the sea, a huge landmass, at least as big as their own world. Not many years before, the people of that world had been as unaware of the existence of the Mayas and the Nahuas as their own people had been of the bearded ones. Then one day a great queen named Isabella, who was dedicated to an all-powerful god, decided to back a sailor who said he could end up where the sun rose by sailing toward its setting. All the educated men of that world said the earth was round, but many thought it was too big for a ship to survive the passage. The people on board would run out of food and water and perish. That would have been true, of course, if the exploring ships had had to sail straight through from Spain to the place they sought, called Asia. They knew that for certain now. But this man, called Cristóbal Colón, had been fortunate indeed: he had stumbled on a New World in the middle of the sea. First he had touched on the Caribbean islands and then the long, narrow isthmus to the west. He thought at the time that these were islands off the southern coast of India, where he had originally been headed, as he had been certain that if the·part of Africa that lay below the Sahara, far to the south of Europe, was inhabited, then in perfect symmetry there must be a comparable world to the south of China, which would be equally full of conquerable societies. Thus he named the people he encountered "Indians." Over the next decade, the Spanish began to settle the largest islands and insisted that the indigenous people there work for them. Dozens of expeditions carrying hundreds of European men had since set off from the Caribbean in all directions, seeking gold and other precious goods. Jerónimo de Aguilar's ship had been wrecked on its way to Darien, a town the Spanish had founded in a place called Panama. Only in the last few years had the Europeans become fully convinced that this was an entirely new world, not a southern leg of Asia, and that what they were now exploring probably was not a larger island but might well be the mainland of a continent previously unknown to them.[10]

Now, almost thirty years since Columbus had first sailed, the expeditions of the two preceding years had convinced the Spaniards living in the Caribbean that they could perhaps still make their fortunes in the New World even though the islands were growing crowded and gold had not proven plentiful. It sounded as though there really was a wealthy kingdom buried in the heart of the mainland. Did the women think so? Yes? That was fortunate, because as they could see, over four hundred men with perhaps as many as a hundred more retainers and servants had set out from the islands with Hernando Cortés to seek their fortunes. Since the entire European population in the Caribbean at the time numbered about five thousand, this was quite an exodus. The men's hopes were at a fevered pitch.

Before they left Putunchan, the Spanish took the time to introduce Christianity to the people; they were proud to think that they did so everywhere they went. Later they even claimed that before each battle they read aloud the *requerimiento*—a statement that informed the natives about Christianity and offered them peace if they would only convert. It is doubtful that they really had the time to make unintelligible speeches before their battles, but they certainly spoke of their religion after their military encounters. Cortés ordered two of his carpenters to construct a large cross on a hill, and he presented the town with a beautifully dressed figure of Mary holding her child. Cortés himself displayed the image of the Virgin on his standard, so his action would have appeared perfectly logical to the defeated indigenous; goddess or queen, her gorgeous raiment would have proven her to be important. Fray Bartolomé de Olmedo said Mass. The Chontal were noncommittal, but some of the Spaniards chose to believe that they had accepted the faith, or at least that they would give up their idols.

Later fray Bartolomé and Jerónimo de Aguilar began to try to explain to Malintzin and the other women the nature of their God in somewhat greater depth. What the friars always explained first about a Marian image they had given as a gift was that this was the mother of God, called Mary; that God wanted his mother honored and revered; and that those on earth must take her as their advocate to speak to God on their behalf. Then they attempted to teach their listeners to recite the Hail Mary in Latin. Jerónimo de Aguilar, who was apparently educated, almost certainly knew what it meant. *Hail Mary, full of grace. The Lord is with you. Blessed are you among women and blessed is the fruit of your womb, Jesus. Holy Mary, Virgin, mother of God, pray for us sinners. Amen.* He may have tried haltingly to put it into the Yucatec Maya he knew. It would not have been an easy task. Later, when a linguistically talented priest first tried to put the oration into Nahuatl, he struggled: "May you be joyful, oh Saint Mary, you are full of *gracia*." He simply could not translate "grace." "God the king is with you. You are the most praiseworthy of all women. And very praiseworthy is your womb of precious fruit, is Jesus. Oh Saint Mary, oh perfect maiden, you are the mother of God. May you speak for us sinners. May it so be done."[11] Later, some Indians would say they thought at first that Mary was the highest god. It would be the same in China and elsewhere when the earliest friars made their halting efforts in a foreign tongue.[12] The Christian god seemed to be a woman. Not a goddess, creator and destroyer, capricious and uncontrolled, as in the Nahua or Maya world. But a perfect woman.

After a few days, the newcomers took to their ships. It was Palm Sunday in the Spanish world, and the men were hopeful. The ocean spray would have struck Malintzin's face as the sails caught the wind. They were soon farther out from shore than she had ever been on any canoe. They were going west, to seek the country of the Mexica. They passed by the mouth of the Coatzacoalcos River, at the base of the Tuxtla mountains she had seen so many times as a child, though from the landward side. That was probably on Wednesday. They continued on until the features so familiar to her receded and were lost from view. Another night came. Midday Thursday, they anchored at a point charted the year before by Juan de Grijalva and labeled by him San Juan de Ulúa. Men scurried, rolling up the sails and preparing to disembark.

In less than half an hour, two canoes approached their fleet. The Aztec king Moctezuma, it turned out, had had the spot watched ever since the strangers had made their appearance there the year before. He knew they merited watching, as traders passing through Xicallanco had told his agents what had happened on the Champoton coast last year. Possibly he—or at least his team of observers—already knew what had happened at Putunchan this year. The paddlers made straight for the largest and most decorated ship, the flagship, on which Cortés and Puertocarrero sailed.[13]

In later years, it would be said that the Nahuas at this point thought the Spanish ships were clouds, or floating mountains or temples, and that they struck awe and fear in their hearts. In fact, they, like the sea-faring Chontal, seem to have seen immediately that these contraptions were boats—albeit far larger and more impressive than their own. A generation later, after dutifully repeating some of the expected hyperbole to the Spanish priests to whom they spoke, native informants explained what happened next in remarkably pragmatic terms: "[The Spaniards] hitched the prow of the [Indians'] boat with an iron staff and hauled them in. Then they put down a ladder." This is not to say that the men in the canoes were not impressed. They undoubtedly were. With the same wood and cotton they themselves had at their disposal, these strangers had built something extraordinary. According to another story told years later, "The Indians boarded the vessel and were amazed at such a powerful structure with its many cabins, decks and other spaces. It seemed a thing more divine than human, a work of genius."[14]

This same narrative reveals a probable explanation for the Spaniards' early belief that the ships had been taken for floating mountains or temples. With their limited ability to understand Nahuatl, early colonizers seem to have misunderstood what the Indians told them they had been thinking. The storyteller says: "The [messenger] described how, when he had been walking next to the seashore, he had seen a round hill or house moving from one side to another." He uses the word "house" again later, which is suspicious, for in Nahuatl, the word for boat translates as "water-house." The word for settlement is "water-hill." This story was originally told in Nahuatl but then summarized for posterity in Spanish. The speaker could easily have said that he saw a round water-hill, a water-house, meaning he had seen a floating settlement, or boat, on the water. This seems likely, for later the speaker elaborates, "This wooden 'hill' [was] so big that it would lodge many men, serving them as a home. Within it they would eat and sleep."[15]

With remarkable aplomb, given the circumstances, and apparently very little panic, the messengers demanded to speak to the leader and announced that they bore greetings from Moctezuma. Cortés demanded that Jerónimo de Aguilar tell him what they said. Under pressure, the friar tried to understand; he could not. He spoke a dialect of Maya, but unbeknownst to him, this was Nahuatl. By his own admission, Cortés was irritated. What kind of translator was this? He had gone to a great deal of trouble and expense to ransom him, apparently to no purpose.

Malintzin could have remained silent. No one expected her to step forward and serve as a conduit. But by the end of that hour, she had made her value felt. Cortés's secretary and biographer later wrote that afterward he took her aside with Aguilar, asked who she was, and promised her "more than her liberty" if she would help him find and speak to Moctezuma. Undoubtedly, he promised her riches; it was what he promised everyone who agreed to aid his cause.[16]

It would be well to pause to consider Malintzin's options. She knew that she could certainly continue in silence as the concubine and slave of Puertocarrero—a man who had once even abandoned a Castilian woman whom he had persuaded to run away with him. When he tired of his Indian girl, or when he was killed, she would be at the mercies of whichever of the Spaniards were left alive—perhaps even their common property, as some of the young women probably had already become. Or alternatively, she could speak aloud, earning the respect and gratitude of all the men present, and especially of their charismatic leader. In that case, she herself would probably live longer, as she might stave off battles with the locals and could certainly help to obtain food. She could not possibly have harbored any loyalty to Moctezuma or desire to shield him from these well-armed newcomers. Any assertion that she should have entertained such feelings would literally have confused her. He and his kind had always been the enemy; the merchants who sold her in Xicallanco almost certainly were numbered among his people. In what way could she be construed as his ally or as owing him her allegiance?

She did what almost anyone in her situation would have done. She worked with Jerónimo de Aguilar to translate conversations between Cortés and the emissaries from Moctezuma. Overnight, she was accorded a new level of respect; some of the men even began to refer to her as doña Marina, just as they referred to noblewomen from Spain. The usage took hold: Spaniards who had known her continued to accord her the title years after her death, even when they were under pressure not to.[17] The next day was Good Friday, and the Spaniards worked all through the hours of light to disembark their goods, including their cannon and horses, and set up a protected camp. Over the ensuing days, Cortés explained to local leaders through his interpreters that he insisted on meeting with Moctezuma. He presented gifts for them to send to him; they said that it would take relay runners three days roundtrip before an answer could possibly be returned. While they waited, a local chief followed orders and had a painting made of Cortés, Aguilar, and doña Marina, together with the ships, horses, dogs, and weapons. They would send this text to Moctezuma, whose assistants would know how to interpret the various glyphs that explained how many of each item were present. To impress the people with their strength and to exercise the beasts, the Spanish galloped their horses up and down the hard-packed sand of low tide. They wheeled and shouted with laughter, their armor glinting in the sun.[18]

The messengers returned. They addressed themselves to Malintzin, who explained their words to Aguilar, who turned to speak to Cortés. The answer was no: Moctezuma could not see them. It would be too difficult for him to descend to them or for their party to come to him. He sent rich presents for them to bear to their emperor when they returned home over the sea, which he was sure they would shortly do. Cortés insisted that messengers be sent again with more valuable gifts and an even more urgent desire on his part to see the Mexica king. This time, while they waited, far fewer Indians came to trade. Food grew short, but the men managed to catch enough fish from the sea to keep body and soul together. The answer came. No, they could not come. It would never work; Moctezuma could not guarantee their safety in the lands between. But he sent even greater gifts to bring to their king, jade and turquoise, the most precious jewels he had at his disposal.

The next morning, not a single Indian remained anywhere near the Spanish camp. There would be no more food and water forthcoming. And the mosquitoes were eating the men alive, preventing them from sleeping well, and leaving them downcast and short-tempered. Some of the men began to say they should return to Cuba.

Cortés, however, had another iron in the fire. Some Indians whom Malintzin could not understand had approached the camp not long before. They were Totonacs. She knew enough about how this part of the world worked to know how to proceed: she asked if they did not have *nahuatlatos,* "interpreters of Nahuatl," living in their midst? They did indeed. So it was, after conversation with these men, with Malintzin there not only to interpret but also to explain, that Cortés learned that Moctezuma had enemies—or at least highly unwilling tributaries—at his own back door. It was just what he needed to know. If he could enlist some of these to join the Spanish cause, he might well be able to proceed to Moctezuma's court even without an invitation. He undoubtedly asked Malintzin if she thought the thing were possible; she would have answered unhesitatingly that there were always those willing to make war against Moctezuma. For indeed, as she herself knew well, the monarch spent most of his time putting down rebellions or trying to force the hand of those not yet conquered.

Before he put his plan into action, however, the Spanish captain needed to make a settlement here on the coast that would allow his forces to remain in touch with ships coming and going from the outside world. And there was another reason as well—as Malintzin would have pieced together bit by bit as she watched the animated debate among her captors and gradually came to understand more of what was passing. According to Spanish law, Cortés was technically not allowed to seek Moctezuma. He had been empowered by the Cuban governor, Diego de Velázquez, only to explore and barter, after which he was instructed to return home with any information he had gleaned. Velázquez intended to use that information to colonize the mainland himself once he had received exclusive rights to do so from the Crown. He had certainly never authorized Cortés to conquer anyone or settle anywhere. And in fact, just before Cortés sailed, word had come at the last moment that even the more general exploration permit had been revoked by a nervous Velázquez, who feared the unruly Cortés might proceed in a selfish manner and try to colonize the area himself after all. The eager would-be conquistador decided to pretend never to have received the message and departed immediately, before he had even finished stocking his ships. Legally speaking, then, Cortés was a rebel. There was, however, a possible way out of this predicament.

According to the *Siete Partidas*, a compilation of laws dating from the thirteenth century, an organic unity of purpose bound king and subjects together for the common good. Thus laws could be set aside at the behest of all good men of the land, if, for example, an obstreperous bureaucrat were not behaving well. If the vast majority were acting for the common good when they refused to obey, then they were not in fact traitors. Cortés therefore needed a citizenry that existed in law to insist that he settle the land. He found one. Or rather, he made one.

He arranged to have the expedition's men *demand* that they attempt to conquer Moctezuma, as it was clearly in the best interest of their king and country to strike now, when all was in readiness. They founded the city of Villa Rica de la Vera Cruz, thus constituting themselves a legal citizenry. They appointed Cortés alcalde and chief justice and insisted that he lead them where they wanted to go. Bernal Díaz remembered, "Cortés gave in, although he pretended to need much begging. It was a case of 'Press me harder' (as the saying goes) 'but I'm very willing.'" What could he do, if this was what the majority demanded of him as their leader?[19]

As soon as the ink was dry on the documents, they set out for Cempoala, the largest of the twenty to thirty Totonac settlements in the vicinity. By previous arrangement, guides had come to get them. In case they were being led into a trap, the Spaniards walked with their muskets and crossbows ready. Mounted scouts went on ahead in a relatively invulnerable cluster.

When the riders saw the sun shining at a distance on a glistening white tower, they came galloping back to say they had seen a city of silver. Bernal Díaz says that doña Marina laughingly explained what the phenomenon undoubtedly really was—a pyramid that had recently been coated with lime.[20] Whether or not she actually made a joke of it that bright June day we will never know, but certainly she and the other women must have laughed to themselves more than once to see these great strong men with their remarkable machines turn out to be more gullible than they had ever known any of their own warriors to be.

Over the next two months, Cortés worked to build an alliance with the Totonacs, such that each side would promise to support the other in war. He claimed to have encouraged them to imprison five arrogant Mexica tax collectors in their midst, and then, in his dealings with the Mexica, to have blamed the Totonacs for the deed, thus cleverly sowing dissension. But no such sowing was necessary. The fed-up Totonacs undoubtedly arrested the tax collectors because they wanted to. It was a good test: they would find out if Cortés backed them as he said he would. If he did not, they could later claim it had all been his idea. They soon told the Spanish that the Mexica garrison at Tizapantzinco was sending out raiders to punish them. When the Spanish got to Tizapantzinco, however, the villagers there told them that the Mexica soldiers had cleared out days before and that the Totonacs were using the protection offered by the Spanish to sack the town. Cortés may have wanted to believe he was manipulating the Indians—or at least may have felt it was important to portray it so in the news he sent home—but the Totonacs clearly had worked out for themselves how they could best use their newfound friends.[21]

To cement what appeared to them to be a good bargain, the Totonacs gave the Spanish eight women—not slaves this time, but the daughters of chiefs. The king told Malintzin to explain that he was offering his own niece to the captain as a wife; thus they would henceforth be kin. In what must have appeared to his men to be a splendidly funny joke, Cortés had the niece christened "Catalina"—just as his wife back home in Cuba was called. With more serious intent, he took the most beautiful young woman and presented her to Puertocarrero, who was probably in need of a consolation prize. Presumably, Malintzin had by then moved entirely out of his orbit.

Despite the rather mundane nature of the early interactions and trafficking between the Spaniards and the Indians, tellers of the story many years later would almost always say that the indigenous had perceived the white men to be gods during these very events. When the story gained currency in the 1560s, the Aztec capital lay in ruins, and Indians were being forced to pay tribute into Spanish hands; it was probably comforting to the Europeans to envision a scenario in which they had not been unwanted conquerors but, rather, warmly welcomed and even worshipped figures. Whether for that reason or some other, the story was a popular one from the 1560s onward. There is, however, very little cause to believe it. The evidence against its being true is far weightier than the evidence for it. Almost no one wrote anything down between 1519 and 1521. Cortés himself was one of the few who did; his letters to the king are the only surviving source from those years, and in them he never claimed to have been perceived as a god.

The reason the story has been taken seriously is that the Mexica themselves offered it up as fact. What is often forgotten, however, is that their statements were made at least forty years later, by the next generation of people living in a completely different context. The children of the Aztec elites—who were those the Spanish taught to write—probably wanted to come up with a reasonable explanation as to why their previously awe-inspiring fathers and uncles had been so roundly defeated. Eventually, they began to claim that there had been terrifying omens before the events, that the god called Quetzalcoatl had long been expected from the east in the year One Reed (1519), and that the Spaniards were therefore perceived to be divine.

The story of the omens appears in Book Twelve of the Florentine Codex—a text prepared under the direction of Bernardino de Sahagún, a Franciscan friar, in the School of Tlatelolco, where Indian noblemen were educated in the Roman alphabet and Christianity. The omens the students mention bear an interesting affinity to those of certain Greek and Latin texts that would have been in the school library. Why, however, would they have been so eager to make the mental leap of believing that similar omens had convinced their forebears of what was to come? We must remember that they came from a culture in which omens were often retroactively sought to explain a recent tragedy. More specifically, as the sons and grandsons of priests and other noblemen, they probably had frequently come face-to-face with popular resentment of—and their own discomfort with—the fact that their forebears had been caught off guard, to put it mildly. One old man put words in Moctezuma's mouth at the end of the century and had him berate the seers and priests who were supposed to have been shepherding the kingdom through potential catastrophes:

> It is your position, then, to be deceivers, tricksters, to pretend to be men of science, and forecast that which will take place in the future, deceiving everyone by saying that you know what will happen in the world, that you see what is within the hills, in the center of the earth, underneath the waters, in the caves and in the earth's clefts, in the springs and water holes. You call yourselves "children of the night" but everything is a lie, it is all pretense.

No wonder the children of such "pretenders" wanted to insist that their immediate ancestors *had* in fact known what was to befall—and that it was their very knowledge that had paralyzed them.[22]

Interestingly, although the Florentine Codex at first uses mystical language and has Moctezuma and his advisers trembling in fear at ominous portents during the time that the Spaniards are on their way, it changes in tone completely when warfare later erupts in the capital.[23] The book suddenly offers a technical and very detailed description of battle scenes. ("At the first shot the wall did not give way, but the second time it began to crumble." Or: "For a little while the Spaniards' boats were grounded. They were there for a short time while they adjusted their guns.") This in fact makes perfect sense: the old men being interviewed as sources in the 1550s would have been young warriors in 1521, participants in the battles, or at least eyewitnesses. On the other hand, they would have had no real idea of what transpired within Moctezuma's inner circle. The king's advisers were old men even in 1519, and most of them died in the conquest. So the writers of the book—the students at the School of Tlatelolco—were free to present whatever scenario they found most satisfying. They turned to portents and prophecies.

The most famous prophecy in which the Indians in general were supposed to have believed was that the god Quetzalcoatl had long ago disappeared into the east and was expected to return in 1519. The messages that passed back and forth from the coast to Tenochtitlan while Cortés and his entourage waited on the beach purportedly concerned this subject. In the codex, Moctezuma sends gifts for four different gods to see which are most welcome to the newcomers. He then determines that it is

Quetzalcoatl who has come. There are, however, serious problems with this story—beyond the fact that it does not coincide at all with Cortés's record of events. First, Quetzalcoatl was not in fact a particularly prominent deity, except perhaps in the altepetl of Cholula. And his depiction elsewhere in the codex as a peace-loving god who abhorred sacrifice has no basis whatsoever in any preconquest sources. Second, in the Florentine, when Juan de Grijalva lands on the coast in what we know was 1518, the writers of the codex assert that the people believed *he* was Quetzalcoatl. So much for the perfect coincidence of 1519.

Anthropologists have analyzed all the existing sixteenth-century references to the Quetzalcoatl story. Through their work, we can see how the narrative gradually came into existence and gained acceptance. There really was, of course, a god called Quetzalcoatl, a feathered serpent, a boundary maker and transgressor, often understood to be the wind. In the calendar, he was tied to the year One Reed, which is correlated to 1519 and other cyclically repeating years. But the Feathered Serpent had not gone away and was not prophesied to return. (Nahua gods never did that; they were an integral part of the cosmos.) In Nahua lore, there was also a wandering mortal hero called Huemac or Topiltzin ("Our Lord," meaning "our nobleman") who figured in various ancient stories. In some narratives, he was exiled, and his return was occasionally expected. The Franciscan friar Motolinia, writing in the 1540s, for the first time gave such a hero the name "Quetzalcoatl" and said he was apotheosized into a god. (Deserving mortals often become gods in European mythology, but they do not generally do so in the Nahua world.) The priest added that when the people first saw the Europeans' white sails, they apparently thought that this same Quetzalcoatl was returning, "bringing by sea his own temples." Then, having heard that all the Spaniards were supposed to have been treated as gods, he quickly added, "When they disembarked, they said that it was not their god, but rather many gods."[24]

In the 1560s, the Florentine Codex (produced, remember, under the aegis of another Franciscan priest) drew all the pieces together into the story familiar to us today, though references to the more traditional god Quetzalcoatl as well as to a separate hero named Huemac still appeared in other volumes in the codex. The writers amplified some, claiming that Quetzalcoatl was actually a Christian saint who had visited their lands years earlier and been exiled. This was a motif that was growing in popularity among Christian friars at the time; later, when they went to China, they would come to believe that a saint had preceded them there as well.[25]

In about 1570, the Nahua author of the Annals of Cuauhtitlan, who was well aware of the project going on at the School of Tlatelolco, included a version of the story in his work, though without the prophecy of a return. It was the first time that a Nahua working apart from Spanish priests and writing in his own language had mentioned it at all. He said that a peaceful king named Quetzalcoatl had so abhorred the idea of human sacrifice that he fled to the east and later was transformed into the planet Venus. In the midst of claiming that the king's priests were the first to invent the grisly practice, the writer suddenly seemed to become uncomfortable. (After all, he himself had penned earlier stories of sacrifice only a few pages before.) Apparently deferring to his friends at the School of Tlatelolco, he said, "That has been put on paper elsewhere and there it is to be heard." Most likely, the author of the annals was attempting to integrate something he had heard elsewhere—and was somewhat invested in believing—into the ancient stories of his people.[26]

Even if we discount the notion of the Indians' having believed that Cortés was Quetzalcoatl, however, the fact remains that except for Cortés, everyone—Spanish and Indian—later insisted that the indigenous did refer to the newcomers as *teotl* (plural *teteo'*), which the Spanish heard as *teul* and translated as "god." What we must ask ourselves, however, is what the Indians really meant by it. They certainly struggled at first to find any appropriate way to refer to the newcomers. In their world, people were labeled according to their altepetl. The Tenochca, for example, lived in Tenochtitlan. The strangers undoubtedly came from an altepetl somewhere on earth, but it was not in the known world. Years later, they would be called Caxtilteca (people of Castile), but that could only come when familiarity with the concept of a Spain or a Castile was widespread. Nor did the strangers at first have a political relationship to anyone. In certain texts, Cortés ceases to be called a "teotl" and is pointedly referred to as a "tecuhtli" (dynastic overlord) or even "tlatoani" (king) immediately after he has vanquished an altepetl and thus has authority over its people.[27] But the real man at first had no such connection to any altepetl. In a world of relationships, these newcomers had no relationship to any place or anyone. What, then, were they to be called?

Malintzin was probably one of the first to use the term "teotl"; she was, after all, doing most of the explaining. According to one story about the first interaction purportedly told by a Nahuatl speaker to a Spanish friar, Malintzin said, "The leader of these men says he has come to greet your master Motecuhzoma, that his only intention is to go to the city of Mexico." In the next interchange, she added, "These gods say that they kiss your hands and that they will eat." Standing there on shipboard, the woman called doña Marina may in fact have used the word "teotl." If she did not, someone else did soon thereafter, and it took hold. What exactly did the word "teotl" mean to those who adopted it?[28]

It could in fact mean what we would translate as a "god"—a capricious immortal over whom mortals had no control. It could also, however, refer to ceremonial human impersonators of such characters. Sometimes god impersonators in religious rites were destined for sacrifice and thus were special, sacred; sometimes they were wise and powerful priests who lived long lives. They wore the most extraordinary raiment and were set apart, owing allegiance to no earthly being. What Malintzin and others were probably trying to convey was something akin to "strange sorcerer" or "representatives of their gods."[29]

In fact, according to Bernal Díaz, after Malintzin first conveyed the nature of the word to Cortés in Cempoala, he laughed and said, "I think we'll send Heredia against them." Díaz explained: "Heredia was an old Basque musketeer with a very ugly face covered with scars, a huge beard, and one blind eye. He was also lame in one leg. . . . So old Heredia shouldered his musket and went off with [the Indians] firing shots in the air as he went. . . . And the caciques sent the news to the other towns that they were bringing along a *teul* to kill the Mexicans who were at Tizapatzinco."[30] The story would be almost incomprehensible if Cortés had been told that a teotl was a glorious and divine being. It makes perfect sense, on the other hand, if he understood that the word encompassed the notion of a weird and awful figure, like the deity impersonators of the ceremonies, who owed allegiance to no one and whose powers could be turned against Aztec overlords.

There is even a document existing in Spain, dictated by King Charles within months of his first hearing of Cortés's triumph, that indicates he had clearly been given to understand that the word "teul" referred to someone akin to a priest, a person with spiritual powers who was accorded authority and respect. "I charge you to take special and primary care to effect the conversion of the *teules* and Indians of those parts. . . . Because the Indians are so subject to their *teules* and *señores* [political lords] and so agreeable about following them in everything, it seems that our first path should be to attempt to instruct the said lords." Later he added, "Because it is just and reasonable that the Indians should serve us and pay us tribute, . . . and we are informed that they are accustomed to paying tribute to their *teules* and *señores*, I order you . . . to find out about the tribute that they have given to the *teules*."[31]

A word connoting some sort of sorcerer or priest would have been an appealing choice to indigenous people who were struggling to understand why these men, who seemed in some regards so foolish and naive, possessed such extraordinary metal equipment and other goods. A teotl might well be blind to certain realities and yet possess magnificent boats, weapons, and animals that he had received as gifts from the gods. Undoubtedly the Indians hungered for some explanation of what they were facing. Malintzin of all people—with her close proximity and her keenness of mind—knew that the Spanish certainly did *not* possess superior intelligence, yet somehow they had gained vastly superior technology. The Europeans could tell themselves they had these things because they were endowed with superior capacities, but the Indians who were intimately acquainted with them knew that such was not the case.

It would not be until the 1980s, more than four centuries later, that scientists would be able to provide information necessary to explain the discrepancy. At that time, it had already been clear for many years that those societies that turned away from hunting and gathering in favor of full-time agriculture saw their populations increase markedly and experienced a variety of other changes. The world's seasonally migrating peoples almost all experimented with cultivation on a part-time basis, but only some of them settled down and made it a permanent, year-round way of life. Those who did began to practice the kind of division of labor that led to the development of technology—transportation devices, calendars, writing, weaponry—and, as an indirect result, a panoply of germs and resistance to germs. The real question, then, was why some ancient peoples chose to settle down and become full-time farmers, while others waited several more millennia or never did it at all. The people of the Fertile Crescent began farming over eleven thousand years ago and their techniques soon spread through Europe; those in Mexico only became full-time farmers about four thousand years ago. The indigenous peoples in California were still hunter-gatherers when white settlers arrived in the nineteenth century. Their choices obviously had nothing to do with the land: California's land is certainly preferable to most of that of the Middle East. In the 1980s improved radiocarbon dating techniques for the remains of seeds provided information that allowed scientists in the 1990s to posit a reasonable explanation: people became farmers when there was a constellation of protein-rich crops available to them. They did not do so when such plants were lacking in the environment.[32]

It is a highly risky endeavor for a people to make the transition from hunting and gathering to farming. Crops may fail before there is a stored surplus, or raiders may steal the fruits of one's labor, and men no longer have much time to hunt. Whether or not it is ultimately worth it depends on the plants. It makes absolutely no sense to turn to farming—except on a part-time basis—for the likes of sugar cane or bananas, for example. People simply cannot live on them. It makes perfect sense, however, to do it for the protein-rich wheat and barley and peas that were present in the Fertile Crescent. In ancient times, there must surely have been people in all parts of the world who experimented, and there were undoubtedly some in each region who resisted experimentation. But statistically speaking, it was no accident that certain continents ultimately saw the early growth of farming—and thus of technology—while others did not.

Mexico, of course, had corn. Why, then, did the Mesoamericans not turn to farming as quickly as the Old World peoples? The ancient ancestor of corn, it turns out, was not nearly so useful as ancient wheat and peas. Indeed, after the millennia of part-time cultivation that it took to turn the nearly useless wild teosinte, with its tiny head of even tinier kernels, into something larger and more filling, and after the gradual realization that corn was more satisfying when eaten together with beans, Mesoamericans became very serious full-time agriculturalists.[33] At that point, though, they were still in the Stone Age, while the Middle Easterners—and the Europeans and Asians who had imported their techniques—had moved far ahead, technologically speaking, having already experienced thousands of years of sedentary living. The people of the Old World were to have a distinct advantage when the continents collided.

All of this, of course, was unfathomable to Malintzin, as well as to the

Spaniards whom she was aiding. In fact, their ultimate advantages not-withstanding, the Spaniards at this point were few in number, and they were scared. In 1519, despite what they said later, they do not seem to have felt convinced that the Indians worshipped them. They slept in their armor. And some of them continued to grumble openly about wanting to go home. When a planned mutiny came to the attention of Cortés, he hanged two of the ringleaders. Then he made a decision. He asked Puertocarrero, as an influential personage, to return to Spain. He could present their case to the king before Diego Velázquez could prejudice the monarch against them and then arrange to send more men and ships. The latter would certainly be needed, for he still planned to attempt to bring down Moctezuma. Five hundred men did not alone have the power to permanently defeat a great indigenous empire, but Spain, taken as a whole, certainly did. To make certain that Puertocarrero arrived safely, he sent Antonio de Alaminos as his pilot, or navigator. Alaminos had more experience navigating the New World than any other man there: he had even been along on one of Cristóbal Colón's original voyages.

When all this had been arranged, Cortés scuttled most of the remaining ships, ensuring that none of the other men would begin to entertain seri-ous thoughts about departing. For some messengers to return was crucial, but in a land populated by millions of Indians, he needed the rest of his men to stay right where they were. Then he demanded that the Totonacs provide him with burden bearers and warriors. At the last moment, he also took some of their chiefs hostage in order to guarantee the safety of the fifty Spaniards who were going to remain behind at the new city of Veracruz when the others set off to visit the Mexica capital.

It is impossible to read the thoughts of the hostage Totonac chiefs or of Moctezuma's spies, who watched from the hills as Puertocarrero hoisted the sails of the flagship and set off, together with the Totonac Indian woman who had been forced to become his new mistress. As of that moment, none of them knew enough to be sure of anything; they would soon learn more about the nature of these strangers. But clearly each man saw the situation from a particular point of view and had his own people's concerns and agenda uppermost in mind.

And Malintzin? She does not seem to have faltered. She was deter-mined, apparently, to make the best of what could have been a very bad situation. There were even aspects of the events that she may have found compelling, given her background. Her feelings had to have been laced with fear to some degree, for many would see the Spaniards' venture as foolhardy in the extreme. But the expedition was not necessarily doomed. Malintzin was familiar with the history of more than one people. In the histories she knew, the ancestors of future kingdoms always traveled from some distant land to the place where they were meant to settle. Their footprints traced a twisting path, past mountains, rivers, and critical junctures where their god helped them. It most likely did not seem incomprehensible to her that this group of strangers was determined to cross the land, find Moctezuma, and attempt to conquer him.

She turned her back to the sea and started to walk.

THREE

One of Us People Here

To the hungry Spanish, the turkeys that the Indian visitors brought to their camp looked appetizing indeed. There were dozens of them trussed together, agitating desperately against their wooden cages. The men who brought the food addressed the handsomely dressed noblewoman who had received them and was to arrange for payment. "O doña Marina," they began. But they spoke in their own language, of course. To add a title of respect to the name they pronounced "Malina" they said "Malintzin," "-tzin" being a typical honorific. And they used a form of address. At home, speaking to someone they loved, they would simply have added a syllable at the end: "Malintziné." But here, wishing to maintain their dignity and avoid any sense that they spoke with affection, they shortened the ending "-tzine" simply to "-tze." "Malintze," they said. The Spanish heard "Malinche."[1]

As the visitors laid their gifts before the young noblewoman, they puzzled over who she was. Her very existence in the Spanish camp initiated the need for a new social category, one that would encompass all people who could be defined in opposition to the newcomers, to the Spanish. Messengers returned to Moctezuma and informed him that the strangers were accompanied by "a woman, one of us people here."[2] Someday in the not-so-distant future, they would be well enough versed in world geography to understand the Spaniards' line of thinking when they used the word "Indians," but at this point, naturally, they could not.

If, however, Malintzin was in some ways to be grouped with the people who had always lived on this side of the sea, in other ways, she clearly was not. In addressing her, the indigenous visitors understood that she represented a foreign entity hitherto unknown to them. The well-armored strangers apparently represented the same entity. When the visitors turned to Cortés and spoke directly to him, despite his lack of comprehension, they addressed him as "Malintze," too. And when another Spaniard eventually began to learn their language and started to converse with them himself, they addressed him by the same title. Later, they would develop their own theories as to whom all three represented. In the meantime, Malintzin was their initial reference point; others in her party took on meaning in relation to her.[3]

For she was the speaker. It was she who had been chosen by the Spaniards to make statements on behalf of the whole group. To the Nahuas, that was the crux of the matter. The word for a ruler—"tlatoani"—meant "he who speaks." She was not a ruler, but there were probably moments when it appeared as though she had comparable powers. In the indigenous world, priests and priestesses were also speakers, uttering the sacred rhetoric handed down for generations, reminding their hearers to follow the way of duty and preserve a universe that would otherwise fall into chaos.[4] In the homes of noblemen, performers sang poems aloud, drums beating, rattles pulsating. They vied to create memorable songs—always relying on tried-and-true patterns, subjects, and imagery but giving them new twists or singing the praises of a new king. Priests and priestesses had pictoglyphic texts to remind them what to say, but songs were memorized without such aids and passed from hearer to hearer. Talented singer-poets could become renowned in their own region, and some of these were women. Nezahualpilli, the tlatoani of Tetzcoco, had recently put to death one of his sons and one of his concubines for flirting publicly in their singing. Or so the gossips said.[5] Thus when the young noblewoman Malintzin spoke, and others around her grew silent to listen, it was an unusual sight, but not unheard of.

Moreover, the visitors soon learned that she was a talented speaker; they could trust her comprehension of their own statements and understand her responses and admonishments clearly. When a European boy who was learning their language began to try to speak to them, they sometimes found his performance came up short and demanded her presence. In one disastrous battle, the Spaniards ended up killing some allies because they couldn't understand them; Cortés admitted on that occasion that they could have benefited from the presence of an interpreter.[6]

Usually when the Spaniards told their tales, they liked to pretend they had not really needed their translators. Cortés must have written parts of his letters to Charles V in Malintzin's very presence, yet he mentioned her rarely and only once by name. He was typical of other Europeans in this regard, desiring those who had never been to the New World to believe so completely in his own heroic capableness that he pretended— or at least implied—that he could simply speak to the Indians himself. Many armchair explorers believed him; the idea of facile communication with the indigenous—whose supposedly simple ways and simple languages theoretically did not need much translation—was one of the great myths cherished by Europeans. One scholar has gone so far as to speak of the "systematic suppression of the native voice" in the colonizer's letters home, beginning with Columbus. Perhaps those doing the writing did sometimes keep silent about their translators on purpose; those credulous people reading the accounts back home, though, were simply enjoying a fantasy, without paying conscious heed to the matter.[7]

In subtle and not-so-subtle ways, however, the Europeans gave away their dependence in their actions and their writings. In their expeditions, they were alone in a vast land where they understood nothing and no one; they were completely reliant on the young victims of kidnapping they had with them or on the likes of Malintzin and accidental translation chains. The Europeans would go to almost any lengths to attain translators; Cortés had waited on the coast for many days to try to make contact with Jerónimo de Aguilar, as he had reason to believe there were shipwreck survivors in the area, and he responded with lightning speed when he saw Marina's capabilities. His biographer Gómara conveyed the sense of the issue years later when he wrote that Cortés asked her to be his *feraute*, or "herald," one who went before him to speak to the Indians.[8] To the emperor Charles, Cortés referred to Malintzin simply as *la lengua*— "the tongue," "the translator"—but in practice he knew her role was a profoundly influential one.

Years later, a man named Francisco de Aguilar, who had been a follower of Cortés but then had renounced worldly wealth to become a Dominican, dictated a brief narrative of the expedition on his deathbed. He explicitly mentioned Malintzin only once—but still demonstrated that she loomed large in his mind. In his first paragraph, Cortés and his followers set out; in the second, they pick up Jerónimo de Aguilar. (Tired and forgetful, the friar called him "Hernando de Aguilar.") In the third paragraph, the Spanish land their weapons at the Río Grijalva and win a major victory; in the fourth, they receive Marina.[9]

It was not simply that the Spanish needed their translators in order to find their way and obtain requisite food and water. They needed them for far more than this—for conquest itself. They *could* win a military victory on their own, and if they only wanted to collect some tribute and pass on, as at Putunchan, then language was not critical. But if they wanted to extend Spain's dominion—and Cortés explicitly did—then a translator had to be present to convey the meaning of the military victory, the new set of expectations, to those who had been conquered. These early translators had to be liminal people, figures who had lived in both arenas and understood something about both worlds, in order to be truly effective. They had to be one of "us people here," and yet not. Children who had been kidnapped and forced to live with the Spanish for years were perfect.

Spanish castaways like Jerónimo de Aguilar would do, but only just: such men had been left to learn a foreign language as adults, with no conduits to help them and with strong psychological reasons to resist becoming thoroughly embedded in the host culture. Aguilar's Christianity encouraged him in such stubbornness, as did the hope of eventual rescue that he clearly cherished.[10] Malintzin, on the other hand, was particularly talented as well as young; she still had her inborn ability to learn languages intact. She also had Jerónimo de Aguilar there to help her learn, to answer her questions. Psychologically speaking, she was not in a position to yearn for her old home or to resist learning to think as the strangers did. She knew that her survival was dependent on the Spaniards' survival, so she was motivated to observe them carefully; undoubtedly her years as a slave had honed her skills in that regard. It is perhaps not surprising that by all accounts she learned Spanish and Spanish ways quickly, that Jerónimo de Aguilar became less and less important and she more and more so as the months passed. By 1524—and probably much sooner—Cortés no longer called on Aguilar at all; by then, Malintzin did all his translation between Spanish, Nahuatl, and Maya.[11]

For Malintzin could do more than repeat what others said in a foreign vocabulary. As a liminal person, she could speak in different registers and thus make a necessary point more effectively. We cannot trust Bernal Díaz to tell us exactly what she said to the Spanish, but we can trust him to convey the impression she had made on him. He liked her; all the Spaniards who depended on her competence seemed to like and admire her. Bernal Díaz communicates her good-humored courage, which they appreciated; he also conveys that she spoke to them archly or coquettishly if need be— in other words, that she knew how to handle her Spanish male audience. Such an approach, however, would never have worked with her Nahua audiences, who were also largely male. With them, she spoke rhetorically, formally, high-handedly. They could accept a noblewoman's having the floor and could even be persuaded by her into action, but only if she spoke like a *cihuatecuhtli*, "a lady of power," not if she spoke like a playful girl. A playful girl should respect her elders, not tell them what to do. She knew this and adjusted her tone accordingly.

She was to need all her skills, linguistic and otherwise, as they marched from the sea to Tenochtitlan. Tlaxcala was the first major kingdom that they passed through. Much has been made of the Tlaxcalans' siding with the Spanish, but on that first day of contact in September of 1519, they threw down the gauntlet and fought for their lives and their autonomy. They continued to fight for eighteen bloody days.

By the time the battles began the Spanish were already tense. The gradual ascent from sea level had worn them down. The days were hot and dry and left them parched with thirst. The nights were cold, and they did not have the right clothing for the climate. A few of the Caribbean Indians they had with them died after a hail- and rainstorm hit and left them all drenched, freezing, and exhausted. When they stopped at a settlement, Cortés asked through his interpreters that the chief give them food and gold and swear fealty to the emperor Charles. The man refused, saying he would not do so without Moctezuma's permission. Cortés was feeling far from invulnerable. "So as not to offend him and for fear that some calamity might befall my endeavor and my journey, I dissembled as best I could and told him that very soon I would have Mutezuma order him to give the gold and all that he owned."[12]

When that incident occurred, they were already near the lands of the Tlaxcalans, whom the Cempoalan allies said would be friendly, as they were the avowed enemies of Moctezuma. Two Cempoalan chiefs went ahead as messengers, but though Cortés waited eight days, they did not return. The outlook was thus doubtful, but Cortés felt strongly—and with good reason—that the only way to go was forward, as any sign of weakness would lose him the allies that he had. They set out and soon came across a nine-foot-high barrier wall built of stone "which ran right across the valley, from one mountain range to the other." It was shaped like a prism, as if it were an extended pyramid: at its base, it was twenty feet wide, and at the top it culminated in a flat walkway a foot and a half wide. They had, it seemed, reached the Tlaxcalan border. Despite the forbidding scene, the Cempoalan allies continued to insist that all would be well, or at least that they were better off crossing this territory than that of Moctezuma's allies.

Cortés passed through an opening in the wall and rode forward to explore with half a dozen horsemen. They saw about fifteen armed warriors up ahead and called out to them. Cortés sent one of the riders back at a gallop in case reinforcements should be needed, and then he and the others approached the Indians. Suddenly, they were surrounded by hundreds. (Cortés reported that it was four or five thousand, to shield himself from blame, but that is unlikely.) Two of the horses were killed and two riders gravely injured before more of the Spanish force approached and the two sides retreated from each other. Cortés had learned a valuable lesson: six armored men were not enough to withstand an onslaught, not even if they were mounted.

Later that day, Tlaxcalan emissaries arrived, saying they regretted the actions of the warriors. The belligerents, they said, had been Otomí, who lived within their territories but took their own counsel. That much was certainly true. The emissaries also said they themselves wanted to be friends and toured the camp before they left.[13]

The Tlaxcalan forces attacked at dawn and fought all day. They suffered far more casualties than the Spanish, but the Spanish were weakening from hunger, exhaustion, and fever. They were surrounded by a sea of enemies. "Any of our soldiers who was bold enough to break ranks and pursue their swordsmen or captains was immediately wounded and in great danger," Bernal Díaz wrote later. "We dared not charge them except all together for fear they might break our ranks."[14] The Tlaxcalans withdrew only when darkness made it impossible for them to see. That night, Cortés took the thirteen horsemen who remained and galloped over the dry, flat plain to the surrounding hills where lighted fires signaled the presence of villages. "I burnt five or six small places of about a hundred inhabitants."[15]

The next day at dawn, the Indian army attacked again, coming in such force that they were able to enter the camp and engage in hand-to-hand combat. It took four hours for Spanish armor and weaponry to drive them back effectively, and they continued to fight beyond the bounds of the camp for the rest of the day. "One thing alone saved our lives: the enemy were so massed and numerous that every shot wrought havoc among them."[16] Many dozens of Tlaxcalan men died that day, each one swept up into the arms of his comrades and carried off the field.

One Spaniard was killed.

That night, in the darkness before the light, Cortés once again led the horsemen in breaking out of the camp and galloping across the plain, this time in the opposite direction. "I burnt more than ten villages." In the largest, he said, the inhabitants fought back, but there were no warriors there to help them, and they did the armored Spaniards little harm.

Over the next two days, the chiefs of Tlaxcala sued for peace. But one young lord named Xicotencatl would not be mollified. He, too, sent messengers speaking of peace, but something or someone alerted Cortés to the doubtfulness of his overtures. Or perhaps he always tested. In any case, he said that he "ordered one of the [messengers] to be captured discreetly, so that the others did not see." Through the interpreters, Cortés threatened him. Presumably, he tortured him, as was routine in European warfare. If Malintzin blanched, she likely hid it. She herself had lived among enemy peoples, in a world in which slaves were as likely as not to have their hearts cut out. She certainly, however, could no longer have believed that the Christian god was one of peace, if she ever had. "I took all fifty [of the messengers from Xicotencatl]," wrote Cortés to his monarch, "and cut off their hands and sent them to tell their chief that by day or by night, or whenever they chose to come, they would see who we were."[17]

They came that night. Cortés said he was afraid they would follow his own example and set fire to the camp "which would have been so disastrous that none . . . would have escaped." So he met them fully armed for battle before they reached the camp. Unable to penetrate the wall of armored Spanish, they retreated.

After a few days of rest, during which the Indians watched him warily, Cortés continued with his strategy, using the speed and power that the horses gave to his advantage:

> Before it was dawn I attacked two towns, where I killed many people, but I did not burn the houses lest the fires should alert the other towns nearby. At dawn I came upon another large town. . . . As I took them by surprise, they rushed out unarmed, and the women and children ran naked through the streets, and I began to do them some harm.[18]

Some men of rank approached and begged for peace, promising to be obedient to the strangers' king. "They would rather be Your Highness's vassals than see their houses destroyed and their wives and children killed," Cortés said matter-of-factly.[19] Bernal Díaz later elaborated: "Cortés told them through our interpreters, who accompanied us on every expedition, even a night foray, that they need have no fear, but must go at once to the caciques in the capital and tell them to come and make peace, since the war was disastrous for them."[20] Surely by now Malintzin, who conveyed something like these words amidst the uproar in the early morning light, was herself convinced that it would do these people little good to continue to fight. Even if she and the group she was with should perish from hunger and exhaustion, she had understood enough of the Spaniards' conversation by now to know that more were coming. Indeed, it was those very arriving hordes whom the current cohort wished to beat to the spoils. However she put it, she put it well: the Tlaxcalan chiefs opted to save their people's lives and ally with the strangers who, she assured them, truly wanted their friendship. The war with Tlaxcala ended that night.

In the days that followed, Tlaxcala became the first altepetl to attempt to construct a permanent working relationship with the Spaniards—one that would placate the newcomers without tearing asunder the worldview and habits of the people. Their kingdom was what is called a "complex altepetl": it was composed of at least four equal states, each with its own tlatoani, each independent, and yet each one part of the greater whole. It reflected, in essence, the typical Nahua social and political arrangement, but on a larger scale. Thus the Spanish dealt with several kings, not one, in their negotiations. The homes of four of the kings, including the two most powerful, were clustered quite near to each other, creating what the Spanish perceived to be the "city of Tlaxcala"; they themselves actually stayed in one quadrant, the settlement surrounding the king's house in Tizatlan, while they conducted their exchanges.[21]

Malintzin literally stood at the heart of these negotiations. Her people in Coatzacoalcos had long been trading partners of the Tlaxcalans, though recently the travel routes had been cut off by the militant Mexica, whose allies now had Tlaxcala surrounded. According to Tlaxcala's cultural memory a generation later, the people had liked and trusted their translator. She certainly loomed large in their memory, appearing in dozens of illustrations of the conquest that proliferated in the city and its environs.

In all the sixteenth-century codices where Malintzin appears, whether in Tlaxcala or elsewhere, she emerges as a significant presence in the indigenous imagination. She is always portrayed as a beautifully dressed and well-shod noblewoman. Her figure is as large or larger than that of Cortés; she commands speech glyphs and receives tribute, both crucial signifiers in the Nahua world. Beyond these commonalities, though, accounts diverge. In some places, like Tlaxcala, she is envisioned as a more important presence and a more positive influence than in other places.[22]

The surviving Tlaxcalan images of Malintzin are worth examining carefully in the order in which they were produced, for they reveal not only what kinds of sociopolitical arrangements good translators made possible, but also how memory of those arrangements faded with time, almost disappearing from the sources in relatively short order and making our understanding of the earliest period of contact difficult indeed. We have tended to look at pictures produced later in the sixteenth century, assuming that they tell us more or less what Indians were thinking at contact, but they do not. Malintzin, in her day, negotiated complexities of which we can only catch glimpses at this point.

Before the conquest, the Nahuas painted (or wrote—they used the same word) on bark or animal skins or paper made of maguey fibers. They produced foldout books as well as individual maps or sheets of records. The books were mostly ceremonial in nature, probably used almost exclusively by priests, but the individual sheets were often very public agreements: they might commemorate the founding of a community, divide up land, outline a calendar, or record the demand for tribute or its payment. Each page was virtually completely covered with brightly colored, two-dimensional, complex interlocking images that contained within them stylized glyphs bearing familiar meanings to those who were trained to recite on seeing them (fig. 1).

FIGURE 1: Stripe Eye's journey begins. Plate 35 of *The Codex Borgia: A Full-Color Restoration of the Ancient Mexican Manuscript,* by Gisele Díaz and Alan Rodgers, with commentary by Bruce E. Byland (New York: Dover Publications, 1993), reproduced with permission of the authors. Historic and ritual journeys are a significant theme in surviving preconquest art. The Codex Borgia originated in the south central highlands.

FIGURE 2: Cortés attacks the people. Detail from the Huamantla Codex, sixteenth century. Probably of Otomí origin, in the region of Tlaxcala. Courtesy of the Instituto Nacional de Antropología e Historia, Mexico.

After the conquest, at the behest of curious Spaniards, many codices were produced in which some of those preconquest glyphs were removed from their context and placed against a blank backdrop for easier identification. Doing so made their meanings appear far simpler than they ever were when they were embedded in complicated and dynamic pages. At the same time, native artists began to learn the techniques required to represent three-dimensional space. As they began to use their new skills sporadically and without having had much practice, their work appeared primitive in a way that it never had in the old days. We must keep all this in mind as we sift through the sixteenth-century visual evidence, lest we unconsciously draw conclusions about relative ability. Later, of course, indigenous artists and craftsmen would produce some of the most beautiful images of the colonial era.

Just east of Tlaxcala, in the altepetl of Huamantla, a painted roll was produced not long after the conquest: its images are strongly reminiscent of precontact forms, though less intricate. The ancestors of the people, probably Otomí, travel along a complex and circuitous historical route, full of prayers, battles, and temporary stopping points. At the very edge of the sheet, the arrival of the Spaniards is shown. This part speaks of particularly bloody battles, of warriors surrounded by mounted Spaniards,

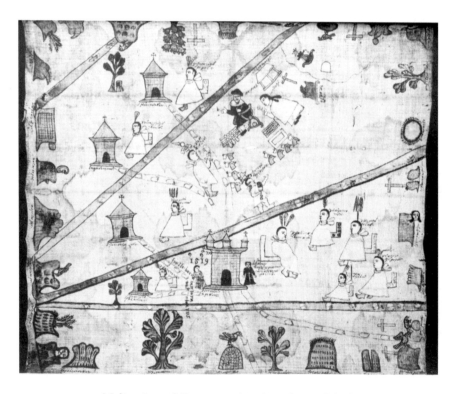

FIGURE 3: Malintzin and Cortés receive the tribute of the local lords. Mapa de San Antonio Tepetlan, sixteenth century. From the region south of Veracruz. The ocean is visible in the distance. Courtesy of the American Museum of Natural History.

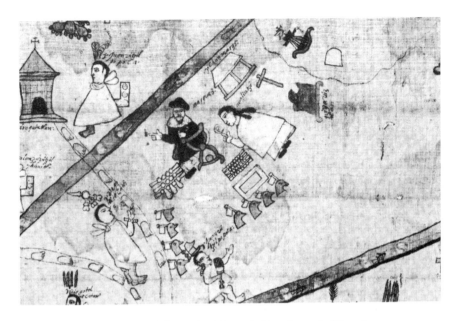

FIGURE 4: Detail from the Mapa de San Antonio Tepetlan.

who are being forced to offer gifts and sue for peace. A bitter military defeat was clearly uppermost in the artist's mind. Malintzin has no place here and there is no reference to her (fig. 2).[23]

At about the same time, in Tepetlan, Coatzacoalcos and Tlaxcala—where apparently no battles were fought—someone else recorded the events of 1519 a generation or so later. The Mapa de San Antonio de Tepetlan offers a warm rendering of Malintzin. Preconquest glyphs appear side by side with a few Spanish-style images of churches; the general arrangement is reminiscent of the old style. Streams and roads crisscross a farming valley, with the sea in the distant background. From different points come the named chiefs or tecuhtli of the four parts of the altepetl to pay their respects to Cortés, who rests on a European seat of power, as well as to Malintzin, who is standing next to him and speaking. They have each received eighty turkeys and some gold jewelry, and she, in addition, has been offered a blanket (figs. 3, 4).[24]

By the 1540s—and probably earlier—Tlaxcalans had begun to represent their own first meeting with the Spaniards in a similar way. They began with the peace negotiations and expunged all references to the initial military resistance; the mediator Malintzin thus plays a starring role. By that time, they were busy defending to all the world a special status granted to them by Cortés in the 1520s and confirmed by the Crown in 1535: as a reward for their services during the conquest, they were to answer directly to the monarch and not be placed under the power of any other Spaniard. Under the circumstances, it little behooved them to mention their initial fierce resistance; it would have been counterproductive to say the least. A set of images reflecting their mid-century memory of the coming of the Spanish was produced—probably having been inspired by some commemorative pictures on the wall of the king's house, or *teccalli*, at Tizatlan—and later was copied and amended so many times and in so many ways that following the story of the various versions of what has short-handedly been called the "Lienzo de Tlaxcala" is itself a daunting task. One relatively early version, now lost to us, was an actual *lienzo*, or painting on a large piece of cloth. It hung on the wall of the city council in the town; copies of it—or of a closely related version—were produced on cloth and on paper, and some of these have survived. The images they contain are familiar to people who read about colonial Latin America, for they have been chosen to illustrate many works.[25]

However, the earliest extant version of the conquest pictorials, probably dating from the 1530s or 1540s, is quite different and is almost certainly closely related to the original images that were painted on the teccalli wall in Tizatlan. It reveals minute details very much in keeping with what we know of altepetl politics: it probably represents a relatively accurate record of what transpired during the peace negotiations, although it may obfuscate or exaggerate in certain regards, in that the paintings were not only designed to seal the pact that had been made but also to emphasize Tizatlan's loyalty and importance to Spain. After all, the members of the chiefly line of Tizatlan needed to offer some reassurances—both to the Spanish and to their own people—as to what the leaders thought they were doing, for it was the aging king's son, Xicotencatl the Younger, who held out longest against the Spaniards.

On a rectangular piece of bark paper that is folded in half and appears to be a fragment of a larger work, there are four scenes. They include precontact glyphs and spatial arrangements, but the people and horses are drawn in the Spanish style. The painter left no room for written words in the Roman alphabet, which were not in common use among the Nahuas

FIGURE 5: Marina and Cortés arrive in Atlihuetzyan.
Scene One of the "Texas Fragment," the earliest known version of the
Tlaxcalan conquest pictorials. Courtesy of the Nettie Lee Benson
Collection of the University of Texas Library.

until at least the 1540s, but someone squeezed some explanations in after the fact, lest posterity forget.[26]

In the first scene, Cortés and his mounted men travel through Atlihuetzyan, in Tizatlan. The traditional sign for travel, a road with footprints leading in a certain direction, has been amended to include hoofprints. Malintzin stands in front, the most visible figure of all, in gorgeous raiment, speaking to the lord Tepolouatecatl, a noble member of Xicotencatl's family. Kings always sent envoys before appearing themselves; the practice demonstrated their own importance. The Tlaxcalan lord offers the Spanish visitors birds, bread, and corn (fig. 5).

In the next scene, Malintzin still stands at the fore, head raised proudly like a true noblewoman. Cortés has dismounted and reaches out to clasp the hand of Xicotencatl—either the king or his son, it does not matter—who has come to greet him in person for the first time. Behind him come five Indian lords whose moving hands indicate that they are speaking to Malintzin, as she signs back (fig. 6).

In scene three, the whole party has repaired to Xicotencatl's home. The two kings sit, each with one hand raised to represent speech, and Malintzin stands before them, speaking to both, both hands moving. On one side the Spanish men wait, their all-important horses tied near them; on the other side are the lords of Tlaxcala's other sub-altepetls. Much of the page is taken up by traditional glyphs representing certain quantities of goods—turkey, quail, corn, tortillas, and eggs. It was a primary purpose of traditional painting to make accurate records of tribute payments or gifts, and the artists seem to have done so here. Perhaps the Tlaxcalans were paid for the food or perhaps not: when a war ended, it was always a matter open to interpretation in later years as to whether gifts had been given voluntarily by an altepetl choosing to opt for peace or were tribute exacted from a defeated political entity (fig. 7).[27]

In the last scene the artists came to the point, just as the actual participants would have arrived at it, in typical Nahua style, after a formal exchange of polite words and gifts. The Tlaxcalans wanted Malintzin to convey that they desired to make Cortés and his men their kin by marrying their daughters to them, just as they would have attempted to end almost any other war. In fact, they offered three kinds of girls—magnificently dressed princesses, well-dressed lords' daughters, and plainly dressed commoners who were probably slaves. The wide array fits perfectly with

FIGURE 6: Xicotencatl comes to greet the arrivals.
Scene Two of the "Texas Fragment."

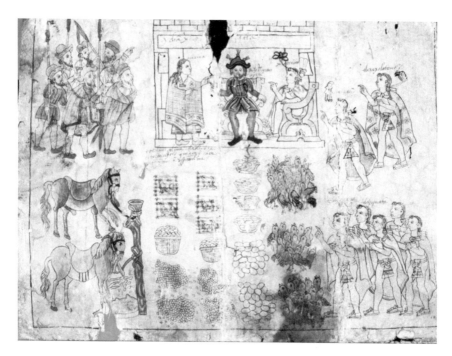

Figure 7: The negotiations. Scene Three of the "Texas Fragment."

what we know of Nahua culture. The kind of women offered at a war's end depended on the kind of defeat suffered and the altepetl's hopes for the future peace. Slave girls could be offered as a gesture of submission, or the king's own daughter could be offered as a marriage partner for the enemy tlatoani in hopes of building an alliance. Sometimes reality was fuzzy, and kingdoms had to do both, uncertain of results. Such was apparently the case here (fig. 8).[28]

Malintzin, who had herself lost her home in a somewhat similar fashion, now found herself in the position of receiving and instructing a passel of girls being given into the custody of her camp, her household. In the picture, she faces five princesses, head thrown back, admonishing them, while they listen silently, hands clasped in the accepted demure fashion. Beneath them, someone later squeezed in the words, "Here are painted [that is, recorded] the noblewomen who were the children of kings who were given to the captain." The person writing could still remember the names of three of them: two daughters of Xicotencatl the Elder, Tlecuiluatzin

Figure 8: The giving of the women. Scene Four of the "Texas Fragment."

and Tolquequetzaltzin, and another girl named Couaxochtzin, probably the daughter of Maxixcatzin of Ocotelolco, the other significant power in Tlaxcala. The first was renamed "doña Luisa" and given to Pedro de Alvarado. The others, Bernal Díaz thought he remembered, were given to Juan Velázquez de León, Gonzalo de Sandoval, Cristóbal de Olid, and Alonso de Avila.[29]

At least two of the other more minor lords' daughters appeared in Spanish legal records later: one was given to Juan Pérez de Arteaga, who was busy trying to learn Nahuatl, and another went to Jerónimo de Aguilar, who was still a crucial linguistic link.[30] Translators were important; Cortés rewarded them. And it was probably not lost on him that living with Nahuatl-speaking women would only help the men improve their language skills. Both sides remember the Spanish as having offered, through Malintzin, elaborate thanks as well as promises that the girls would be treated well, according to their station. In fact, however, these women, the daughters of tlatoani and tecuhtli, would spend the rest of their lives seeking marriage and the legitimization of their children; only a very few would get what they wanted, what their fathers had envisioned when they gave them away. When, however, the earliest version of the conquest pictorials was painted, the Tlaxcalans clearly still believed in the significance of the politically motivated marriages and wanted to advertise them at home and abroad.

The Tlaxcalans may have made such a picture to accompany their 1535 petition to the Crown to have the special arrangement Cortés had offered them formalized. In 1552 their city council records tell us that they prepared a new version to accompany another petition concerning their political status. At that point, the leaders were no longer making a statement partly to their own people but, rather, were addressing themselves entirely to the Spanish, whom they now knew quite well. In the beautiful and lengthy lienzo dating from this era, the political marriages between Spanish men and Indian women have disappeared. In one image, the byline says, "They gave them gifts," and a large cluster of indistinguishable young women appear next to other gifts of jewelry and textiles. The substance of the conversations that took place in September of 1519 has been obliterated (fig. 9).[31]

What is remembered instead is Malintzin herself, and with her the process of negotiation, the period of mutual aid between Tlaxcalan and

FIGURE 9: The Indians give the Spaniards gifts. Plate Seven of the Lienzo de Tlaxcala, mid-sixteenth century. Reproduced from *El Lienzo de Tlaxcala*, ed. Mario de la Torre (Mexico City: Cartón y Papel de México, 1983).

Spaniard. Malintzin appears in eighteen out of the forty-eight scenes of the first part. She is beautiful, larger than life—most often larger than Cortés. She is rich, wearing a gorgeous new huipilli and skirt in almost every town she passes through, along with European footwear, though the indigenous noblemen wear sandals. She expertly supervises the collection of tribute on the Spaniards' behalf. The Tlaxcalans fight everywhere alongside the Spanish, and their alliance is symbolized in the person of Malintzin herself: the men wear the twisted red and white headbands that all Tlaxcalan noblemen purportedly wore, and she wears red and white as well, often with a red and white twisted border on her cloak or skirt.

When she stands next to Xicotencatl's daughter, doña Luisa, their identical skirt decorations are particularly noticeable. In scene after scene, the Spaniards are in the capable hands of Indians. If there were ever pictures made by the indigenous that could elicit gratitude from the Spanish, these were those pictures.[32]

Clearly there is an agenda here; we cannot take this text at face value. But there is also truth embedded in it. The conversations about political marriages have been lost, but the Spanish really were dependent on Indians at this point, and Malintzin really was a beautiful and eloquent woman who had been given many gifts and undoubtedly wore sturdy footwear. If the Tlaxcalans had loathed her, they could not have produced such a work only one generation later. We are still catching glimpses of the difficult days of 1519 and 1520.

But not for long. By the end of the sixteenth century, the Spaniards who had actually known Malintzin were dead; the colonists by that point had lost sight of the desperate need for translators and gifts of food that their forebears had experienced. When the Tlaxcalans prepared another set of images to send to Europe in the 1580s, Malintzin was reduced to a relatively minor presence in comparison to earlier versions. In her place in almost every scene stands the cross, which the Tlaxcalans in the pictures eagerly accept. By the 1580s, the Tlaxcalans' best claim to fame was their early Christianization and their support of general conversion.[33] When we look at this source, even though it dates from the sixteenth century, we cannot learn anything about what really transpired at first contact.

Yet although the specifics of what Malintzin talked about or did were lost with the passage of time, the deep impression she made on her indigenous audience lasted. In the 1560s, the Nahua informants for the Florentine Codex mentioned her a number of times even when the Spanish priest editing their words did not think the matter important enough to include in his translations of what they said. At the turn of the seventeenth century, an indigenous historian descended from a tlatoani mentioned her as "la lengua" every time he had the chance, even noting that she was the intermediary when the Spanish received gifts of women. Another indigenous scholar reading the reference to her in the work by López de Gómara scribbled in the margin that she was called Tenepal, conveying the sense of "la lengua."[34]

These were educated Indians, familiar with Spanish traditions, but it was not only among the educated that memories of Malintzin survived. Stories about her passed from hand to hand, far beyond the circle of those who were witness to her actual translations. Some said that a famous "skull rack lord," a sorcerer who could make predictions, long known for having had four sons and then a fifth one who was to be their leader, had also given birth to a daughter. Her name was Malintzin. "And she too was a skull rack lord." A character named Malintzin also made her way into many folktales and came to be associated with la Llorona, an ancient female presence wailing in the wind. Perhaps she was the figure who eventually caused the green-skirted volcano near Tlaxcala, from which the rains descended, to be renamed "Malinche."[35]

To this day, a mythical Malintzin figures in countless local indigenous dances across Mexico: interestingly, someone named doña Marina is Cortés's translator while the woman named Malintzin has quite another role. She is a powerful consort, sometimes paired with Cortés and some-times with the indigenous king. In the stories of ancient times, founders of kingly lines attained legitimacy from a consort or a mother who was a goddess, or was named for a goddess, just as, in the world Malintzin inhabited, royal heirs needed to be born of royal mothers. In some of these dances, the character Malintzin does indeed have all the attributes of a goddess; in one, there is even a human impersonator who wears her skin, just as in the ancient ceremonies of sacrifice.[36]

There is also some sixteenth-century written evidence that the notion of Malintzin reverberated strongly with the concept of a legitimating con-sort. Her name is sometimes paired with that of Cortés in indigenous sources. In the Annals of Tlatelolco, one of the earliest Nahuatl documents we have, the two are treated as a couple. Cortés has implicitly married into the Aztec culture. A Mexica nobleman calls Malintzin *nochpochtzin* (my daughter) and she calls him *motlatzin* (my uncle). Others address her as *cihuapilli* (noblewoman). Furthermore, there exists a sixteenth-century picture on native paper—one that includes numerous native glyphs—that shows Cortés seated on an indigenous-style throne, demanding tribute, and in front of him a native woman on a similar seat, speaking, mak-ing the gestures that Malintzin makes in many another codex. But she is not exactly Malintzin, rather an altepetl's leading noblewoman working in concert with Cortés: the words "doña Isabel" have been inserted over her head.[37]

Or perhaps the reason the idea of Malintzin reverberated so strongly was that she was associated with Mary. The reverential form of the name "María" before the *r* sound was familiar would have been "Malitzin"—which, in a world where an *n* was often silent at the end of a syllable, could easily have been heard in the same way as "Malintzin." Indeed, in a mid-sixteenth-century census of Tizatlan, the part of Tlaxcala that doña Marina had visited, an indigenous woman who had apparently been named for Mary Magdalene styled herself "Magdalena Mallintzin."[38] Everywhere she went, everywhere the Spanish paused, Malintzin was asked to translate as a priest offered an explanation of Mary and ceremoniously presented an image of her to the town. For generations, of course, Santa María has been quite distinct in every Mexican's mind from Malinche, and from rather early on, the friars referred to Mary in particular ways—as a *santa* or with Nahuatl phrases meaning "our precious mother" or "ever virgin." But in those early months, before such conventions had been worked out, there could easily have been some slippage. At the very least, addresses to the flesh-and-blood Malintzin would probably have resonated strongly once people had been told about Mary. The human Malintzin could easily have been understood to be a ceremonial god impersonator for the Spaniards' own obviously powerful deity, or simply have been thought to represent her, to be named for her, or to be part of a people who were named for her. Indeed, Cortés and the other Spanish men could also have been thought to be her emissaries. They carried her image on their banners and spoke of her at every opportunity. Perhaps it was in that sense that they, too, were addressed as "Mali[n]tze" and referred to as "teotl."

One anthropologist has done a careful study of what sixteenth-century Nahuas seem to have thought about Mary once they had time to come to know her better. Nobody left a disquisition; the evidence must be circumstantial, as we know only what they were taught about her and to which elements of the story they themselves most often alluded. They certainly found her deeply appealing, more so than the Father, the Son, or the Holy Ghost. She was human, yet close to God. She spoke for the people, or on their behalf; she protected them. She was humble, yet all-powerful. She was a liminal figure who could signify different things to different people. "The Spaniards' conquistadora, shifting shape, becomes the mother and advocate of the conquered."[39] And this was exactly the role of the legitimating consort, historically speaking. A woman married with a dangerous outsider and, in so doing, tamed him, or at least bore children who signified peace. Spanish priests and their indigenous assistants worked together to create a literature about Mary that would be meaningful to Indians. In an early text written in an indigenous hand, for example, it is Mary's ability to speak when still a girl that marks her as special:

> There is nothing that is such a marvel as the way she would pray. The way she would speak, she made the words quite clear. She would say, "Thanks be to god," the way we do today. There wasn't yet anything like those words. It was all quite wonderful, how she would speak. There was nothing as wonderful as her words were when she was on the earth.[40]

It would hardly be surprising if in the initial chaos of attempted communication, there was some blurring of identities between the woman who spoke about Mary and the subject of her discourse: with or without the linguistically variable *n*, Malintzin had all the right qualities to be either herself (Malina, Malintzin) or a representative of the Virgin (Malía, Malitzin) about whom she spoke. Fragmentary evidence of this blurring seems to lie in some of the songs from the period that were passed from performer to performer before being written down sometime in the second half of the century. In one, Malintzin was called "Malía," and in another, where she was directly paired with Cortés, she was given a name that sounded like *tonan,* either meaning "our mother," or else representing an early attempt to use the Spanish word "doña" as a title for a great lady. The latter example presents a certain mystery: the little phrase is rich with ambiguity and could stem equally well from an early association with Mary or from a perception of Malintzin as a political consort. Perhaps the two notions sometimes reinforced each other.[41]

Whether the astute Malintzin ever played on the association between her own name and Mary's, or ever actually presented herself as wife to the powerful Spanish captain, we will never know. She was probably far too pressed at this point even to take the time to consciously consider the matter. For having arranged with the Tlaxcalans to provide military reinforcements (perhaps as many as five thousand), the Spanish were once again on their way. They were headed for Tenochtitlan by way of the altepetl of Cholula, known far and wide for its beautiful architecture and its temple to Quetzalcoatl.

Moctezuma had sent emissaries to try to stop the Spanish. "They told me," Cortés wrote to Emperor Charles, "that they had come on behalf of Mutezuma to inform me how he wished to be Your Highness's vassal and my ally, and that I should say what I wished him to pay as an annual tribute to Your Highness in gold and silver and jewels as well as slaves, cotton, clothing and other things which he possessed; all of which he would give, provided I did not go to his land, the reason being that it was very barren and lacking in provisions [just then]."[42] Most likely Moctezuma believed this would end the matter. In his experience, people attempted to conquer others with just such objectives in mind. As the most powerful tribute collector in all the land, he had hoped to avoid having to make such an arrangement, but if the newcomers could defeat the Tlaxcalans, then they were strong indeed, and now they had rendered his old enemies the Tlaxcalans a force to be reckoned with as well. It was time to cut the matter short and give them what they wanted, rather than have them appear at his doorstep and make him look vulnerable. But it didn't work. Moctezuma would try the same tactic several more times before the Spanish made their way into his presence, upping the ante each time. To no avail.

The Spanish pushed forward, determined not to show weakness by hesitating. The Tlaxcalans counseled against passing through Cholula, as they had recently fought a war against the Cholulteca and the altepetl had allied itself with Tenochtitlan in order to protect itself. Cortés, however, liked the idea of pausing in Mexica territory to test the waters.

Once there, he had to admit, he wondered about the wisdom of his course. Despite an initial show of politeness, it was obvious that the Spanish were not welcome. Each day, the locals brought less food to sell to them, and the lords spent less time conversing with them. The Tlaxcalans predicted doom and gloom. In an odd sentence in his letter home, Cortés implied that Malintzin made it her business to find out how things stood. "Being somewhat disturbed by this [treatment], my interpreter . . . was told by another Indian woman and a native of this city that very close by many of Mutezuma's men were gathered, and that the people of the city had sent away their women and children and all their belongings."[43]

They purportedly planned to attack the Spanish on their departure as they passed through certain ravines near the city. That was why, Cortés explained, the Spanish and the Tlaxcalans suddenly fell on the Cholulans, killing many hundreds who had gathered in the town square and burning and looting the settlement.

Historians still do not agree on whether or not Cortés told the truth about having uncovered a plot. In his own lifetime, his critics argued that his actions were needless as well as being brutal. Historians have surmised that he may simply have wanted to terrorize the people in order to make a point to Moctezuma. There is a serious problem with such a theory, however: the Spanish were not yet in a strong enough position to choose to make a point in such a way. Cortés and his forces were still very vulnerable, as he himself admitted elsewhere. He had no way of knowing as yet if such battles would convince Moctezuma of anything or if they would in fact be counterproductive.

There must certainly have been some sort of an indigenous affair afoot. Moctezuma really did have good reason to attempt a military confrontation just then. That the Cholulans were not old and staunch allies would have been a positive, not a negative. He certainly would not have wanted to risk his reputation for strength closer to home. But while the newcomers were yet on the other side of the mountain range, in Cholula, he could still attempt to use violence to persuade them to leave, with little regard for the fate of the people who lived there. And he could blame the Cholulans if the attempt failed, both in his dealings with the Spanish and with his own people. On the other hand, because the Cholulans were recent allies, it would have been extremely difficult for him to persuade them to take such a risk on his behalf. What seems more likely is that it was the Tlaxcalans who wanted to punish Cholula: until recently they had been Cholula's allies, and Cholula's recent realignment with Tenochtitlan had left them more vulnerable than they liked. If they could bring down the current chiefly line, the one that had orchestrated the change, and bring back one more sympathetic to Tlaxcala, it would obviously be to their benefit. That a number of chroniclers either doubted the need for Cortés's military actions or mentioned the Tlaxcalans as being the ones who predicted some sort of an attack makes this scenario seem the most likely. However it was, the Spanish and the Tlaxcalans combined their forces in a brutal rampage. "The destruction took two days," commented Andrés de Tapia.[44]

Gómara and Díaz both followed Cortés in mentioning Malintzin as the source of the Spaniards' information, and the story has come down through the ages. They said that the Cholulan noblewoman with whom Malintzin supposedly chatted so intimately offered her a home if she chose to abandon the Spanish but that she loyally stood by the conquistadors.[45] If a Cholulan noblewoman ever really approached her—and the story seems highly unlikely, given that the events were almost certainly engineered by the Tlaxcalans—Malintzin would have had no reason to trust promises from such a person and every reason to believe she would be sacrificed if she stayed in Cholula. She had arrived as an enemy and may well have been perceived as a ceremonial god impersonator. Either was more than enough reason to have one's life force offered up to the universe. Even if she could avoid that fate, she could never hope to be more than a particularly vulnerable concubine, for she had no family ties to render her marriageable or make her the mother of heirs. *If* Malintzin joined the Tlaxcalans in speaking of a conspiracy, and *if* she mentioned any offer to stay, she did so only to remind her purported masters of her loyalty thus far and of their dependence on her continuing goodwill. For if she valued her life at all, there could not have been any contest in her mind about remaining behind anywhere that the Spanish went.

Their business done, the Spanish and their apparently satisfied allies moved on, climbing upward toward the mountain pass that would lead them to the great city of Tenochtitlan. Snow-capped Popocatepetl (Smoking Mountain) towered on one side and Iztaccihuatl (White Woman) on the other. Once at the top, the flat, marshy valley stretched before them, dotted with settlements. As they proceeded, messengers and even noble representatives sent by Moctezuma continued to intercept them and offer regular tribute if they would only turn back. Some towns offered them gifts and sold them food. At night, Cortés was convinced, "spies" approached the camp. At one point, he had some nocturnal visitors shot with crossbows, lest anyone had forgotten the havoc that his people's weapons could wreak.

Close to the very center of the valley, the densely populated towns were built on lakesides and islands, sometimes even partly over water. The various sections were connected by causeways; the architecture grew increasingly complex and beautiful. Many people came crowding to get a good look at the strangers—but their degree of interest paled in comparison with that of the Spaniards. Bernal Díaz would never forget the scene that met them:

> When we saw all those cities and villages built in the water, and other great towns on dry land, and that straight and level causeway leading to Mexico, we were astounded. These great towns and cues [pyramid temples] and buildings rising from the water, all made of stone, seemed like an enchanted vision from the tale of Amadís. Indeed, some of our soldiers asked if it were not all a dream.[46]

When the men stopped to rest at the town of Iztapalapa, they were stunned. The lord's palace there rivaled buildings in Spain. Behind it a rose-filled garden cascaded down to a lovely pond:

> Large canoes could come into the garden from the lake, through a channel they had cut. . . . Everything was shining with lime and decorated with different kinds of stonework and paintings which were a marvel to gaze on. . . . I stood looking at it [all], and thought that no land like it would ever be discovered in the whole world, because at that time [the] Peru [of the Incas] was neither known nor thought of.[47]

Perhaps as he wrote these words in his old age, Bernal Díaz remembered the scene through the glow of nostalgia. But he had good reason to grow misty-eyed; his people had not been generous to so fine a land, and he knew it well. At the end of his paragraph, he suddenly added a very different kind of sentence: "Today all that I then saw is overthrown and destroyed; nothing is left standing."

At the time, however, Malintzin and the Spaniards and the other Indians who accompanied them had little idea where events would lead. Leaving Iztapalapa, they started down the wide causeway that led to Tenochtitlan. Coming toward them, they had been told, was Moctezuma himself.

Many myths have since grown up around that historic moment. The morning of November 19, though, must have seemed all too real to the straight-backed Malintzin as she traversed the cleanly swept roadway, the blue waters of the lake shining in the sunlight all around her. A new world was going to be forged over the course of many years and via countless attempted translations and mutual misunderstandings. But the *longue durée* would not have been visible to her then or seemed particularly relevant if it had. That morning, there was only Malintzin herself. She alone was responsible for being an effective channel to Jerónimo de Aguilar and all the Spaniards. She carried a heavy burden, in the imagery of her people. For she knew that whatever the great lord Moctezuma was to say to the strangers in that first encounter, and they to him, would have to pass through her.

FOUR

Tenochtitlan

THE PROCESSION OF ARMED SPANIARDS STOPPED AT A GREAT GATE WHERE hundreds of dignitaries had gathered to greet them. "Each one performed a ceremony which they practice among themselves; each placed his hand on the ground and kissed it," wrote Cortés a year and a half later. In true Nahua style, each segment of the polity accomplished its part separately. "And so I stood there waiting for nearly an hour until everyone had performed his ceremony." Then the foreigners were led across a bridge and found themselves looking at a long, open avenue that made the mazelike medieval cities of Europe seem ramshackle indeed. "[It] is very wide and beautiful and so straight that you can see from one end to the other. It is two-thirds of a league long and has on both sides very good and big houses, both dwellings and temples." Down this corridor proceeded Moctezuma with a large retinue. Cortés said that when they were within a few paces of each other, he dismounted from his horse and moved forward to embrace the king, lord to lord, according to European custom, but that the men on each side of the tlatoani quickly stepped forward to stop him. That is probably exactly what happened: the indigenous accounts of the event written years later are replete with references to the Spaniards making free with the sacred person of their lord. Cortés presented the monarch with a necklace of pearls and cut glass. Moctezuma immediately sent a servant to fetch an equally magnificent gift: a necklace of red snail shells, hung with beautifully crafted golden shrimp. Then he ushered Cortés into one of the halls, where they each sat upon special seats that betokened political authority. In the presence of their leading men, they began to talk. Malintzin stood between them.[1]

Moctezuma addressed his uninvited guests in the elaborate courtly speech that was always used with ambassadors. It had its own grammar and relied upon a code of polite inversion that all elite Nahuas understood. A prince might address his social inferiors as "my grandfathers" and they might call him "my child." He might say to them that he was unworthy to receive the honor of such a visit, when they were to understand that they were lucky he was taking the time to see them at all. According to the memories of that day that the nobles passed down to their sons in their own tongue, Malintzin understood Moctezuma's courtly language perfectly but responded with brutally direct speech, devoid of honorifics or polite reversals.[2]

We will never know what Moctezuma really said. The following year, Cortés reported to Charles V that he had immediately volunteered to cede his entire realm to the Spanish monarch. For many years the story was taken literally, until certain savvy historians began to note that Cortés had strong motivations for making this claim, and his European readers had equally good reason for choosing to believe him: according to Spanish law, the Spanish king had no right to demand that foreign peoples become his subjects. But he had every right to bring rebels to heel. In order for the Spanish to define the indigenous as rebels so they might make war against them, it was important to insist that the Indians had at first declared their loyalty. Cortés, naturally, was only too happy to tell His Majesty King Charles what His Majesty needed to hear.[3]

It is preposterous to think that the most powerful warrior king in all the land, who had ruled successfully for seventeen years, would suddenly and immediately relinquish his domains without further ado. In believing it for so many years, Western historians have only showed ourselves to be more naive than Moctezuma ever was. Still, parts of Cortés's account of the speech do ring true. And the indigenous account written in the 1550s contains some of the same elements—though, of course, it might have been written under the influence of the Cortesian version, which appeared in book form in Spain in 1552 and made its way across the sea relatively rapidly. The conquistador put these words in the tlatoani's mouth:

> For a long time we have known from the writings of our ancestors that neither I, nor any of those who dwell in this land, are natives of it, but foreigners who came from very distant parts; and likewise we know that a chieftain, of whom they were all vassals, brought our people to this region. And he returned to his native land and after many years came again, by which time all those who had remained were married to native women and had built villages and raised children. And when he wished to lead them away again they would not go nor even admit him as their chief; and so he departed. And we have always held that those who descended from him would come and conquer this land and take us as their vassals. . . . We believe and are certain that he is our natural lord, especially as you say that he has known of us for some time. So be assured that we shall obey you and hold you as our lord.[4]

That the Indians "believed and were certain" that the Spanish king was their "natural lord" was pure legalese, of the kind that Cortés was invested in providing, and the idea of the return of the son certainly smacks of Christianity. The account of Chichimec history, on the other hand, seems remarkably accurate: Nahuatl-speaking men had invaded the central valley on more than one occasion, each time marrying into the local cultures, each time facing difficulties later with more invaders from the same northern regions. How would Cortés have known what the Mexica history accounts said, if not from Moctezuma? Perhaps Malintzin had heard such tales chanted in her father's central courtyard, but that is unlikely, as her father's people were no friends of the Mexica. Even if she had, though, in what other context would she have had the time and energy to tell Cortés such tales? And it is certainly true that the indigenous were preoccupied from very early on with the question of how the Spanish had known of their existence; the Europeans' knowledge, like their weaponry, implied a technological superiority that promised to be a problem. Moctezuma might well have used exaggeratedly polite speech to explain away a phenomenon he felt needed explaining and to attempt to incorporate the outsiders into his vision of world history, all in an attempt to reassert—albeit indirectly—his own dominance and his own worldview.

The children of the indigenous chiefs later recounted Moctezuma's speech this way:

> O our lord, be doubly welcomed on your arrival in this land; you have come to satisfy your curiosity about your altepetl of Mexico, you have come to sit on your seat of authority, which I have kept for a while for you, where I have been in charge for you, for your agents the rulers—[the dynasty of Mexica kings] Itzcoatzin, the elder Moctezuma, Axayacatl, Tizoc and Ahuitzotl—have [all] gone. . . . It is after them that your poor vassal [myself] came.

Stripped of the distractions provided by courtly speech, Moctezuma's comment reads quite differently. In the words of a modern historian, "It is a rhetorical artifice meant to convey the opposite—Moctezuma's stature and multigenerational legitimacy—and to function [at the same time] as a courteous welcome to an important guest."[5]

Interestingly, Cortés wrote that Moctezuma then insisted to his Spanish audience that he was not a god and did not possess extraordinary wealth. "I know that [my enemies] have told you the walls of my houses are made of gold, and that the floor mats in my rooms . . . are likewise of gold, and that I was, and claimed to be, a god. . . . The houses as you see are of stone and lime and clay," quoted Cortés. "Then he raised his clothes and showed me his body, saying, . . . 'See that I am flesh and blood like you and all other men.'"[6] The last statement certainly has biblical overtones and could well be a product of Cortés's active imagination. On the other hand, a Mexica speaker would have been more than likely to use both "floor mats" and "blood" as important metaphors. They did so frequently in their songs. It is difficult to think of a good reason for Cortés to have thrown in this particular paragraph if it had no basis whatsoever—but Moctezuma himself had every reason to make the statement. In true Nahua style, he worked his way around politely and indirectly to his punch line: he did not believe that the Spaniards were gods or in any way superior to other men. Such an interpretation seems even more reasonable when we realize that it is apparently the way the Spanish themselves understood what they were recording, judging from the style in which other Spaniards described the incident. Bernal Díaz, for example, claimed that Moctezuma dismissed the stories of his own divinity in this interesting way: "You must take them as a joke, as I take the story of your thunders and your lightnings."[7]

Ultimately, however, all analyses of Moctezuma's statements are conjectural; we can never know how faithfully he was represented by his would-be conquerors. Such analyses are worth making only in order to undermine any easy acceptance of the utterances as fact and to remind ourselves how easily the Spanish may naively or willfully have misinterpreted whatever he really did say. The reality is that if we want to consider what Moctezuma was thinking as he sat there and listened to Malintzin's words, we essentially have only his previous and future actions to go on. We know that he had spent the preceding months intently gathering information. After the sighting of the first ship in 1517, he had the sea watched. When the 1519 expedition made landfall, he sent painters to make a full record of all that they saw. Then, as the Spanish began their ascent toward Tenochtitlan, he organized a veritable war room. Men who had been young at the time later remembered: "A report of everything that was happening was given and relayed to Moctezuma. Some of the messengers would be arriving as others were leaving. There was no time when they weren't listening, when reports weren't being given." Cortés also mentioned that Moctezuma's messengers were present in every altepetl that they visited, including Tlaxcala, watching every step the newcomers took. Bernal Díaz said that by the time the Spaniards got to the capital, the religious sermon that Malintzin had translated frequently along the way had been repeated so many times to Moctezuma that he asked them not to give it again, as the arguments were by now quite familiar to him. Despite his intelligence-gathering apparatus, however, Moctezuma still had the problem that his frame of reference was not as wide as that of the Spanish: in what may well have been an apocryphal tale, an elderly man later said that Moctezuma called for priests and sages from different parts of the kingdom to consult their libraries and their traditions and tell him who these strangers were. But they could find nothing of any relevance amidst their stores of knowledge. Only one seer said something useful, in that he accurately described the power of the Spanish and said that the first explorers were merely there to scout out a route and that others would soon arrive.[8]

Now, after having apparently orchestrated at least one failed attack on the Spanish and having had his people try unsuccessfully to block up the roads, Moctezuma had decided to let the strangers and their hated Tlaxcalan allies enter within his precincts. A generation later, bitter and perplexed young people in Tenochtitlan went over and over the situation in their heads. "Moctezuma did not give orders for anyone to make war against them or for anyone to meet them in battle. No one was to meet them in battle. He just ordered that they be strictly obeyed and very well attended to."[9] Historians, likewise, have looked in horrified fascination at Moctezuma's supposedly great mistake. Recently, in lieu of traditional assessments that he was either a coward or a fool, scholars have proffered more reasonable explanations. He may have thought it would be easier to kill the Spaniards once they were in his keeping; it would also be safer, in that it could be done in secret so that their distant king would never know. Then again, as king, it was his responsibility as it was no one else's to proceed cautiously and to "diagnose [the situation] in cosmic terms." Furthermore, he often allowed tributary lords to visit his city, even ones he later made war against, and if he did plan to make war, he would have had to wait until the dry season.[10]

There is, however, a central explanation for Moctezuma's decision, which is often overlooked. By now, he knew that the Spaniards generally won their battles. Even if he had gathered and armed every warrior in the valley so that he might surround and destroy the Spanish with the sheer force of numbers, he himself would have been politically destroyed. The casualties would have been immense, beyond anything anyone had ever seen, and right in his own backyard. The heartland of the empire accepted the arrogance of their Mexica neighbors in exchange for peace and the privilege of living close to power. If the Mexica could not deliver a quick victory on the outskirts of their own capital, they were politically doomed. If the emperor's army could not win quickly and easily here—and he knew for certain from his spies and generals that it could not—then they could not fight. At the time, Cortés did not understand the political situation well enough to grasp this fact. Not so those who wrote a few decades later. López de Gómara wrote: "It seemed unfitting and dishonorable for him to make war upon Cortés and fight a mere handful of strangers who said they were ambassadors. Another reason was that he did not wish to stir up trouble for himself (and this was the truest reason), for it was clear that he would immediately have to face an uprising among the Otomí, the Tlaxcalans, and many others." Said Bernal Díaz: "Moctezuma's captains and *papas* [highest-level priests] also advised him that if he tried to prevent our entry we would fight him in his subject towns."[11]

Almost certainly, Moctezuma was disposed to attempt to gather information through Malintzin, just as the Spanish wanted to learn about him. It seems to have been his hope that they would eventually leave of their own accord, and he could then maintain a nominal tie to their distant king. A few months later, a young Spanish carpenter would send word home that up to the present, the Indians had been content to deliver food to the captain, believing that the Christians would soon leave.[12] In the meantime, Moctezuma would have reasoned, it was best to cement the peace and learn as much as possible. Perhaps we have tended to make too much of this moment, under the circumstances: it was not the first time that a beleaguered native king had been forced to allow armed Europeans and their indigenous allies into his domain, and it would not be the last.

That night, Malintzin slept in fine quarters in the finest city of her known world. The brightly painted walls and stairwells were alive with carved animals and the images of gods, the floors and beds lined with the softest mats. It was the city of her people's enemies, a city that lived by making war, a city full of captive women—as she had once been herself. But she was no longer one of the expendable, invisible ones. Servants now brought her succulent foods. Everyone sought her out; she alone could resolve the difficulties that arose as living arrangements were sorted out between two groups of people who could not understand each other at all.

In the following days, the Spanish—always armed and armored—toured the city. The streets were wide, hard packed, and swept to the point of burnishing. Between and around them lay a network of straight, well-tended canals alive with the traffic of passing canoes. The white lime-coated houses, many of them two storied, had flowers and greenery cascading from their flat roofs. Pyramid temples punctuated the cityscape at every turn: each neighborhood held its own religious complex, but in the central area rose the two greatest towers, dedicated to Huitzilopochtli and Tlaloc, the gods of warfare and of rain. At the southern edge of the crowded town, food grew in pretty gardens called *chinampas* that were efficiently planted in raised beds within the lake itself. An aqueduct carried fresh water to the town. Perhaps most memorable of all, in the gardens of one of Moctezuma's houses there was an aviary and a zoological garden, both staffed by men whose only occupation was to feed and care for the many fascinating inmates.

In Tlatelolco, the neighboring Mexica altepetl that had only recently been forced to become a part of the Tenochca polity, the Spanish found a market larger than any they had dared to hope for. In a region of a quarter of a million people, many thousands came here to trade each day. The visitors saw gold, silver, copper, precious stones, seashells, bones, and feathers—both in their natural state and made into stunning ornaments. They saw stone, adobe bricks, tiles, and lumber, firewood, charcoal, matting, and bedding. Animals abounded—birds of every description, rabbits, and small dogs. "There are streets of herbalists where all the medicinal herbs and roots found in the land are sold. There are shops like apothecaries', where they sell ready-made medicines as well as liquid ointments and plasters. There are shops like barbers' where they have their hair washed and shaved."[13] The Spanish also found cotton, deerskins, furs, paints, dyes, pottery, and obsidian mirrors. The foodstuffs were perhaps the most appealing to the tired travelers—fruits and vegetables of all stripes, honey, syrup, bird eggs, corn, and a kind of wine, as well as pies, salted fish, and even ready-made tortillas.

Cortés was taken up into the great temples, but for the first time, apparently, he was parted from his translator. "No woman is granted entry nor permitted inside these places of worship," he commented briefly.[14] Perhaps Malintzin did not want to make the climb in any case. There must certainly have been moments in her troubled past when she had wondered if her heart would soon be taken from her. Inside the recesses at the top of the pyramid there was little light and one could not see clearly, but the chambers certainly still held the blood of sacrificed prisoners of war. The hair of the priests was matted with it, a discordant sight in the midst of so much elegance and splendor, at least as the Spanish experienced it.

What happened over the course of the next few months is the subject of debate. Cortés claimed that at the end of the first week, he took Moctezuma hostage and began to rule through him. This step certainly did reflect an ancient practice of European warfare, but at the end of seven days, the tense and vastly outnumbered Spanish, who still knew almost nothing about the city, were hardly in a position to arrest the emperor of the realm—not, at least, without bringing on a state of chaos, as later events proved.

There is strong evidence against Cortés having arrested Moctezuma after only one week in the city, above and beyond the implausibility of it. First, although he was supposedly in full control of the kingdom from November to May, Cortés made no effort to inform anyone in the outside world of his extraordinary success. Secondly, his story contradicts itself in places and is seriously undermined by the statements of others. Cortés himself experienced some discomfort over the first issue and claimed that because he had scuttled his ships he had to await the return of the one he had sent home. But he failed to explain why he did not immediately assign anyone to rebuild one of the old boats or to construct a new one. He did have at least one shipbuilder with him, as is revealed elsewhere in the letter. The secretary who later wrote his biography saw the awkwardness of the thing and so wrote at this point in the plot, "Now that Cortés saw himself rich and powerful, he formed three plans: one was to send to Santo Domingo and the other islands news of the country and his good fortune." He then implied that unfortunately Cortés had never quite had the time to see to the matter. By the chronicler's own account, Moctezuma continued to live in various palaces, to go on hunting expeditions, to meet regularly with his advisers, and to give all orders regarding the operation of the kingdom. And except when Malintzin was present, his supposed captors never knew with certainty what he and his companions were talking about.[15]

None of the other conquistadors ever denied Cortés's statement about the early arrest—they would have been fools to do so, for their own reputation for daring depended on it, as did Spain's "legal" right to govern—but their stories are full of inconsistencies. "While I stayed, . . . I did not see a living creature killed or sacrificed," wrote Cortés, who was trying to show that his power had been absolute. Bernal Díaz, on the other hand, said, "The great Moctezuma continued to show his accustomed good will towards us, but never ceased his daily sacrifices of human beings. Cortés tried to dissuade him but met with no success."[16] In the midst of describing Moctezuma's palaces, Francisco de Aguilar suddenly seemed to recall that he was supposed to be describing a prisoner: "[His servants] brought him river and sea fish of all kinds, besides all kinds of fruit from the sea coast as well as the highlands. The kinds of bread they brought were greatly varied . . . The plates and cups of his dinner service were very clean. He was not served on gold or silver because he was in captivity, but it is likely that he had a great table service of gold and silver." Aguilar went on to say (as had Cortés) that the arrest had taken place because the Spanish had learned that Moctezuma had plotted against them, had even ordered some of the men left in Veracruz to be killed. Aguilar and Andrés de Tapia had been sent to the coast to ascertain the truth of the matter. But de Tapia's own account says Indians were sent on that errand. Concerning Moctezuma's arrest, de Tapia wrote, "He never told his people he was a prisoner but continued dispatching matters pertaining to the government of his people." We must ask ourselves if Moctezuma was really a prisoner if the Spanish were the only ones who thought so. Indeed de Tapia casts even more doubt on the matter in describing the five-month period of purported Spanish control: "In this manner we stayed on, the marques [Hernando Cortés] keeping us so close to our quarters that no one stepped a musket-shot away without permission." A priest who arrived in 1523 and knew most of the conquistadors personally discreetly skipped over this period in the narrative, as did the men who were questioned in various kinds of court cases later in the decade.[17]

Several indigenous sources, produced in the 1550s and even later, do contain some version of the story of an immediate arrest—sometimes even placing it on the first day—but we must remember that these texts also repeat the story of Quetzalcoatl's expected return, which they were probably hearing from the Spanish. Only one text, the Annals of Tlatelolco, provides an exception. It seems to have been written in the 1540s, possibly based on a narrative that had been memorized in the 1520s, and thus is the earliest known indigenous record of the conquest. According to this source, in the early months after the arrival of the Spanish, the people provided the Spanish with food, water, and firewood, just as they would have for any honored guests. Only later did the Spanish attempt to manhandle Moctezuma.[18]

Certainly Cortés must have been mulling over the possibility of attempting to take Moctezuma hostage. This was a tried and true practice in European warfare and had already been used in the Caribbean; later on he definitely did put it into practice. It is also clear that at some point toward the end of his stay, he captured and put in irons the tlatoani of Tetzcoco, who had been critical of Moctezuma's pacifist policy regarding the newcomers. In the meantime, though, he and his men behaved like the honored guests they almost certainly were. They explored the city further, consulted with Moctezuma's tribute collectors and royal mapmakers, sent contingents out to visit other areas, demanded gifts, and then cataloged their newfound wealth—all of which would have been exceedingly difficult if they were coup-staging interlopers. In addition, by all accounts, Moctezuma provided them with plenty of slave women to add to their comforts.

Tellingly, the king allowed the Spanish to have contact with at least three of his daughters, including one who was of great social importance. Her Nahuatl name was Tecuichpotzin, or "Lord's Daughter," the kind of name one gave to the child of a wife of rank, and she later held high political stature among her people. In Tenochtitlan, power did not necessarily pass from father to son. In fact, the leading contender for the inheritance was often the nephew or cousin who managed to marry the current king's most prominent daughter. Tecuichpotzin, at age ten, was already betrothed—or perhaps even married to—a nobleman named Atlixcatzin, whom everyone expected to succeed. Thanks to Malintzin, apparently, the Spanish understood the girl's importance. They christened her "Isabel" in a pointed reference to Queen Isabella. If Moctezuma had been living in a state of fear, he could easily have arranged to have his most beloved and precious children—to use his people's imagery—hidden from these marauding strangers, who could not tell people apart and did not speak the language. Clearly he did not want to. He even sent for one daughter as a possible bride for Cortés. Moctezuma was apparently covering all possibilities: he was choosing to attempt to build an alliance in this time-honored fashion. The royal sisters, presented in all their finery, would have kept their eyes cast down and maintained a perfect and respectful silence as their elders made the requisite rhetorical speeches and Malintzin translated. In private with Malintzin, the lady of Cortés's household, young Tecuichpotzin would have spoken formally, using the scrupulously polite and self-deprecatory courtly speech, "Oh, lady, I do not wish to disturb you, bring illness upon you, or cause you stomach pains [with my presence]."[19] We can never know to what she or any of the girls may later have been subjected at the hands of the Spanish men with whom they now lived side by side. That they were not happy over the ensuing weeks seems certain, for later, when they had the chance, they fled.

All that, however, lay in the future. For now, the Spanish continued their project of gathering information about Moctezuma's territories and resources. Cortés had his host send for mapmakers so that they could give him a report on all possible ports, and he soon learned that the River Coatzacoalcos was the only waterway with the length and depth he was looking for. Though they had never seen it, his men were so well apprised of its location that a troop of them were able to find it with no difficulty when they set out to do so. They were so convinced that it would be worth their while to take the area that they came back with glowing reports—choosing to ignore the fact that what they had actually explored thus far was swampland and would never make a good port.[20] All this at first seems inexplicable, until we remember that Malintzin was in the room, very much in control of what was said on both sides, and that she may well have had a stake in ultimately returning to her home. If so, she was to be disappointed at this stage.

In April of 1520, Moctezuma received news from some of his runners that must have appeared extremely interesting to him. At least eight hundred more Spaniards in thirteen great ships had arrived on the coast: eyewitness observers had prepared painted records for him to peruse.[21] When he eventually told Malintzin, who turned to tell Jerónimo de Aguilar and the other Spaniards, Cortés was visibly shaken.

When Alonso de Puertocarrero and a companion named Francisco de Montejo had sailed away from Veracruz just as Cortés was about to turn inland, they had promised to make straight for Spain and speak to the king himself. They were to take an unusual route, passing along the north coast of Cuba without stopping. Montejo, however, had lands on the coast near the settlement of Havana, and he longed to anchor within site of his old home, arrange his personal affairs, and show off a bit to those who mattered most to him. They stopped for three days in October of 1519 and used the time to replenish their food and water supplies. A trusted man who worked on Montejo's lands boarded the ship and saw some of the riches they were taking to Spain. He was suitably impressed and, after they sailed away, told others what he had seen. No one relished the thought of being accused of treachery to the Crown at some later point, so the locals sent word to the Cuban governor of what had happened. The irate Diego de

Velázquez flew into action. After first making a useless effort to overtake the scofflaws on the high seas, he brought anyone who had learned anything during the ship's brief stopover to Santiago de Cuba for questioning. There he supervised the production of lengthy legal documents based on the witnesses' testimony and fired off letters to everyone of importance with whom he had any connection in Spain. Velázquez, who had once led a brutal conquest of Cuba's indigenous people, suddenly expressed himself to be extremely concerned about the violence that Cortés had employed on more than one occasion. Cortés, he had learned, had kidnapped Indians—even including noblemen, two of whom had been seen on the ship with Puertocarrero. This kind of thing, Velázquez assured the king, was not in Spain's best interest, as it would stir up trouble for the emperor in his acquisition of the new lands. He would send an expedition of his own to Mexico. It would be led by Captain Pánfilo de Narváez. Narváez had been his second-in-command in the taking of Cuba and had just returned from Spain with a permit from the king for Velázquez to conquer the mainland. The members of the new expedition would seek out Cortés—an obvious troublemaker—cast him in irons, and proceed with the conquest of the New World in a more appropriate way.[22]

The first missives of the infuriated Cuban governor arrived in Spain not long after Puertocarrero and Montejo themselves; other documents continued to arrive while the two representatives of Cortés's forces did their best to convey their side of the story to the royal court. The delivery of the treasure they carried with them spoke volumes on their behalf. The king was most happy to receive it. What had not been melted down for deposit in the treasury went on tour for exhibition throughout the realms of the emperor. In July of the next year, for example, the artist Albrecht Dürer saw some of the remarkable objects in the town hall in Brussels. "All the days of my life, I have seen nothing that rejoiced my heart so much as these things, for I have seen among them wonderful works of art, and I have marveled at the subtle intellects of men in foreign parts." And the stories traveled even faster than the exhibit. Puertocarrero's ship had first docked in Seville on Saturday, November 5, two weeks before Malintzin began to translate the words of the Mexica emperor on the causeway. From the time the ecstatic sailors disembarked with their news and precious cargo, Spaniards began to mention the matter in letters, some quite accurate, some full of hearsay and wild exaggeration. "For a crystal that is worth two maravedis, the Indians gave five hundred pesos of gold, and in this manner all other things in proportion. They speak of so many marvels that one cannot write [about them]." Soon some of the letters would be printed, translated, and printed again, thus passing into the hands of an even wider audience. Excitement gradually spread throughout Europe.[23]

The name "Hernando Cortés" was on its way to becoming a household byword, but this did not satisfy Martín Cortés, Hernando's father. Puertocarrero and Montejo had brought a missive for him, too, carrying a very specific plea for help. He immediately wrote to the king on his son's behalf. His letter went beyond the subject of that energetic young man's right to proceed with the conquest without interference from Narváez. He also felt it incumbent upon him to mention that delay of any kind would certainly "produce damage and detriment to the Spanish settlement and its people for lack of supplies and provisions."[24] He himself began to pour resources into fitting up a ship. There was no time to be lost. If Old World technology were to be victorious now rather than later, they would have to use some of it immediately and send more support.

In the meantime, across the sea, Moctezuma wondered if the increasingly obvious divisions among the Europeans would provide an opportunity for him to gain the upper hand. He was an expert at the adroit manipulation of feuding peoples. In his letter to the king, Cortés insisted that because of the great love Moctezuma had for him, the Indian king was only too eager to help him drive the interlopers from the land, but all Spanish accounts produced later insist that at this point, Moctezuma reversed his previous policy and began to prepare his people for war.[25] Whether he did or not, Cortés was well aware that this latest development was not good news for him. If the newly arrived ships had come in such numbers and so very quickly, then they undoubtedly came from Diego de Velázquez with orders to arrest him.

There is strong evidence that Cortés took Moctezuma hostage—literally put him in irons—at this point.[26] Desperate times call for desperate measures, after all. Only with a knife to Moctezuma's throat could he assure the recently arrived Spaniards that he was in control of the kingdom and thus possibly win their allegiance, and probably only in that way could he stave off a violent rejection on the part of the Indians. Numerous sworn witnesses in later court cases mentioned that the Spanish guarded Moctezuma round the clock in this period. One text—in Spanish, but claiming to summarize the narrative of an Indian—mentioned eighty days of confinement, putting the arrest to within days of the arrival of Narváez. Naturally, Cortés and his men could not admit to their desperate predicament; they needed to portray their control of the area as long term, not as the result of a recent incident. Fray Diego Durán later wrote, "A conqueror, who is now a friar, told me that though the imprisonment of Moctezuma might be true, it was done with the idea of protecting the lives of the Spanish captain and his men."[27] This was to be a secret, though. The "conqueror who is now a friar" was almost certainly Francisco de Aguilar, who, in the statement he prepared for public consumption, said that Moctezuma had been arrested early on for his betrayal of the Spaniards of Veracruz, not as a desperate ploy designed to save Spanish lives in a crisis.

Meanwhile, the representative of Charles V who governed the Caribbean in its entirety had sent another ship with a royal official to hear both sides of the dispute—that of Cortés and that of Narváez—in order to prevent a fratricidal struggle between Spaniards. At the settlement on the coast, Lucas Vázquez de Ayllón questioned a young Spanish carpenter who had been on the expedition to Coatzacoalcos. Francisco Serrantes, asked how he knew that Moctezuma was in the power of Cortés, did not say that he had seen him imprisoned but, rather, that he had seen that Moctezuma always did what Cortés asked him to.[28]

Narváez had no patience for this kind of investigation. It probably did not occur to him to doubt the security of Cortés's hold over Moctezuma. Instead, he accused the annoying royal arbitrator of disloyalty, arrested him, and packed him off to Cuba. Then he prepared to fight his rival, whose men, he thought, would certainly come down from the mountains soon. In this he was right.[29]

Gonzalo de Sandoval, whom Cortés had left to govern the newly founded Veracruz, had early on in the game arrested the messengers who came to him from Narváez's camp and sent them up to Tenochtitlan under guard. Cortés had wined and dined them and given them rich gifts with promises of more; from them he had learned all he needed to know about the situation on the coast. It became clear what he needed to do. He would go himself with some of his men, leaving another force to hold Moctezuma hostage. Malintzin would accompany him. Those left behind in the city might face difficulties without their talented translator, but they would manage, due to the good offices of Francisco, a Nahuatl-speaking Indian boy whom Grijalva had kidnapped on the coast nearly two years ago and who was beginning to learn some Spanish. There was no question but that Malintzin would go with Cortés, even though his mission involved a confrontation with Spaniards, not Indians. To a large degree, his powerful and charismatic presence depended on his ability to understand what was going on around him and to obtain food and sleeping quarters for his men with very little trouble; traveling without her was thus unthinkable. All the other women, however, would stay behind. He rode out on horseback, but most of the expedition's members, including Malintzin, retraced their path back down through the pine forests on foot.

The Spaniards who had been taken by force to Tenochtitlan were released when they reached the coast. They soon spread the word throughout Narváez's camp that there was, after all, enough wealth to go around amongst them all and that Cortés did in fact seem to have the region under control. Cortés followed up by offering liberal bribes to as many people as possible and making a show of wanting peace with Narváez. At the end of May, under cover of darkness, his much smaller force attacked the enemy camp positioned at Cempoala, the layout of which he and his men still remembered well. Perhaps, as is sometimes claimed, the newcomers had been lulled into a false sense of security because of their greater numbers and in their slackness could not withstand the daring onslaught of Cortés and his men. Or perhaps they did not really want to fight other Spaniards in this awe-inspiring and even terrifying land where they did not speak the language and had no other obvious allies. The latter explanation must be construed as most likely, since Cortés himself lamented that Narváez's men received word of his being on the move a full half hour before his forces were able to arrive, despite the effort they made at speed and stealth. For whichever reason, Cortés's men managed to capture Narváez with the loss of only two of their own number and about ten of the enemy's. With the obstreperous Narváez out of the way, most of his subordinate captains came round almost immediately and made arrangements to join their erstwhile foes.

Cortés suddenly had approximately eight hundred more men, eighty more horses, and several ships' worth of supplies at his disposal. Now, indeed, control of the kingdom was within his grasp. They even had wine with which to celebrate. The merrymaking had to be cut short, though, for as Malintzin explained, the huge Spanish force quite literally had eaten the locals out of house and home, and there would be no more food forthcoming in the immediate vicinity. Cortés began to divide the men up, some to go to Veracruz, some to the Coatzacoalcos area, and some to Tenochtitlan. He worked as quickly as possible to make the necessary arrangements and write creative reports on recent events that were sure to incriminate Narváez when they were sent back to Spain. He himself planned to lead the main force back to the Mexica capital and win everlasting fame.

But on the twelfth day, some Tlaxcalan Indians brought Malintzin some shattering news. She who had been astute enough to comprehend far more subtle realities would have recognized its import at once. It was more than possible that the beginning of the end had come: the people of Tenochtitlan were in rebellion. The Spanish were holed up in a palace that they had turned into a fort. For several days, they had been under attack, and then a deadly quiet had ensued. The food was certainly all but gone; their water supply was limited. The next day, in the midst of the panic that had ensued when she made her communication, two more Tlaxcalan messengers made their way to the camp. These carried a letter from the besieged Spanish that had been smuggled out by some of the Indians who had thrown in their lot with them. "I saw the messenger that they sent from Tenochtitlan begging the captain for help," Jerónimo de Aguilar later swore. Cortés remembered reading the letter. "I must," he recalled, "for the love of God come to their aid as swiftly as possible."[30]

He gathered together all who were not too far dispersed and they set off almost immediately. It was an eerie passage up the mountains. "Not once in my journey did any of Moctezuma's people come to welcome me as they had before. All the land was in revolt and almost uninhabited, which aroused in me a terrible suspicion that the Spaniards in the city were dead and that all the natives had gathered waiting to surprise me in some pass or other place where they might have the advantage of me."[31] He would later learn that a group of Narváez's more recalcitrant captains, whom he had sent under guard up to the city before the new tidings reached him, had in fact been surprised at a mountain pass and killed to the last man. His own force, however, was huge and therefore relatively invulnerable. They were not molested.

When they reached the city, they made their way through silent streets to the building the Spanish were calling their fortress, which had once been the palace of Moctezuma's predecessor, Axayacatl. "The garrison received us with such joy as it seemed we had given back to them their lives which they had deemed lost; and that day and night we passed in rejoicing." Cortés so loved to tell a dramatic story that he was even willing to include an occasional detail that reflected poorly on his judgment: "The next day, after Mass, I sent a messenger to Vera Cruz to give them the good news of how all the Christians were alive and how I had entered the city which was now secure. But after half an hour this messenger returned, beaten and wounded and crying out that all the Indians in the city were preparing for war." As indeed they were.[32]

By now Malintzin had heard the gist of what had happened in her absence. The resentment of the locals had become evident when food supplies stopped being delivered to the Spanish. A young woman who had been doing their laundry for pay was found dead, the first victim of the witch-hunt mentality that was to haunt the beleaguered city for the next year. The Spanish began to send armed men to the market to buy food and they made careful efforts to store some as well. Meanwhile, the city people were preparing for one of their most important holy days, the celebration of Toxcatl, in which the altepetl's greatest warriors danced before a huge figure of Huitzilopochtli. Pedro de Alvarado, who had been left in charge, said that he began to fear they were planning to use that day to launch an attack. He seized three Indians and had them tortured until they "confessed" that such was indeed the plan. His only interpreter was the boy whom the foreigners called "Francisco." But he had been slow to learn Spanish, and, in addition, he was a commoner and thus probably had never heard Nahuatl courtly speech until the last few months.[33]

That there was no plot seems certain: the Mexica warriors were far too experienced as tacticians to attempt such an attack in the midst of a festival. They knew of better ways to render the Spanish vulnerable, as events would later prove. Alvarado, however, followed an old maxim in deciding that he who attacked first would be victorious. A generation later, the story of the festival of Toxcatl was etched in the city's memory:

[T]he festivity was being observed and there was dancing and singing, with voices raised in song, the singing was like the noise of waves breaking against the rocks. When . . . the moment had come for the Spaniards to do the killing, they came out equipped for battle. They came and closed off each of the places where people went in and out [of the courtyard]. . . . And when they had closed these exits, they stationed themselves in each, and no one could come out any more.

When this had been done, they went into the temple courtyard to kill the people. Those whose assignment it was to do the killing just went on foot, each with his metal sword and leather shield. . . . Then they surrounded those who were dancing, going among the cylindrical drums. They struck a drummer's arms; both of his hands were severed. Then they struck his neck; his head landed far away. Then they stabbed everyone with iron lances and struck them with iron swords. They struck some in the belly, and then their entrails came spilling out. . . . Those who tried to escape could go nowhere. When anyone tried to go out, at the entryways they struck and stabbed him.

But some climbed up the wall and were able to escape. Some went into the various calpulli temples and took refuge there. Some took refuge among . . . those who had really died, feigning death. . . . The blood of the warriors ran like water.[34]

By the end of the day, war cries rose in the air. The Spanish retreated to their "fortress" and the Mexica attacked en masse, but to no avail. Crossbows and steel kept them out. Then for more than twenty days, they left the Spanish in dead silence and uncertainty. Indian men who had been young at the time remembered clearly what they had been doing, though the Spanish were as yet unaware. "The canals were excavated, widened, deepened, the sides made steeper. Everywhere the canals were made more difficult to pass. And on the roads, various walls were built . . . and the passageways between houses made more difficult."[35] They were preparing for a great urban battle.

As soon as Hernando Cortés and his men had joined their brethren in the trap that had been prepared for them, the Tenochca attacked. The battle lasted for seven days. Often the Indians seemed to be about to take the fortress or burn the Spaniards out of it, but then their armored enemies would focus so much power at the vulnerable spot—using crossbows, harquebuses, iron bars, and lances—that they were forced to withdraw again.

Somewhere in the melee, Moctezuma was killed. Most of the Spaniards said he was stoned by his own people when he tried to address them from a rooftop. Most Indian sources insist that the Spanish killed him themselves. In any case, he was by then no longer the de facto leader. Power had passed by consensus to a younger brother, the militant Cuitlahuac of Iztapalapa.

Cuitlahuac's views of the situation soon became known to the Spanish. Cortés claimed to have parleyed with the new king's captains from a rooftop. Perhaps he did. Or perhaps he interrogated prisoners. In either case, it was Malintzin, as usual, who actually exhorted the Indians to make peace and save their own lives, Malintzin who passed on to Cortés their response, though he put it in his own terms:

> They were all determined to perish or have done with us, and . . . I should look and see how full of people were all those streets and squares and rooftops. Furthermore, they had calculated that [even] if 25,000 of them died for every one of us, they would finish with us first, for they were many and we were but few. They told me that all the causeways into the city were dismantled—which in fact was true, for all had been dismantled save one—and that we had no way of escape except over the water. They well knew that we had few provisions and little fresh water, and, therefore, could not last long because we would die of hunger if they did not kill us first.[36]

Some indigenous later said that before he died, Moctezuma had made an opposing speech from a rooftop, pleading with his people to lay down their arms; others claimed that he had a representative do it for him. Whether he ever really made such a speech during the heat of the battle, we will never know. But what the people remembered him as saying certainly represented thoughts he had at least entertained during his months of deliberation and may well have represented his conclusions. And there were definitely other experienced leaders who agreed. His words as they come down to us stemmed from an existing school of thought:

> Let the Mexica hear! We are not their match. May they be dissuaded [from further fighting]. May the arrows and shields of war be laid down. The poor old men and women, the common people, the infants who toddle and crawl, who lie in the cradle or on the cradle

board and know nothing yet, all are suffering. This is why your ruler says, "we are not their match; let everyone be dissuaded."[37]

These were the same images of widespread tragedy that the Nahuas used in speaking of natural disasters like droughts and pestilences. The old, the babies, the unarmed farmers, all would suffer. In this case, the overwrought pride of the most stubborn warriors might make the unavoidable calamity worse. A responsible king would work with both sides to make peace. The oldest Nahuatl account of the conquest says of the period of battle: "The ruler Moteucçoma of Tenochtitlan, accompanied by . . . [a lord of] Tlatelolco, was trying to hold the Spaniards back. They said to [the Spanish], 'O our lords, let it be enough. What are you doing? The people are suffering? Do they have shields and war clubs? They go unarmed.'"[38]

There is strong evidence that Malintzin was of the belief that it would be counterproductive to continue to fight the war machine she had observed firsthand. And many in her Indian audiences agreed with her. The same early text that spoke of Moctezuma working for peace has Malintzin ask angrily about Moctezuma's successor, "Is he such a small child?"— meaning, "Is he so irresponsible, so uncaring?" She goes on to explain: "He has no pity on the children and women; the old men have already perished."[39] In another Nahuatl account, Malintzin exhorts—quite on her own—a Tetzcocan lord to work peacefully with the Spanish. He goes to speak to his brother, Coanacochtzin, who was the tlatoani, but the belligerent Coanacochtzin ignores Malintzin's warnings and has him killed. The old man telling the story years later—to his own young people, not to Spaniards—seems almost audibly to sigh as he comments:

> If Coanacochtzin had done what the Captain said, great benefit would thus have been done to the altepetl and the commoners. For it is the task of rulers when dangers befall the altepetl to try to determine where indeed they may save the commoners, so that it may be well with the altepetl and so that the commoners do not, as it were, flee along the roads. [Coanacochtzin] endangered the altepetl and the commoners.[40]

Years later, after Malintzin's death, old conquistadors on various occasions would remember that one of her greatest skills had been her ability to convince other Indians of what she herself could see clearly—that it was useless in the long run to stand against Spanish metal and Spanish ships. "She had a great wisdom and manner with the Indians to make them understand that the Spanish were a big deal [*gran cosa*], so much so that even though they might all unite against them, they would not be able to destroy them [in the end]." "She used to talk to the Indians without the Marques [Cortés] being present, and then would make them come in peace."[41]

But at this juncture, apparently, Malintzin's skills failed her. She was now dealing with enraged young warriors who did not have Moctezuma's sense of responsibility, long-term perspective, and wide experience. Nor had they spent hours listening to all that she had to say concerning the Europeans' technological capabilities. Instead she was dealing with people who were understandably hot for vengeance. And in the short term, they could have their vengeance, as she well knew. She remained right about the long view. More Spaniards might arrive—certainly would arrive—next year. But by then, those of this first contingent—and all those people from this part of the world who had been swept up into their company—would probably be dead. Still, she had faced death before, and she had learned to keep her feelings to herself. To outside eyes, she appeared undaunted.

The Spaniards who were with her in this emergency turned on each other with vicious accusations of cowardice and grave misconduct. Cortés, for example, was supposed to have taken a final opportunity to rape the sister of the king of Tetzcoco; the men who had come with Narváez were said to have behaved like self-pitying madmen, regretting their decision to believe the fools who had led them to this place.[42] But none of the Spaniards, with one exception, ever turned on Malintzin or said anything disparaging about her. The exception was Jerónimo de Aguilar: his own early importance had been diminished due to the extraordinary speed with which she learned Spanish, and his friends also hinted in later years that he had been romantically interested in Malintzin, but without result. He was the only one ever to have implied that doña Marina had not behaved nobly on all occasions. The others, who were dependent on her and knew that she had certainly not always succeeded at everything she attempted, chose to remember her unfailing courage and good humor in all circumstances. Bernal Díaz is famous for having written glowingly of her. He was not alone in his feelings. "After Our Lord God, it was she who caused New Spain to be won." "Without her, we couldn't do anything." "If it wasn't for her, we wouldn't have won this land."[43]

Yet at the moment, Malintzin could do nothing for those with whom she found herself facing death, save offer them her calm example. Escape offered the only hope of survival; they determined to attempt it. There was one causeway still leading from the island to the mainland. They would have to take it. Yet the bridges connecting its separate segments were undoubtedly destroyed. Men worked all night constructing a portable bridge. Others packed the most important tools and valuables, including treasure that had been set aside for King Charles.

Before midnight, they broke suddenly through the gates in what was at first an organized body, racing down the avenue that became the causeway over the lake as quietly as possible. The bridge served its purpose at the first place they faced the water, but they were never able to pick it up and move it to the next location where it was needed. They went forward with only some wooden beams from the palace to help them make the other crossings. Warriors in canoes descended on them from all sides: they were intent on destroying the makeshift bridges and stabbing upward at the armored horses who were vulnerable from below, for they recognized the horses as the Spaniards' most valuable weapon. They killed fifty-six of the eighty horses that night. At the second place the causeway was broken, the fugitives drowned in droves. The Indians told what the Spaniards never did: "It was as though they had fallen off a precipice; they all fell and dropped in, the Tlaxcalans . . . and the Spaniards, along with the horses and some women. The canal was completely full of them, full to the very top. And those who came last just passed and crossed over on people, on bodies."[44]

Approximately two-thirds of the Spanish died that night and perhaps an even greater proportion of the Tlaxcalans: about six hundred Spaniards and an unknown number of Indians. One Indian observer remembered with particular horror the sight of the women who were drowned. They were highborn ladies who had been taken as concubines by the Spaniards. Now their beautifully dressed forms floated lifelessly in the fetid water. Almost all of the men who had come with Narváez were killed, for most of them were in the rear. Those who survived were largely in the first wave and had surprise on their side to some extent; they were at least able to make it past the wooden bridge and the second canal before those places became disaster zones. Bernal Díaz was among those ordered to guard the temporary bridges and see that those in the rear could make it through. As an old man, he still struggled with his conscience, for he had not done so: "I declare that if the horsemen had waited for the soldiers at each bridge, it would have been the end of us all: not one of us would have survived. . . . The lake was full of canoes. . . . What more could we have attempted than we did, which was to charge and deal sword thrusts at those who tried to seize us [from below], and push ahead till we were off the causeway?"[45]

The treasure and the big guns were gone, of course, along with most of the horses. That went without saying. Cortés did not even ask about them as his forces gathered on the other side of the causeway. He did ask if the shipbuilder, Martín López, had made it across and was told that he had. The Spaniards believed that a son of Moctezuma's and his several daughters, who were to have come along as hostages, had all been killed, abandoned by their guards as quickly as the gold and larger weapons had been abandoned. In fact only the son and one daughter had died. Tecuichpotzin and two of her sisters had been recognized and escaped into the arms of their people. A guard of thirty Spanish soldiers and a large Tlaxcalan contingent had escorted Malintzin and doña Luisa, daughter of Xicotencatl, the Tlaxcalan chief upon whose aid the Spanish now depended. Whatever his flaws, Cortés was no fool. He knew that these two women were his most valuable asset; in the near term they were even more important than horses and steel. One Spanish woman had also traveled in their company and so survived. It is even possible that all three were given breastplates and helmets to wear. Malintzin and the *castellana,* María de Estrada, were said to have worn them on other occasions, and there was surely no occasion like the present one. Amidst all his self-doubts, Bernal Díaz did remember something good about that night—and it was the joy he felt on the other side when he suddenly caught sight of the faces of Marina and Luisa in the rainy dawn.[46]

FIVE

Water-Pouring Song

WHEN THE LAST OF THE SPANIARDS WHO HAD FAILED TO ESCAPE HAD BEEN killed, the people of Tenochtitlan began to celebrate. Men who were young at the time later looked back wistfully, "It was thought that [our enemies] had gone forever, that they would never come back." Those who thought differently were silenced. Tecuichpotzin and her sisters watched happily as their people swept away the debris left by the Spanish with a fervor that was as much religious as it was political. Together the city folk set to work refurbishing the altars to their gods. Tecuichpotzin, who carried the royal line within her person, had learned that her first consort had died, but she was soon married to Cuitlahuac, thus conferring legitimacy upon him as Moctezuma's successor.

The happy weeks were few. In a matter of months, Tenochtitlan was struck with the most terrible disaster within living memory. A great pestilence came. It came as a secret enemy, traveling from the east. A person exposed to someone who was sick felt no effects at all for the first ten days and remained unaware of mortal danger. Then the high fever and wracking pain set in, lasting for days. Toward the end came the pustules. They spread over the body in great hideous sores. "People could no longer walk about, but lay in their dwellings and sleeping places, no longer able to move or stir. . . . they called out loudly [in their pain]." There weren't enough healthy people remaining to gather food and water, cook, or bury the putrefying bodies; the population weakened and starved. Of those who survived, many were left blind or disfigured for life. When the epidemic began in the city with just a few people, it seemed to everyone that no illness could be worse, but even then, though the healthy were sensitive to the horror experienced by the ailing, no one imagined the extent of the disaster, the numbers of people who would eventually contract the disease. It was unfathomable. The wave of death rose ever higher, week after week, for sixty days. Then suddenly it abated and moved onward in the direction of Chalco.[1]

Tecuichpotzin and her sisters, who were among those who always had access to food, survived. But their city was desolate. Cuitlahuac had died; the noblemen who were left alive met to decide who would be the next tlatoani. They chose Cuauhtemoc, a young kinsman of Moctezuma's. He, too, married Tecuichpotzin, as a sign of the legitimacy of his rule, and began to act as king. But it would be several more months before the living rallied and attempted to resume their lives as best they could.

The devastated people had no way of knowing what it really was that had occurred. A microbe had arrived in one of Narváez's ships. It was another weapon, albeit an unintended one, in the European arsenal—invisible and deadly, destroyer of worlds. It was *la viruela,* "the smallpox," and it had a long history. Technology produces some unexpected results. For many centuries, Old World peoples, in living with their farm animals, had exposed themselves to dangerous viruses. Trade and transportation had only made the problem worse. The Mediterranean had long served as a grand thoroughfare connecting Europe with North Africa and Asia. People on all three continents worked to perfect the ships that scudded over the blue waters, the pulleys and machinery used to load and unload the boats, the armaments employed to protect the cargos, and the maps, star charts, and equipment used to guide the craft in and out of ports. And in doing so, they unintentionally perfected another weapon, for those boats carried microbes. The citizens of the Old World developed a hideous menu of diseases, as sickness spread more rapidly and efficiently from port to port than in any other way, with new germs attacking previously unexposed populations. There was an important silver lining behind this dismal picture. Those who did not die of a particular pest were usually immune for the rest of their lives, and mothers could even pass some of their own antibodies to the children they nursed at their breasts. Thus the Spanish not only carried the smallpox germ to Cempoala but brought their own relative immunity as well. The indigenous, on the other hand, had no such defense.[2]

The Spanish might theoretically have seized the moment of Tenochtitlan's grisly epidemic to reenter the city and take it without a fight. They could not do it, however. For it was not only the Spaniards' enemies who fell before this new onslaught but their friends as well. With great difficulty, Cortés and the other survivors of the *noche triste* ("Night of Sorrows" as they called it) had managed to retreat to Tlaxcala, where they desperately hoped to meet with a friendly reception. With doña Luisa still alive and supposedly married to Pedro de Alvarado, the leaders of the two groups remained kin, figuratively speaking. When the fugitives arrived, they found that the pox had preceded them. Maxixcatzin, king of the sub-altepetl of Ocotelolco, was dying of it, along with thousands of his people. In years to come, the Tlaxcalans would keep up their tradition of passing on their history. The year 1520 was important in their accounts, not because the Spaniards came back, which almost no one mentioned, but because the deadly sickness arrived. It was also the year, the native writers occasionally added, when the Tlaxcalans learned to build great ships.[3]

How that came about is part of a longer story. The Spanish had returned to Tlaxcala in desperate shape. Mexica warriors and their allies had harassed them throughout the retreat. Out in the open, however, the Europeans could still defend themselves effectively. They had moved together toward their destination in a great amoebic mass—with those who were still able to fight and those on horseback on the outside edges of the formation. The relatively few Tlaxcalans who still survived guided them on their journey. They stopped in abandoned towns and ate the scraps of corn they found; they also ate a horse that died.[4]

The Tlaxcalans, needless to say, were divided over the question of what they should do with the Spanish once they arrived. Many saw them as a plague of hungry locusts who had descended in a time of sickness, or as warmongers who had already been responsible for the deaths of many fine Tlaxcalan warriors. Some, therefore, were for allying with their old enemies in Tenochtitlan and finishing the job the Mexica had started. But others reminded these hotheads that the remaining four hundred

Europeans and twenty-odd horses could still do extraordinary damage, as the Tlaxcalans already knew from their own experience, and that more of the strangers would probably come. Probably doña Luisa told them that she knew for certain more were coming. They would do best, reasoned many, to stay the course and use their alliance with the armored ones to gain the upper hand over Tenochtitlan. They could bargain with the Spanish, demanding a promise that they would never have to pay tribute to whoever ended up ruling in that city. It was this school of thought that eventually won out.[5]

For twenty days, while the discussions and negotiations continued, the Spaniards ate, rested, and tended to their wounds. Gangrene set in here and there, and some more men died. Cortés had to have two fingers on his left hand cut off. Once he was able to ride again, he knew what he had to do: either Malintzin had explained it all to him, or else he could see the lay of the land himself—probably both. Retreating to the coast, however tempting in the short term, would never do. It would only make their problems last longer. They had to demonstrate the strength of their weapons again immediately. Thus they made it their business to begin mounted attacks on smaller altepetls that were not friendly to them. The prisoners they took were branded on the cheek and set aside to be sold into slavery in the Caribbean. It was not long before several states sued for peace or came forward to ask to become allies. "They see," wrote Cortés in the midst of the fighting, "how those who do so are well received and favored by me, whereas those who do not are destroyed daily." The Mexica, meanwhile, offered one year's tax relief to those who refrained from going over to the Spanish, but that was a distant carrot compared to the immediate threat of mounted lancers riding through town. When the altepetl of Coatinchan received Tenochca emissaries, the Spanish torched their villages. "On the following day three chieftains from those towns came begging my forgiveness for what had happened and asking me to destroy nothing more, for they promised that they would never again receive anyone from Tenochtitlan."[6]

It has become commonplace to assert that the Spanish could never have attained victory if the Mexica empire had not been riddled with conflict, that they needed their indigenous allies in order to win. That is clearly true. The earliest Spanish to arrive would have been crushed by greater numbers had they not worked with Indian allies, "special forces" style.

sacrificed, many of the Spaniards' allies withdrew again. It has often been said that they returned only when the Nahua priests' predictions of a great Tenochca victory to occur within the ensuing eight days did not come true. Cortés, though, outlined events as follows: first, messengers arrived from Veracruz telling of the arrival of yet another ship and bringing more powder and crossbows to prove it, and then, in the next sentence, "all the lands round about" demonstrated their good sense and came over to the Spaniards' side.[9]

Thirty years later, some of the young Nahua men who worked for the Franciscans at their school in Tlatelolco asked the old men who still remembered the embattled months of 1521 to come and talk to them about their experiences. They led their guests through dark, quiet rooms bordering the church courtyard to a place where they could work, and then asked them in polite and respectful Nahuatl to consider themselves welcome, to take care to preserve their good health, to seat themselves. As the old ones spoke of what they remembered, the young ones dipped their feather quills in black ink and tried to write it all down on the large, thick paper they had before them. Their actions made a peculiar scratching noise. In the old days, the elders knew, the writing would have been different, and the scribes would never have used black ink alone, but red and black together, on the same page. These young men remembered little or nothing about those times, however, having spent so many years of their lives with the Spanish friars.

The old men said the first attack on the city had come suddenly. Like lightning in the storm season, they had known it was coming, and yet when it came they were somehow stunned. The Spanish had been moving in the area for months; they had been seen assembling their boats across the water in Tetzcoco. Then one day they came rapidly across in a body toward the neighborhood of Zoquipan on the island's shore. The indigenous had not known how fast those great boats could go when in full sail with the wind behind them. The people ran about frantically, calling desperately to their children; they grabbed them, tossed them in their canoes, and paddled for their lives. The water grew full of their craft. The Spaniards and their allies thus took an uninhabited quarter and looted it.[10]

There was a pattern to the events that the old men went on to recount;

as they spoke, the strategy the Spanish had employed became clear. The foreigners repeatedly used their cannon to knock down the walls that the Mexica had built as obstructions and even to bring down whole buildings. Then they would send in their indigenous allies to fill in the canals in the area with rubble or sand, while the long-range crossbows and guns guarded them. Once the Spanish had a flat, open space before them they could take control of it relatively easily with their horses and lances. They also had constant access to food supplies; the Mexica, on the other hand, did not, for they were surrounded.

And yet despite their advantages, the invaders found it tough going. For close to three months the Indians contested every foot of ground. At night, the city folk were sometimes able to reexcavate the filled-in canals. Famous warriors performed death-defying deeds and sometimes managed to topple a horse and bring down its rider. Twice the Mexica managed to isolate and capture large groups of Spaniards. They knew exactly what to do with them, how best to terrify their enemies. "When the sacrifice was over, they strung the Spaniards' heads on poles; they also strung up the horses' heads." In this case, they wanted to be sure their enemies saw the sacrifice victims from afar—which they did. Normally, the Mexica did not kill Spaniards in this way, for it gave them too much honor. The natives preferred to strike them on the back of the head, like ignoble criminals.[11]

Events involving Spanish losses were etched in Mexica memory because they had provided fleeting moments of extraordinary pride, for the battle was ultimately unequal, and Spanish defeats were unusual in the grand scheme of things. Every day, it seemed, the Spanish killed dozens more of the Mexica; once, several hundred died in a single day. "Bit by bit they came pressing us back against the wall, herding us together."[12]

The indigenous used their ingenuity in every way possible. Early in the campaign, they secretly opened a dike and nearly managed to trap the Spanish on an island that was connected to land only by a single narrow causeway. Usually, however, they were left in the position of needing to decode Spanish tactics and technology as quickly as possible, rather than showing off their own. They made keen observations:

> The crossbowman aimed the bolt well, he pointed it right at the person he was going to shoot, and when it went off, it went whining, hissing and humming. And the arrows missed nothing, they all hit

someone, went all the way through someone. The guns were pointed and aimed right at people. . . . It came upon people unawares, giving them no warning when it killed them. However many were fired at died, when some dangerous part was hit: the forehead, the nape of the neck, the heart, the chest, the stomach or the abdomen.[13]

Even when the Mexica seized Spanish weapons in combat, they found them difficult to use. At one point, some captured crossbowmen were apparently either forced to shoot at other Spaniards or to give lessons to Mexica warriors; in either case, the arrows went astray. And the guns of course would not work without powder and shot. When the Indians captured a cannon, they recognized that they had neither the experience nor the ammunition necessary to make it useful to themselves. The best they could do was to make it impossible for the Spanish ever to regain it: they sank it in the lake. They learned to make extra long spears, like those of the Europeans, and to zigzag so rapidly in their canoes that the brigantines could not take aim at them as effectively as they had at first. Yet what they could do in this regard was limited. Their tactics could not bring them victory; they could only hinder the Spaniards for a time. The old men did not want to bring themselves to say this in so many words, but one of them apparently came perilously close, or else one of the younger men interpolated: "In this way the war took somewhat longer."[14]

As frustrated as they were by their technological shortcomings in comparison with their enemies, however, the warriors never seem to have been awestruck. At one point, the Spanish decided to build a catapult. Cortés wished to believe that the Indian observers were petrified.

Even if it were to have had no other effect, which indeed it had not, the terror it caused [would be] so great that we thought the enemy might surrender. But neither of our hopes was fulfilled, for the carpenters failed to operate their machine, and the enemy, though much afraid, made no move to surrender, and we were obliged to conceal the failure of the catapult by saying that we had been moved by compassion to spare them.[15]

Little did he know that, in Indian memory, the incident would border on the humorous:

And then those Spaniards installed a catapult on top of an altar plat-
form with which to hurl stones at the people . . . They wound it up,
then the arm of the catapult rose up. But the stone did not land on
the people, but fell [almost straight down] behind the marketplace at
Xomolco. Because of that the Spaniards there argued among themselves. They looked as if they were jabbing their fingers in one another's faces, chattering a great deal. And [meanwhile] the catapult kept
returning back and forth, going one way and then the other.[16]

As usual, the indigenous had a rather straightforward view of what the
Spanish had and had not accomplished.

Two elements of the Spaniards' power seem to have stood out in the
men's memories above all others: the metal that the foreigners used to
make weapons and armor, and their information network. And indeed,
these were the very arenas in which the additional millennia of sedentary
living in the Old World had made the greatest difference. It certainly was
not the ancient Indians' fault that wild corn in its early form was not nearly
as rich in protein as wheat was and that they therefore had not rushed to
become full-time farmers. In continuing to rely largely on hunting and
gathering for several thousand more years, they were only doing what
made sense. But now, in 1519, they were just barely exiting from the Stone
Age, while their enemies had left it behind long ago. The elderly speakers
used the word *tepoztli* (metal, iron) more than any other in describing the
Spanish: "Their war gear was all iron. They clothed their bodies in iron.
They put iron on their heads, their swords were iron, their bows were
iron, and their shields and lances were iron." Each succeeding reference
became more specific: "Their iron lances and halberds seemed to sparkle,
and their iron swords were curved like a stream of water. Their cuirasses
and iron helmets seemed to make a clattering sound." When the Spanish
entered the city, the men's description of the metal weaponry filled whole
pages. They noted every detail. "As they came, the iron crossbows lay in
their arms. They came along testing them out, brandishing them. But
some carried them on their shoulders. . . . Their quivers went hanging at
their sides, passed under their armpits, well-filled, packed with arrows,
with iron bolts."[17]

"Packed with arrows, with iron bolts." These were meaningful words
to Indians, who lived by the bow. In their own histories, they spoke of the

power of their ancestors' arrows: "They had bee sting arrows, fire arrows, arrows that followed their prey. It is even said that their arrows could seek after [what they wanted to kill]." Indeed, the arrows of the ancients were so marvelous that they could change course midflight. "If the [hurtling] arrow saw nothing [in the sky] above, it would suddenly shoot downwards on something, perhaps a puma, or an ocelotl." But the same people who told wonderful stories of ancient arrows that could seek out their prey fully recognized that they were not living now in the realm of magical tales. They were living in a world of real quivers strapped onto real shoulders and filled with iron bolts, and they knew it. The remainder of their narrative offered a realistic, even technical description of the battles of 1521 and the weaponry used in the skirmishes.[18]

The elderly speakers' second preoccupation—perhaps more unconscious than their first, but equally important—was the Spaniards' ability to share information with each other across time and space. From the beginning, apparently, although the Indians had not known who the Spanish were, Spaniards who had never been to Mexico before had known enough about the world to decide to seek out Moctezuma. The indigenous writers had Cortés say almost immediately: "I want to see and behold [the Aztec city], for word has gone out in Spain that you are very strong, great warriors." The Spanish asked many questions and continued to demand to see the king. "When they saw [a Mexica war leader] they said, 'Is this one then Moctezuma?'" On the causeway, Cortés greeted the monarch: "Is it not you? Is it not you then? Moctezuma?" And Moctezuma at last answered, "Yes, it is me."[19] The Spaniards had somehow used their knowledge to make their way to the heart of Mexica power, but the Mexica could not begin to envision a similar expedition to the seat of Charles V. They all knew about the ships, but only a few—only those who had been able to spend time talking to people like Malintzin, who knew the strangers well—had seen the compasses, the technical maps, and the printed books that made all of this possible. The rest of the people were only beginning to piece together an explanation. It is a tribute to them that they saw so clearly that this is what needed to be explained.

Some said the fighting went on for seventy-five days, some for ninety-three. It depended on where one started to count. In any case, it went on far longer than the Spanish would have thought possible, given the effects of the smallpox and the starvation to which their enemies had been reduced. Malintzin and Jerónimo de Aguilar sometimes went with Cortés to the front lines to attempt to parley. Once, after more than a month of battling, the Tenochca warriors shouted to the Spaniards' allies that they wished to speak to the woman, she who was one of the people from here. She came, and they offered a full peace, but only on the condition that the Spanish would return to their home across the sea. "While we stood there arguing through the interpreter," Cortés remembered, "with nothing more than a fallen bridge between us and the enemy, an old man, in full view of everyone, very slowly extracted from his knapsack certain provisions and ate them, so as to make us believe that they were in no need of supplies." There must have been more specifics mentioned by the Mexica—most likely an offer of an annual tribute—for they stood in conversation with Malintzin for some time without having her translate each sentence. She was to summarize the situation afterward. "We fought no more that day, for the lords had told the interpreter to convey their proposals to me," said Cortés.[20]

Malintzin translated several other conversations that lasted hours— one with a high-level prisoner of war and one with a noble emissary who came voluntarily. The talk of compromise came to nothing, how- ever. Despite her many skills, there was absolutely nothing Malintzin could do to change the situation. The Spanish were only interested in capitulation, and the Mexica warriors, who had been feared by all the world only months before, were determined to die rather than capitu- late. Most of them did die. On August 13, presumably when there was virtually no one left to go and fight, Cuauhtemoc allowed himself to be taken. The Spanish believed they had taken him unawares—or at least so they said—but in the indigenous accounts, he chose to go forward and offer himself up. Even the Spanish account can really be taken in no other way: the Europeans said they came upon a certain canoe, and when they were about to kill the occupants, one of them shouted out that the tlatoani was in the boat. Even with the world falling in shambles about them, the Mexica could have hidden the king's canoe from the Spaniards' large vessels had they wanted to; instead it ventured into the very path of the enemy.[21]

Cuauhtemoc asked for protection for his wife, Tecuichpotzin, and his household of women and requested that the remaining city people—almost all women, children, and old people—be allowed to leave, to go find food in the countryside. Malintzin explained his demands, and the Spanish agreed to both. Word spread with a rapidity in proportion to the people's hunger. They had already eaten everything they had, down to their leather goods and the lizards in the gardens. For more than two days, there were people on the roads, carrying their most precious property out toward other altepetls where they had friends and relations. There were still some young children alive, carried on the backs of their mothers and older siblings. But no babies cried; they had died long ago. Those of the men interviewed in the 1550s who would have been among the children remembered a feeling of joy that day as they made their way out of the stinking city, toward the food that awaited them in the countryside; yet they also remembered hearing the sounds of lamentation.[22]

The Mexica said that even then, in their filthy and starved state, some of the indigenous allies still attacked them—not yet having fully settled old scores—and that Spanish men kidnapped some of the young women. Indeed, Cuauhtemoc soon asked Malintzin to arrange to have all the Mexica women living in the Spanish camp released. It was a complicated issue, however, as even a European observer could see:

> [Cortés] gave the Mexicans permission to search in all three camps, and issued an order that any soldier who had an Indian woman should surrender her at once if she of her own free will wished to return home. Many chieftains searched from house to house and persevered until they found them. But there were many women who did not wish to go with their fathers or mothers or husbands, but preferred to remain with the soldiers with whom they were living. Some hid themselves, others said they did not wish to return to idolatry, and yet others were already pregnant.[23]

In the end, apparently, only three were returned to their families in this way. Perhaps others simply slipped away from the Spanish camp more quietly. Perhaps not, however. Their family members who were left alive were starving, as the captive women knew all too well. And even if there were enough food to go around, to return to a father or husband pregnant with a Spanish child would bring untold trouble. Whereas by staying in the Spanish camp, it was possible that the women would have access to resources and could help those they loved.

It seems clear that Malintzin played an integral role in the unfolding negotiations, that without her, the defeated Mexica would probably have fared worse, finding it nearly impossible to express themselves to the victors. We should steer clear, however, of any romantic notions: no one thanked her for her efforts. On the contrary, the Mexica saw her as they saw any other conqueror. Theirs are the only indigenous records demonstrating subtle hostility toward her. This is hardly surprising. She hailed from a distant region they deemed a land of barbarians; she was a former slave, and now she gave commands to men who only a few years before would have thought no more of her than they did of any other pretty prisoner of war. The old men speaking in the 1550s described her as having loudly—almost violently—passed on Cortés's demand that they locate the gold that had been lost in the canals during the noche triste. At length Cuauhtemoc presented some treasure through his second-in-command, whose traditional title was *cihuacoatl*:

Malintzin replied, "The Captain says, 'Is this all?'"

Then the Cihuacoatl said, "Perhaps some of the common folk removed it, but it will be investigated. Our lord, the Captain, will see it [again]."

Then again Malintzin replied, "The Captain says that you are to produce two hundred pieces of gold of this size." She measured it with her hands, making a circle with her hands.

Again the Cihuacoatl replied, saying, "Perhaps some woman put it in her skirt. It will be sought; he will see it."[24]

Earlier in the purported dialogue, the cihuacoatl has already been snide to the Spanish. "Let the *teotl*, the Captain, pay heed," he lectures Cortés, before telling him that they do not have the gold. That he does not mean to call him a god in using the term is quite evident. The more politic Cuauhtemoc interrupts him, "What are you saying, Cihuacoatl?" Then, as an example to the would-be rebel, he refers to the Spanish as *totecuioan*, meaning "our governing lords." More than one historian has suggested that the obviously angry and indiscreet cihuacoatl is making a sarcastic joke at Malintzin's expense when he refers to a woman hiding gold under her skirt—gold that is to be offered to Cortés. If the real cihuacoatl did not actually say this in 1521—and expect Malintzin to translate it—then the men who recounted the incident were telling an apocryphal story, one that demonstrates their own attitude toward Malintzin as they looked back on that time.[25]

Various references to Malintzin in the Florentine Codex portray her as screeching from rooftops and making demands. In another source, she fares worse: there is a postconquest indigenous document from Coyoacan, located next door to Tenochtitlan, that depicts the Spaniards using dogs to attack indigenous leaders. Cortés and Malintzin calmly look on, he making a peaceful hand gesture and she holding out a rosary. It is extremely unlikely that Malintzin would have stood publicly praying with a rosary at such a moment, but the point is that such was the impression left in the minds of those who felt they had reason to resent her.[26]

About the same time as the students of the Franciscans were interviewing elderly men who remembered the battle for Tenochtitlan, other friars were supervising the transcription of some of the old Nahuatl songs that had come down through the years. For centuries, the songs had evolved with each new generation; they were malleable, constantly reflecting the new experiences of the singers and their audiences. By the 1550s and 1560s, many of them contained references to the Christian god and to other elements of life with the Spanish. One of the songs written down at that time was called the "Water-Pouring Song." Reading it now, it is clear that some of its motifs are ancient. In the first lines, the Mexica reach the turquoise-green waters where they choose to make their home. They touch the source of life, the water's flowing-out place. For a number of lines, the song continues in this vein, then it is swept up into more recent events, and water takes on new meanings. Cortés arrives at the shores of the lake, as the Mexica before him had done. Moctezuma goes to meet him and says, just as he does in the Florentine Codex, that he will be his poor, suffering vassal. The great Moctezuma is to be reduced to a tributary. "In Mexico, princes pour out water," run the words of the singer. Even Moctezuma is hauling a great vat of water, and the Tlaxcalans come to marvel—and to gloat. It is Malintzin who gives the imperious orders, though she bears a name reminiscent of the Virgin (*Malía teuccihuatl*). "The lady María comes shouting, María comes saying, 'O Mexicans, let your water pitchers come in. Let them be carried in, lords.'"[27]

In the midst of the song, the central metaphor shifts again: the beautiful water pitchers of the Mexica are broken, shattered. They never thought it would be so, living in a world of blue-green flowing water, waters rushing, waters pouring forth. Yet even with their pitchers shattered, their world is not destroyed. "I seek the lords who drew the water," intones the singer. For they have left something of their world, those who were lords, who once had the water carried to them. Those who wept at the moment of defeat were indeed the lords and rulers. But much that is beautiful still remains in this watery world. Now, baptizing bishops sprinkle water on the city, and ships plow the teeming ocean: these new images of water continue for pages. The poetic images that we can still understand are arresting, both before and after the moment of conquest, but by the end, the song has moved far from where it began. Reading it now, we cannot help thinking that something has been lost.

And indeed, something more than an original song was irrevocably lost. Among the Mexica, those who were lords, those who once had water carried to them, were brought low, displaced. Malintzin—an interloping noblewoman from another altepetl—gave orders to the most powerful lords the world had known up until then. There could be no clearer statement of the Mexica people's ultimate loss. It is no wonder that their warriors were willing to fight to the death.

Many of them died as heroes, their stories living on to make their people proud: "Axoquentzin pursued his enemies; he made them let people go, he spun them about. But this warrior Axoquentzin died there [in the battle for Tenochtitlan]; they hit him with an iron bolt in the chest, they shot an iron bolt into his heart. He died as if he were stretching out when going to sleep."[28]

Axoquentzin was a great hero. Perhaps, though, his was not the only kind of heroism. As the women filed out of the city with those of their parents and children who were still alive, they relinquished the symbolic right to have water carried to them; they chose survival instead. As others had done before them, they found the strength to do what was needed, to carry on. "If someone asks you, 'Mother, why are you crying?' Tell them, 'the firewood is green, and makes me cry with so much smoke.'" That afternoon and evening, the rains came as they always did in that season. In the gray-wet dusk, wherever they found a welcome, the Mexica women helped to pat corn dough into tortillas. They fed the children, many of whom would now live to grow up after all. In the months to come, they would return to their city and carry on with their lives, practicing their crafts, reopening the market. From time to time, they might sing the "Water-Pouring Song." If the Spanish ever heard it, they would not understand its mysteries. For it was part of the world of "we people here"—a world that was, after all, still theirs.

SIX

Reed Mats

A FEW MONTHS LATER, IN NOVEMBER OF 1521, LICENCIADO ALONSO SUAZO sat working excitedly in his chambers in Santiago de Cuba. Suazo, a well-reputed judge from Segovia who had been sent to the New World in 1518 to conduct an inquiry into the treatment of the indigenous, had just met with one of Cortés's companions, Diego de Ordás, who was racing back to Spain with treasure and with news. Suazo was eager to share all that he had heard with a high-ranking priest who was one of his patrons back in Spain. He had gotten some of the specifics confused, but he had retained a great deal of what Ordás had told him: "There are great lords," he wrote, "whom they call in their language *tectes*, especially one whom they call Monteuzuma, who is lord of all the province of Mexico; and he resides in a city that they call Tenestutan, founded over the water on a salt lake which measures more than thirty leagues in circumference; they cross over the lake to the land by means of certain bridges of two to three leagues, even of four." Ordás had also shown off some of the treasures that he had aboard the ship. Suazo had seen, for example, some warriors' costumes made to resemble ferocious animals. "They are so aptly put together that not even Circe . . . in her time could have managed to turn men into beasts more effectively." He waxed on enthusiastically about the goods he had been told were for sale in the market and about those that he had seen himself. "There is even silver that the Indians have made into large vessels in our own style."[1]

To Suazo's mind, the Mexicans had all the marks of a great civilization—most especially, a pronounced social hierarchy, and besides that, skill in artisan crafts and a thriving marketplace. Perhaps he found himself discomfited at the thought that these people were to be reduced to a kind of serfdom—were even now being so reduced—for he shifted his tone very suddenly. "Every day they sacrifice a live human," he claimed. And he went on to describe a grisly prison for those captured in war—a house of horror where men and boys were kept caged until their hearts were cut from their bodies. Suazo thus reassured himself that these people were, after all, barbarians, in desperate need of Spain's humanizing influence.

Alonso Suazo did not know that even as he wrote, the indigenous were experiencing Spanish customs as barbaric in the extreme. Surviving Tenochca nobles, including Cuauhtemoc, were being submitted to torture as the Spanish sought still more gold. Hot rods were applied to the soles of their feet. The Europeans had carried some of their victims about on poles and hanged several of the most recalcitrant publicly. In a variety of other cases—in Tetzcoco and Xochimilco, for example—they loosed their giant dogs and let the mastiffs seize men by the necks and kill them.[2]

Indeed, the Spaniards seemed to be in a veritable frenzy to amass riches. By the middle of 1522, they had gathered together thousands of pesos worth of gold and collected other goods that would fetch a price back home—cacao, cotton, obsidian mirrors, jade jewelry, certain kinds of shell necklaces, and exotic feathers. One-fifth of all goods (or the profits thereof) were purportedly sent to King Charles. In the accounts prepared for the monarch, the colonizers proudly entered the sum of 5,397 pesos as the royal share of the funds that had been raised by selling into slavery the branded prisoners of war taken in the environs of Tenochtitlan. There was at first a heady atmosphere of wheeling and dealing among the Spanish, an expectation that their fortunes were made. Even small men became big spenders. Pedro Hernández, a tailor, decided to return to Spain with the 1522 shipment, taking his 200-peso share of the spoils with him. In the port of Veracruz, or perhaps onboard the ship, he either lost money gambling or made some splendid purchases, for he had only 140 pesos left by the time he reached Seville. In fact, the Spanish in general were beginning to find their newfound wealth to be finite after all. When the treasure troves the conquerors were able to extract from the defeated polities began to dwindle, they did not hesitate in many cases to sell more Indians into Caribbean slavery, claiming that they did so only in the case of those who had been enslaved before the Spaniards ever arrived.[3]

In this atmosphere, Malintzin saw firsthand the fate that might have awaited her, had she not been fortunate enough to manage to take matters into her own hands. The victorious Europeans seemed to see Indian women as theirs for the taking, without understanding any of the social rules that had formerly governed the giving of women at the end of wars. To start with, they assumed that young girls and wives were hiding treasure. "The Christians searched all over the women; they pulled down their skirts and went all over their bodies, in their mouths, their vaginas, their hair." And it was not long before the Spanish were also accused of holding women by force and using them for sex. Pedro de Alvarado later defended himself from such charges. He condescendingly implied that there were more than enough desperately impoverished women available and that he had no need to use force. "[I let] that Indian woman return to her land [her people]; since there were so many Indian women about, just as there are now, I had no need of her." Despite the Spaniards' usually cohesive attitude regarding the indigenous, some of the conquerors were scandalized at their peers' behavior and lodged complaints, causing Charles V to make a special plea in January of 1523 to cease the abuses of the women.[4]

Despite the appearance of a free-for-all in the early months, however, Cortés actually did have a plan. In the words of the oldest Indian narrative of the conquest, "The altepetls all around were distributed. The altepetls everywhere were given to the Spaniards as vassals."[5] Though he did not officially have royal permission to do so until Diego de Ordás returned from Spain in October of 1523, Cortés began almost immediately to distribute the altepetls to his followers as *encomiendas,* as had been done in the Caribbean. Each Spaniard was—in theory—to guard the spiritual welfare of the ethnic state (or part thereof) he had been assigned; in exchange he had the right to demand that the people there pay him tribute and that they labor on his behalf.

When the vanquished altepetls in the immediate vicinity had been given out, Cortés sent his forces outward and organized the conquest of any states that chose to resist. The Tlaxcalans and other native allies were instrumental in this project. After the battles were over, the negotiations carried on in Nahuatl were the next crucial step: at first Cortés relied on Malintzin to help him make all necessary political arrangements. Often a belligerent noble family had to be ousted and replaced by a rival family more amenable to the Spaniards' agenda, and only a translator who could understand the subtleties of local politics could be helpful in this regard.

Several decades later, an old man in Tetzcoco gave an account of how Cortés had proceeded in his altepetl. There had long been tensions between rival factions of the chiefly family. In the aftermath of the war, Cortés proposed to have a young man called Ahuachpitzactzin—the younger brother of the former ruler—installed as king, but he met with resistance. Few even came to meet with him:

> After some time the Captain came to the palace at Ahuehuetitlan. And there in the pumice stone house was Ahuachpitzactzin. Coanacochtzin [the former king] had not yet gone away. The Captain spoke; Marina interpreted. She said to Ahuachpitzactzin: The Captain says, Why is it thus? Have the noblemen, the lords, the chiefs, the seasoned warriors, gone away somewhere? Is the altepetl to which I have come not very large? Are there not very many people?[6]

In Nahuatl, the answer to such rhetorical questions was meant to be a resounding "No!" The great Tetzcoco, the Paris of the Nahuatl-speaking world, clearly was not to be mistaken for a small and insignificant altepetl. If the current tlatoani could not or would not muster a large audience in support of the Spanish, then he would not be allowed to continue to rule. Malintzin continued: "Apparently no one is here. Apparently there is no reed mat [of authority]. Why has Ixtlilxochitl the steward held everything back? Shall I not just depose him? Coanacochtli and Ixtlilxochitl have done wrong." They pressured Ahuachpitzactzin to assent to the execution of the former king, Coanacochtli, his elder brother, who had sided against the Spanish in the war, but Ahuachpitzactzin maintained a stony silence.

At first the story told by the old man from Tetzcoco seems confusing: Ixtlilxochitl, another of the king's brothers, was known to the Spanish for being one of the few true enthusiasts for their cause. Later he would be among the very first—if not the first—to accept the Christian sacrament of marriage. Why hadn't he arranged for more people to come to this public event, and why did he join the others in maintaining an angry silence? This was undoubtedly what Cortés himself wanted to know.

Malintzin knew what he did not: the question of who should occupy the reed mat, the symbol of political authority, had long been a vexed one in Tetzcoco. The Spaniards had stumbled into an inflammatory political situation whose roots were generations old. The problem was a familiar one to the girl from Olutla: it was the old issue of half siblings who hated each other. Nezahualcoyotl, one of the greatest kings of the Nahua world and a renowned poet, had had sons by different wives. There had been tensions over who should inherit the kingship. Eventually—and unsurprisingly—Nezahualpilli, whose mother was from Tenochtitlan, won out. He, too, had sons by multiple women, and they, too, ended up fighting a civil war. Something like eleven sons were born to him by a niece of Tizoc, who was then the king of Tenochtitlan. Later, however, when Moctezuma became king of the Tenochca, he married his sister to Nezahualpilli and wanted her son, Cacama, to inherit the Tetzcoco rulership. Reasons were found to execute several of the older boys, but at least two of them survived the bloodbath, among them Coanacochtli and Ixtlilxochitl. The latter waged a war against Cacama, Moctezuma's favored nephew, and he had the backing of so many people that the altepetl split in two.

When the Spanish came, Ixtlilxochitl saw a marvelous political opportunity and went to ally himself with them, hoping to gain control over the entire kingdom. After the Spanish arrested and then killed Cacama, Coanacochtli—Ixtlilxochitl's full brother—was able to replace him as king of the southern part of the altepetl, the part still known as Tetzcoco. He did not share his brother's desire to ingratiate himself with the powerful strangers; he simply hated them. When the Spanish tried to influence a younger brother by another wife and used him as a messenger, he had the young man killed; probably the boy came from a branch of the family that had sided against him and his own full brothers in days gone by. Then Coanacochtli went off to Tenochtitlan to join the Mexica in fighting the strangers. He was imprisoned at the end of the war along with Cuauhtemoc. During the battles of 1521, the Spanish, who were encamped at Tetzcoco, had appointed another younger brother to rule—Tecolcoltzin, whom they called "don Hernando"—but he had died, probably of smallpox, and now needed to be replaced. The obvious choice was Ixtlilxochitl, but he preferred to publicly acquiesce to the Spaniards when they chose yet another younger brother, Ahuachpitzactzin. Ixtlilxochitl himself would act as steward. Almost certainly this was because he did not want to be the one to oust his own full brother, Coanacochtli, with whom he had survived the horrors of their troubled youth. He had sided with the Spanish for reasons of expediency in order to defeat another branch of the family; now suddenly he found himself pressured to accept Coanacochtli's execution. It was probably not what he had had in mind. His old loyalties ran deeper than his new ones.

If Malintzin imagined that the past lay heavily over the people whom she was addressing, she was not wrong. The old man telling the story years later alluded to it himself, saying that memories of two great kings were with them that day: all that was spoken was said "in the presence of all the sons of Nezahualpiltzintli and the noblemen who were Nezahualcoyotl's [other] grandsons and the lords their fathers." Either Malintzin or someone else speaking through her apparently conveyed the situation to Cortés. After some negotiating, he reversed himself and said that Coanacochtli need not die if he would leave the altepetl and live under virtual house arrest. Coanacochtli then put the tensions to an end by accepting the proposition: "'Do I not understand? The lord has now generously agreed to let me go.' This is all Coanacochtzin said. Then he arose and went forth through the palace gate." His earlier determination to fight had already been the cause of enough problems for his people, and now an acceptable peace would be offered to them, if he were out of the way.[7]

Here in Tetzcoco, as elsewhere, a very young man who had begun to learn Spanish was apparently found to help the new king and his steward to govern and bring the labor levies to their destination. His Christian name was Tomás:

[I]n Ixtlilxochitzin's absence, the Captain spoke to all the field people whom Ixtlilxochitzin was taking with him. He said to them: You no longer belong to Ixtlilxochitl. You are to construct my house in Mexico. Ixtlilxochitl will favor peace. And if he brings no one [to labor], I shall therefore become angry; I shall hang him for it. He will no longer give things to anyone [as chiefs do]. The interpreters were Marina and Tomás.[8]

Between them, Marina and Tomás found a way to convey to the commoners why it was in their own best interest to do as Ixtlilxochitl asked and agree to work for the Spanish.

In the ensuing years, the new king, Ahuachpitzactzin, whom the Spanish had renamed "don Carlos" (after their own monarch) in order to convey their belief in his political authority, did not always do what the Spanish wanted. He lost power. Eventually, Ixtlilxochitl simply ruled himself. He was later replaced with a commoner, to the horror of the nobles. But in 1521, the Spanish did not yet have the power to take such a step, as Malintzin knew well. The nobility became restive enough when she told them that Cortés was appropriating Coanacochtli's lands—not only those that supported the rulership and were his while he was chief, but also those that he had amassed privately with the intention of leaving to his sons and nephews, the next generation of the nobility. "Don Hernando Cortés really mistreated the noblemen of Tetzcoco and the rulership," lamented the aging man who recounted this story, himself one of the descendants. Then he remembered to be tactful, and he added, "The Captain did not think he was doing that."9

Meanwhile, as the noblemen steeled themselves to accept what they had no power to change, the commoners were taken in large groups to labor in the capital and elsewhere. Within a few years, they had easily learned a whole new style of construction. In the words of a Mexican historian, "Building European style houses turned out to be child's play for the indigenous artisans, once they had chisels and iron hammers."10 The Plaza Mayor in Mexico City was built over one of the great central squares of Tenochtitlan. Where Moctezuma had had his palace, Cortés ordered that his own home be constructed. Where the great temple had been, the Spanish demanded a cathedral. The main government building was the first project to be finished. It had a massive facade, with a battlemented tower at each end. There were three small windows in the front and a column on each side of the main door, but these did not alleviate the almost oppressive heaviness of the palace, which contrasted strongly with the tall, elegantly tapering and colorful pyramids of days gone by.

There was new construction everywhere. Members of the first generation of conquistadors received land grants in 1522 in the vicinity of the Plaza Mayor and brought Indians from their encomiendas to begin to build Spanish-style houses. The indigenous residents of the city worked on repairing their homes, their water-borne gardens, and the giant market at Tlatelolco. The Mexica silversmiths, goldsmiths, jewelers, mosaic makers, and feather workers ceased to practice their trades in the old ways, but some of them—or their surviving family members—turned their hands to related Spanish crafts. The indigenous who produced such things as foodstuffs, herbal medicines, textiles, clothing, mats, ceramics, maguey paper, and the alcoholic drink called pulque found their work more than ever in demand.

At first, the Spanish did not live in the city but only supervised its construction. "We were still all alone," remembered an indigenous speaker from Tlatelolco. "Our lords the Christians had not yet come to settle [here]; they gave us consolation by staying for the time being in Coyoacan."[11] The people of Coyoacan, on the other hand, experienced no such consolation. They had always envisioned their home as nestled in a lovely world rich with chinampas, fish, and waterfowl; surrounded by a network of flowing streams that cut across land perfect for growing corn, maguey, and nopal cactus; rising up to forests that generously provided human beings with wood. The Spanish, on the other hand, merely saw good, relatively level ground with an abundance of fresh water and at least six thousand houses full of people who could work for them. They had staged the battle for Tenochtitlan from here, and they decided to stay until they were ready to move their capital to Mexico City proper, which turned out to be in 1524.[12]

In Coyoacan Malintzin lived with Cortés, probably in the palace that had once belonged to the local king. She not only helped him with the political negotiations that were necessary for each and every altepetl but also orchestrated the collection of tribute from far and wide. This role was in fact what many indigenous remembered most clearly in their pictorial accounts of their relationship with her. Jerónimo de Aguilar, whose own importance dimmed as hers grew, later commented sourly that there was a secret door to the house in Coyoacan, where she received extra tribute, outside of that which was officially recorded for Charles V, so that Cortés might avoid paying the royal fifth. Aguilar said that he had used his abilities as interpreter to stop Indians in the street and ask them where they were going with such abundant goods, and they would tell him they were on the way to Marina's house. The story sounds suspicious in itself and is the more so when we remember that Aguilar never spoke a word of

Nahuatl, the language of the city's residents; his importance had lain in his ability to understand Yucatec Maya. Still, there may have been a kernel of truth behind his accusations: Malintzin clearly was a skilled tribute collector and may well have worked behind the scenes to enrich herself and Cortés. Significantly, in 1529, when the conquistador learned that Aguilar's charge was to be officially brought against him by the Crown, he did not completely deny it. Rather, he countered that there were indeed "extra" goods brought to his house in Coyoacan, but that these were gifts from indigenous polities intended for Malintzin, not himself. They brought her fruits, herbal incense, and tobacco, which he said she liked to smoke. Tobacco and foodstuffs were women's special province in the Nahua marketplace, so it is very possible that Malintzin was running a business. Despite her present power, she was still vulnerable, and it would only have been wise for her to amass whatever wealth she could.[13]

Malintzin knew well that the political situation was hardly stable, and beyond this, she had to cope with personal tensions in her relations with Cortés and the constant threat of a crisis. In later years, an enemy of her daughter's would claim that she was known for her dalliances with various men, but not a single witness could be found to corroborate this assertion. Instead, three men referred to Jerónimo de Aguilar's having been interested in her, and to Cortés's raging suspicions concerning the other men. The witnesses believed that nothing had ever happened, but the captain apparently began to rely more and more on Malintzin alone to translate.[14]

Cortés would have been a difficult man to live with for any length of time. His passionate self-righteousness knew no limits. Both friends and enemies said that he was constantly throwing himself on his knees to pray. He was absolutely sure he had God on his side. His ebullient self-confidence had always been remarkable, and since the victory over Tenochtitlan it had only increased. He was so certain of his own talents and of the righteousness of his cause that he saw no discrepancy between his religious avowals and his occasionally duplicitous actions or his womanizing. His friend and devoted follower, Diego de Ordás, explained to another friend, "Cortés has no more conscience than a dog."[15] That was undoubtedly how Ordás saw him—as a large, enthusiastic, extravagantly happy, and easily angered creature whose quick movements often hurt those near him.

Others saw him in a less positive light. In 1529, during an investigation into his previous conduct, many men spoke of the numbers of women he had had in the house in Coyoacan. To what degree they were jealous and to what degree truly disapproving it is difficult to say. Certainly his accusers fed off of each other, increasing the extent of their exaggerations with each passing day of the proceedings. At first, one man mentioned— perfectly accurately—that Cortés had committed the misdeed of having relations with closely related women, with both a mother and a daughter, in one case, and with more than one daughter of Moctezuma. Then someone said on a succeeding day that he had slept not only with Marina but also with her niece. No, someone else said, it was Marina's daughter. In fact, added another, he had had forty Indian women at his disposal in his home in Coyoacan. Indeed, continued a different man, many of them were indigenous princesses, and Cortés was insanely jealous whenever they looked at another man. He even had sex with nuns, said one of the last witnesses. Then, perhaps remembering that there had been no nuns in Mexico at that time, the witness added quickly that he had heard it was so but had no proof.[16]

The embittered Jerónimo de Aguilar also mentioned the purported existence of Marina's niece, relying on its being known that he had worked closely with her in order to be believed. But then he gave himself away when he said he did not know the niece's name, perhaps it was "Catalina." No one who worked so closely with her would have been unaware of something like that, even if it were true that a slave girl had been given away with her niece, which is itself virtually unimaginable. To their credit, the judges worked hard to get to the bottom of these stories. It turned out that in 1523, a woman named Catalina González called on Cortés to demand restitution (in the form of an encomienda) for his having deflowered her young daughter back in the Caribbean. He responded that he would think about it and that it was time for his siesta. He lay back on his pallet and then suggested that the woman—who was probably only in her early thirties herself—join him. The irate Catalina repeated the story everywhere, and the source of the other rumors suddenly becomes evident, for her daughter's name was Marina.[17]

What Malintzin thought of the captain's behavior we will never know. Certainly she was accustomed to a high chief's having access to more than one woman. But she would not have been accustomed to intemperate behavior or to loud, blustering self-righteousness or to a man's thinking that literally any woman was his for the asking. She might have encountered such a pattern in an indigenous individual, but the phenomenon would certainly have been rare, as that kind of behavior was considered socially inexcusable. Self-mastery was of all traits the most sought after by the Nahua nobility; wildness was deeply wrong, the opposite of everything good. Knowing Malintzin, it seems likely that she hid her private thoughts, whatever they were, and learned to read the new cues with her usual adeptness. She clearly proved herself able to handle Cortés on a long-term basis. But however difficult she found the situation to start with, it only grew worse: in July of 1522, Cortés received word that his wife had arrived in Mexico from Cuba and would shortly make her way up from the coast.

He had married doña Catalina Suárez as a young man in Cuba—against his will, as the story went. Her father, Diego Suárez Pacheco, was, like Cortés, an hidalgo without particularly high status, but he had married doña María de Marcaida, a Basque woman of noble extraction. In 1509 Diego Suárez traveled with his wife, son, and three daughters to Hispaniola in order to serve the viceroy's wife, as such work was very desirable for gentlefolk. Later the family removed to Cuba. Catalina's brother, Juan, received an encomienda in partnership with Cortés. Soon Cortés had seduced Catalina. He promised to marry her in order to gain his ends but then proved recalcitrant. Her family asked the governor, Diego Velázquez, to apply some pressure, which he very effectively did. Cortés married Catalina and remained close enough to Velázquez to receive the appointment to lead the expedition to Mexico several years later.[18]

The house in Coyoacan was not a peaceful place after doña Catalina's arrival. Within a few months, people were saying that Hernando Cortés had murdered his wife. And perhaps he had. At first glance, the charge seems unfair: over the years, many envious people accused Cortés of many misdeeds, including murder on more than one occasion. Some would later say, for example, that he killed the royal official whom the king sent over to take his place as governor. That story is palpably ridiculous. Never would he have been such a fool; nor is there any evidence. That he may have killed his wife, however, is impossible to deny.

In October, on All Saints' Day, Cortés hosted one of the many parties he loved to give. That night, at dinner, Catalina made a remark about all that

PHOTO 2: The chapel of La Concepción in Coyoacan. An eighteenth-century building on the sixteenth-century foundations of a chapel commissioned by Cortés. Across the street is a house where doña Marina is rumored to have lived. It, too, is an eighteenth-century building, but there is a kernel of truth to the story: both buildings are in the vicinity of the indigenous settlement where Cortés set up his temporary residence in 1521. Photo by John Graham Nolan.

she would accomplish with "her" Indians. "*Your* Indians?!" guffawed her husband. "I'm not at all interested in what's yours!" The double entendre was evident to his mostly male audience, and he got the laugh he had hoped for. Catalina swept away in high dudgeon. In a few hours Cortés joined her in the chamber they shared. One of the Spanish women she had brought with her as a companion later said that she knew Catalina had suffered from jealousy ever since her arrival, given Hernando's many women. Another claimed Catalina had said that they often fought, that he was violent, and that she was afraid of him. It is possible that the lady-in-waiting said this for effect, but the story is likely to have been true, in that it offers a realistic picture. In general, medieval Europeans were not well versed in the psychological patterns of battery and would have been more likely to speak of a sudden crime of passion occurring on a single evening, yet this witness described a long-term phenomenon that we know today is often very real. Certainly a man who did not flinch at torture, who believed women existed for men's convenience, who had been drinking—and who probably had threatened his wife before—might have ended by strangling a spouse who harped on his bad behavior.

In the middle of the night, Cortés himself called out for help, announcing with agitation that his wife was dead. Soon the Spanish women who were living in or near the complex had gathered to do what they could. One man mentioned that Malintzin came, too. Several witnesses said they saw thumb marks on the dead woman's neck. Others, however, did not observe them. Still others said that Catalina had a heart condition that had undoubtedly brought about her demise. At first Cortés said nothing. Later he would say that he had found her dead, that she had apparently died of an unusual malady from which she suffered. Probably no one else, including Malintzin, was ever absolutely certain of what had transpired.[19]

It is very likely that Malintzin was living at some remove from the death scene. In two later, unrelated court cases, statements were made that implied she then maintained a household of her own. Two men mentioned that she was receiving tribute from the Indians of Tepexi and Otlazpa at this time—both altepetls near Mexico City. In a completely different context, a young Nahuatl-speaking nobleman declared that he had been raised by her as her *criado*, or "dependent," beginning after the conquest; he referred to living with her in Coyoacan.[20] It is not to be wondered at if Malintzin did not share Catalina's home. Tensions would have been rife. For Catalina had been childless, and by now Malintzin either was in the advanced stages of pregnancy or had just given birth to Cortés's first acknowledged son. That Cortés himself was invested in the child is clear: he named him Martín, after his father.

Malintzin had conceived within a few months of the victory over Tenochtitlan, after more than two years of living with Spanish men. A modern historian has made the interesting suggestion that Cortés may have refrained from placing sexual demands on her until his position was relatively secure; he may have been aware that he could not afford to have her weakened by pregnancy or risk losing her entirely in childbirth. For this to have been the case, however, Cortés would have had to be one of the most unusual European men to have been reared in the late 1400s. He would have had to be sensitive to the rigors of pregnancy and the threat of death that it always brought—and conscious of these to such an extent that he could master his desires. It seems more likely that Malintzin had not been free from sexual demands, certainly not from Puertocarrero, and probably not from Cortés. Most likely, the extreme conditions in which she had lived for the preceding two years—involving poor diet, sleep deprivation, and psychological strain of the acutest kind—had been enough to prevent conception.[21]

Those days, however, had ended in August of 1521. So after the victory Malintzin had watched the Spanish reveal their temperaments and unveil their plans as her belly swelled with the captain's child. In her own mind, the fact of her pregnancy would certainly have changed her relationship to the future world the Spanish were in the midst of forging. In her world, to become the mother of a high chief's child was to become someone of importance, even if she herself were later cast off as a sexual partner. Now she could not dissociate herself from the new reality even if she wanted to: political maps in the indigenous world showed a range of people with the right to sit on reed mats of authority connected to each other by a network of umbilical cords. She was now intertwined with the new state in the most intimate of ways.

Or she would be, that is, if she lived. When she first became aware of labor pains, she called them *nomiquizpan* in her own mind, "my moment of death," "my place and time of death."[22] She lived within the Spanish orbit, and there were some Spanish women present in the colony, but all of them were served by indigenous women, so surely at least a few of the latter were with her, holding her, speaking to her in Nahuatl. There is no doubt that as the pains escalated, reducing all the horrors that she had experienced before to mere nothings, her incoherent thoughts came to her in her native language. It is always the tongue of childhood that surfaces at such moments.

Indigenous attendants were accustomed to helping a woman try to rally toward the end of labor. "Beloved daughter," they would say, "exert yourself! What are we to do with you? Here are your mothers. This is your responsibility. Grab hold of the shield. My daughter, youngest one, be a brave woman. Face it . . . bear down, imitate the brave woman Cihuacoatl Quilaztli."[23] If she were with Spanish women, they, too, in their own language and their own way exhorted her to surpass herself. But they would also have told her to put her faith in God, to pray for help, even for mercy. These were not messages she would have been able to hear, even if she recognized the Spanish words. All her life, she had thought of a woman giving birth as a warrior, a hero who had the opportunity to win honor, not as someone who begged for mercy in the face of a great punishment being inflicted by the deity. She was to seize the shield and fight for her life, to call upon all her powers and do the great work herself. If she succeeded, she would have taken a captive, a soul, from out of the very cosmos and brought it home to receive the highest honors. But if she failed, and she herself died, there was no shame in it. She would become a thing divine; brave warriors would beg for a relic from her body, a talisman that would give them courage forever after.

Malintzin fought the battle, and won. The child came diving down from the cave within her, headfirst into the light, like a god emerging from one of the caverns in the ancient stories. It was a boy, the youngest and most special child in the world at that moment. "You have arrived on earth, my youngest one, my beloved boy, my beloved youth."[24]

If Malintzin had not been sold into slavery as a child, if she had been surrounded by friends and family at this moment, prayers for this latest branch of the ancestral tree, this latest chip off the great stone, would have been joyously offered up. But as it was no one around her envisioned the child as the culmination of all their hopes; no one was there to praise her to the skies for having made it all possible. To the Nahua way of thinking, this would have been a bitter draught to swallow. That Cortés welcomed the child, and named him for his father, was likely deeply comforting. For otherwise there was no one other than herself to call the child a treasure—a precious necklace, a precious feather, a precious green stone.[25]

In this crucial moment, she could find common ground with the Christians in other matters as well. They joined her in hoping that the babe be allowed to live for more than just a little while here on earth, but they baptized him quickly, in case the Lord should take him sooner rather than later. It was a familiar worry. "It may be that thou hast come only to pass before our eyes," the Nahua midwives used to lament. "It may be that we catch but a glimpse of thee."[26] As Malintzin regathered her strength after the birth, she heard the Spaniards around her praying in their own language and in Latin, mouthing words she had been taught and now understood well. "Hail Mary full of grace," they murmured. "The Lord is with you. Blessed are you among women and blessed is the fruit of your womb."

The next year, in 1523, dozens more Europeans arrived. They came in the entourage of Francisco de Montejo—who had left with Puertocarrero back in 1519—and the returning Diego de Ordás. They brought with them the good news—from the Spanish point of view—that Cortés did after all have the king's formal permission to distribute the labor of the indigenous in encomiendas. More translators were now needed. Numerous Indians were quickly becoming bilingual, but the Spanish especially wished to find people of their own kind who could speak Nahuatl. There had been a Spanish boy whom they called Orteguilla, the son of one of the original conquistadors, who had gained some fluency in the language, but he had been killed in one of the ongoing battles after the triumph. Another child named Alonso de Molina arrived about this time. He rapidly began to learn the language from his indigenous playmates. Later he would be taken in by the Franciscans and join their order; he would grow up to write an extraordinary Nahuatl-Spanish dictionary. In the meantime, Cortés found that some Spanish men who entered into permanent, monogamous relationships with Indian women were taking the time to learn something of their language, or at least were willing to ask their *compañeras* for help with translation. Cortés rewarded Juan Pérez, who had married one of the Tlaxcalan noblewomen, with rich encomiendas. Pedro de Alvarado, on the other hand, never bothered to learn Nahuatl from his Tlaxcalan partner, doña Luisa. She, however, clearly learned some Spanish and he kept this most useful woman nearby. In 1523 Cortés sent him to explore and conquer Guatemala, and he took Luisa with him.[27]

It is no easy task to glean a sense of all that was occurring in this period. A seventeenth-century fire later destroyed most of the notarial records from the 1520s. Those that do survive tell us that the decade was a chaotic one, as the Spanish struggled to gain control of a world that was not their own and to dominate a people whose language they did not speak. Cortés was certainly the strongest figure present, but he was surrounded by people watching closely for any signs of a weakening in his position, either in relation to the Indians or to Emperor Charles. His ability to talk to the indigenous—through Malintzin—kept him relatively safe in the one regard, and his advocates back in Spain tried to help in the other. The king waffled a bit in his support, not wanting to take an irremediable step, but over time he and his advisers came to recognize the passionate conquistador as a most effective man. In 1525 the monarch actually wrote to Cortés that his detractors were merely jealous. In order to satisfy the vitriolic critics, he also ordered Cortés to come to Spain so that his conduct could be investigated but then affably allowed him to ignore the order.[28]

Cortés, meanwhile, was taking no chances with the Indians. His ability to speak to the indigenous would remain useful only insofar as they were afraid of him and of his people. The Spanish could not afford to rest on the laurels of their previous victories. There were, after all, still millions more Indians than Europeans in this vast land. In March of 1524, Cortés promulgated very clear ordinances insisting that the colonizers keep themselves armed to the teeth. Every Spanish citizen was required to own a dagger, sword, and lance, as well as a shield, helmet, and breastplate. He who did not acquire them within six months and then appear on military parade on command would be subject to stiff fines. Those who received encomiendas of up to five hundred Indians also had to arrange to purchase either a crossbow and bolts or, failing that, a firelock gun and all the ammunition and equipment necessary to shoot two hundred times. If a colonist received between five hundred and one thousand Indians, he was required to purchase a horse as well, though he had more than six months to do so. He had a year to make the purchase, as horses were only gradually being shipped in from the Caribbean. The new law continued in great detail: the greater the size of the encomienda, the greater the number of military items that were demanded. *Encomenderos* risked increasing fines if they failed to meet these requirements; if they ignored three warnings, they stood to forfeit their grant altogether.[29]

On one level, Cortés's intentions are clear enough: he worked to install tlatoani who were amenable to a Spanish agenda on the altepetls' reed mats of authority, and he nurtured indigenous perception of Spanish strength by insisting that the Europeans keep themselves well armed. The plan worked effectively to make chiefs willing to try to meet demands for encomienda labor. It is unclear, however, if Cortés also entertained the strategy of attempting to change the way the Indians thought or if, as a pragmatic man, he recognized to some degree the hopelessness of any such desire. He certainly wanted to have the indigenous baptized, but since this could mean sprinkling holy water over hundreds at a time, he may simply have wanted to do what he viewed as being morally right—which is far different from seriously expecting the indigenous to make profound internal shifts or to consider realignments in their deepest loyalties.

The church fathers, on the other hand, were definitely optimistic in these latter regards. They were certain they could win over all the souls of the New World, and enthusiasm spread throughout their circles in Europe. In 1523 three Franciscans arrived on Mexican shores—two priests named Juan de Tecto and Juan de Aora and one lay brother named Pedro de Gante, who would later be a strong advocate for the indigenous. They stayed with the Ixtlilxochitl family in Tetzcoco and began to teach a few of their sons. In 1524 Cortés welcomed with great fanfare a large Franciscan mission headed by Martín de Valencia. He arrived with twelve other friars. About two weeks later, they held a meeting and agreed to divide themselves up and begin to proselytize in four densely settled altepetls where Cortés was sure of the political climate—Tenochtitlan, Tetzcoco, Tlaxcala, and Huexotzinco. Surviving indigenous annals from those places record the coming of the friars.[30]

Before the twelve dispersed to their various destinations, however, they demanded to hold colloquies with the indigenous leaders of the Mexica capital. Notes were taken in Spanish. Years later, the eager Bernardino de Sahagún—he who supervised the writing of the Florentine Codex—apparently translated some of these notes back into Nahuatl, in order to create a text about the errors of the ancien régime that would be useful for religious instruction. That text survives today. It is called the Coloquios and purportedly describes what occurred at a single major event. In the 1520s, the Spanish never mentioned such a uniquely grand affair, but the notes undoubtedly do reflect the kind of dialogue that unfolded on numerous occasions.[31]

In the past, historians have expressed doubt as to who in 1524 could have translated such subtle thoughts as are expressed in the Coloquios. We have every reason to believe, however, that Malintzin could have. She was obviously a gifted linguist and by now had been living among the Spanish for five years. Motolinia, one of the twelve original friars, comes close to telling us that she played an active role in such projects. He directly praised her contributions in the early days more than once and implicitly gave her credit when he raved about Cortés's extraordinary ability to converse effectively with the indigenous in this period. Given the context, it seems beyond doubt that she was the intermediary in exchanges of this kind on more than one occasion.[32]

In reading over the Coloquios, we learn that the indigenous did not simply allow themselves to be harangued, that they certainly did not accept everything they were told, and that they made their disagreements known: their quarrels with the Spanish were not lost in translation. According to the text that we have, the noblemen (*teteuctin*) and high chiefs or kings (*tlatoque*) were summoned to meet with the twelve Franciscans. The friars first introduced themselves, explaining that they were messengers coming on behalf of Charles V and the pope, who were concerned about the souls of the people of the newly discovered world across the sea, and that they brought with them God's words. Then they launched into a lengthy overview of the basic tenets of the Christian faith; according to the text we have, their speech would have taken at least two to three hours to give. When they had finished, one of the leaders present stepped forward and answered in courtly language that the twelve were most welcome, that the altepetls were there to serve them. He knew they had come from afar, from a land beyond the mists, and that their words were a great treasure, like precious green stones, like precious feathers, emerging from a chest, a lovely reed hamper. To be polite, he went on in this vein for quite some time. Then he made a shift. "What gives us anguish now is that our wise men who were prudent and skillful in our kind of speech and who were in charge of the principality [who held the reed mats, the thrones] are now dead. If they had heard from your mouths what we have heard, you would have a most agreeable salutation and reply. But we who are inferior and less wise, what can we say?" The speakers insisted that they were doing their best to govern in their predecessors' stead, but they had no experience. It would be better, they insisted, if they called together those priests who still survived, as they would know better what answer to make.[33]

That evening, the governing noblemen made the necessary arrangements, and the next day numerous priests of the old order came to hear the strangers. The spokesman of the day before again addressed the twelve, introducing the priests. "Here they are. They have come. We have told them all you said to us yesterday. . . . So that they may be fully satisfied [or informed] please tell them again from the beginning all that you said to us yesterday, though we know it is tedious for you to do so." And tedious for them to hear it again, they may have wanted to add. The Christians responded positively. "One of the twelve, using the interpreter, repeated everything that they had said to the lords the day before." If the interpreter was growing tired, there was no mention of it.

Finally one of the leading priests arose and began to speak. In true Nahua fashion, he spoke at length of how honored he and his peers were to be allowed to look on the faces of such valiant personages. Truly his people were not worthy of such an honor, he said—intending most likely to underscore his belief in the moral superiority and greater wisdom of his own people. They were impressed by—even amazed by—the words of the Spanish. Then, as any Nahua would have expected, the speaker changed his direction:

> You have told us that we do not know the One who gives us life and being, who is Lord of the heavens and of the earth. You also say that those we worship are not gods. This way of speaking is entirely new to us, and very scandalous. We are frightened by this way of speaking because our forebears who engendered and governed us never said anything like this. On the contrary . . . they taught us how to honor [the gods]. . . . And they taught us all the ceremonies and sacrifices that we make. They told us that through our gods we live and are, and that we are beholden to them. . . . They said that these gods that we worship give us everything we need for our physical existence: maize, beans, chia, etc. We appeal to them for the rain to make the things of the earth grow.

The speaker went on to spell out all the myriad reasons they had to be grateful to their deities. He concluded, "It would be a fickle, foolish thing for us to destroy the most ancient laws and customs left by the first inhabitants of this land." And if the priests were so fickle and foolish as to announce that all that they had ever preached was wrong, there would probably be trouble in store for the Spanish. The man spoke as if he was giving a friendly hint, though he was indirectly making a threat. "You should take great care not to do anything to stir up or incite your vassals to some evil deed. . . . Watch out that the common people do not rise up against us if we were to tell them that the gods they have always understood to be such are not gods at all." Rural peasants are not famous in our own day for being flexible in religious matters, nor were they then. The spokesman insisted that it would be best to act slowly and with deliberation, that the priests were not fully convinced of what the Spaniards claimed—though it gave them pain to say so and to cause their visitors any chagrin. Then he came suddenly to the crux of the matter: "All of us together feel that it is enough to have lost, enough that the power and royal jurisdiction [the reed mats, the thrones] have been taken from us. As for our gods, we will die before giving up serving and worshipping them. This is our determination; do with us what you will. This will serve in reply and contradiction to what you have said. We have no more to say, lords."

In Nahuatl, the priests closed by saying something that, if translated literally, would have been on the order of, "That is all with which we return, with which we answer, your breath, your words, O our lords."[34] It fell to the interpreter to organize the phrases and make necessary adjustments—sometimes amplifying, sometimes shortening—so that the priests' statements would be understandable to the Spanish. Malintzin—or someone else who had learned exceedingly rapidly, watching her technique—had both the deftness and the courage to do the job. Motolinia and his companions got the point, and they did not like it.

Beyond the confines of the capital city, the situation was largely the same. In many instances, new men sat on the reed mats of authority—either because of the epidemic or because the Spanish had ousted old families in favor of new ones. In their annals, the indigenous recorded the coming of the Spanish, the fall of the Mexica, and in some cases, the installation of a new chiefly line in their own altepetl. Daily business, however, went on much as usual. Of course, tribute was now to be paid to the Spanish, rather than the Mexica. And in some places, the Franciscan brothers arrived and began to speak of a new god. Few people, however, were willing to reject the old ways. They let the priests sermonize but were not necessarily persuaded.

In fact, often they did more than ignore the Spanish: they generally found the newcomers quite easy to manipulate, and occasionally they took great pleasure in doing so. Not long after the Franciscans arrived, Cortés, Malintzin, and a large retinue set off on a major expedition to the southeast. They disappeared into the jungle, and rumors began to circulate that they were dead. In 1525 Diego de Ordás set sail to Xicallanco with a Nahuatl speaker to see if they could get to the bottom of the matter in that town, through which all news supposedly traveled. Oh, yes, the Indians there responded. Cortés and all his company had indeed been killed—by Mayas living further east, of course, not by Nahuas in the immediate vicinity. The indigenous had swarmed them, burned them out of their camp, and captured them. Knowing the Spaniards' fear of sacrifice, the tellers of the tale went on in gory detail: the indigenous allies had all been eaten after their hearts were cut out, but the bodies of the Spanish, known to have a dreadful taste, had been dumped into a great lagoon. Gloomily, the messengers returned to Mexico City with the news, and the royal accountant who was acting as governor wrote up an official report and sent it to Charles V.[35]

He would later regret his hastiness. The credulous Spaniards had been duped, as they so often were. Cortés and Malintzin were quite well. They were encamped on the Atlantic coast of Honduras, looking down on the blue waters of the Caribbean.

SEVEN

The Concubine Speaks

WHY MALINTZIN LEFT COYOACAN IN 1524 TO HEAD FOR THE CARIBBEAN SEA, and what happened to her en route, is a tale that needs telling, for hidden in the details are some significant clues as to what she may have been thinking in the earliest years after the fall of Tenochtitlan. In the decisions that she made, we can almost hear her speak. Importantly—from her point of view—she had married a Spaniard during the course of the journey. She had united herself to Juan Jaramillo, one of Cortés's original captains, "as ordained by the Holy Mother Church," publicly and before witnesses. That had been in October or early November of 1524, near the start of the trip. They were in the small Zapotec state of Tiltepec, not far from the river that marked the edge of the Nahuatl-speaking altepetls of the Coatzacoalcos region. In other words, Malintzin married a Spaniard just before she crossed the border into her childhood homeland. Afterward, the company continued on to Guaspaltepec and thence across the water to Olutla, the place she had been forced to leave behind so many years before. The river was swollen with water in that season, and they had to use canoes to make the crossing. Two of them, loaded up with unwieldy baggage, overturned. A chest full of plate and clothing belonging to Juan Jaramillo—much of which he had undoubtedly just received as wedding presents—was swept away by the current and lost forever. The distraught observers could not even attempt to rescue their property, for the water was full of waiting crocodiles.[1]

The stop at Olutla was brief. The company immediately passed on to Coatzacoalcos, and there they paused for a week—so that, in the words of Cortés, he could "settle certain matters." Numerous Spaniards later swore under oath that everyone knew Malintzin hailed from the area. Bernal Díaz said that all the local indigenous lords and kings were summoned and that Malintzin addressed them. He claimed to understand exactly what she said in her Nahuatl speech, which renders his story suspect. He also said she had words with a half brother and with someone who stood to her as a mother, which seems quite plausible. Whether Díaz was fabricating the story in its entirety, or only embellishing, we will never know. It almost does not matter whether the Spaniards were looking on at an emotional scene, and if so, what the indigenous players said, with or without the Europeans' comprehension. What seems clear is that during the week that the company passed in Coatzacoalcos, Malintzin would have seen at least some of the people she wanted to see, and she would have had the power to say what she wanted to say. It was a luxury rarely granted to those who had been given into slavery as children.[2]

Knowing little or nothing of what was passing through Malintzin's mind at this juncture, numerous Spaniards, both then and later, rushed in to fill the silence, interpreting her thoughts as they chose. And historians of all nationalities have done the same ever since. Most often, commentators have envisioned Cortés as pawning off a woman of whom he had grown tired on a slightly unwilling subaltern. According to this scenario, Cortés had no desire to marry an Indian—or even to keep her available as a mistress, apparently—so he got rid of her in this way; Malintzin, it is implied, passively accepted his decision, shedding her tears in private. These ideas first took root during Cortés's lifetime. Even his usually rather dutiful biographer, López de Gómara, wrote, "Juan Jaramillo married Marina while drunk. Cortés was criticized for allowing it, because he had had children by her." (In fact, of course, he had had only one.) Not everyone saw the marriage this way, however. People who were actually there at the time certainly did not. Bernal Díaz, writing his own account years later with Gómara's book open before him, scowled and insisted that it was "not how the chronicler Gómara says." He added forcefully,

"Doña Marina was a person of great presence [importance] and was obeyed without question by all the Indians of New Spain." He meant that she was hardly someone who would or even could be forced to accept a drunken and bumbling husband whom she did not want to marry.[3]

In recent times, modern scholars and Mexican nationalists—for understandable reasons—have tended to accept Gómara's vision, ascribing less than good motives to the conquistador and compliancy and vulnerability to the indigenous woman. It seems plausible, however, that it was Bernal Díaz who came closer to the truth. It is possible that Malintzin was seizing an opportunity to gain something that she wanted—that she was attempting to grab hold of enough power to protect herself and her children, and conceivably even certain other people in Olutla. This can never be proven beyond a shadow of a doubt since Malintzin did not leave us a record of her thoughts. But the contextual backdrop to her marriage, when carefully pieced together in its entirety, offers some powerful circumstantial evidence for such a scenario, and virtually no evidence for the more traditional version of the story that has tended to be accepted without question.

There are several possible beginnings to the story. Even before the conquest of Tenochtitlan, while the Spaniards were the guests of Moctezuma—and eventually his captors—they sent out emissaries to explore the Coatzacoalcos River basin, having learned about it in some way without ever having seen it themselves. After the fall of the city, Cortés began to send large groups out to colonize distant areas beyond the central valley. It was early 1522 when he sent the first such expedition, which was headed first to Tochtepec (a major trading city on the way to the coast) and then to Coatzacoalcos. The leader was Gonzalo de Sandoval, and Bernal Díaz was among those who accompanied him. Though the indigenous along the Coatzacoalcos River had been friendly back in 1520, they were quite hostile now, in face of the Spaniards' having arrived overland with the clear intention of staying. The Spanish founded a town anyway, as that was always the first step in establishing a new colony. They called their settlement Espíritu Santo and proceeded to distribute the region's Indians in encomiendas—which were at that point more theoretical than real. The would-be conquerors had to do battle every step of the way and did not manage to extract tribute consistently by any means, as no victory in that region seemed permanent. The Indians continued to regroup and fight against them again and again.[4]

Whatever Malintzin had or had not told the Spanish about the area, they could see for themselves at this point that Coatzacoalcos was not going to make anyone rich anytime soon. The reality must have been especially galling just then, when the dense populations of the central valley were acquiescing to the Europeans relatively peacefully. We must ask why in fact any of the Spaniards were at all interested in staying. There is documentary proof as to the identity of only five of these initial Coatzacoalcos encomenderos. All five were of the kind to be "left out" in the great carving up of central Mexico. Lorenzo Genovés and Gonzalo Gallego had been part of Cortés's original company but were a mariner and a caulker, respectively, and thus had little social standing. Another, Pedro Castellar, did not have the loyalty of the original group, as he had come with Narváez. Pedro de Bazán was of significantly higher social standing: he would later marry the niece of the rather credulous royal accountant Rodrigo de Albornoz, who wrote to the king about Cortés's supposed death during the expedition to the Caribbean. But Bazán had not arrived in Mexico until just before the expedition to Coatzacoalcos departed and thus had no claim to any of the previously vanquished territories. The status of Bernal Díaz is debatable, but he himself said he did not receive a just reward in central Mexico because he was related to Cortés's archenemy, Diego Velázquez. The prognosis in Coatzacoalcos certainly was not good, but at this early stage, the Spanish had little choice but to follow whatever leads they had received. It was not yet at all clear to them where else they might go in order to meet with better fortune. In frustration, some of the colonizers, including Bernal Díaz, eventually set off for the jungles of Chiapas, but they wisely soon returned to Espíritu Santo and gradually began to establish some minimal control.[5]

Whether Malintzin ever thought of traveling there herself at this point we will never know. It seems unlikely. The zone was in chaos, and traveling with only a small group of Spaniards she would have been in the same danger they were. In Coyoacan, on the other hand, she was needed as a translator and her position was thus still relatively secure. Cortés continued to be enchanted by the child Martín. He said he intended to have him legitimized by the pope, and several years later he did pay the necessary fees and have it done. If Cortés never had a son in wedlock, Malintzin's child would almost certainly end up becoming his heir. That sort of thing had happened before in Spain, where it was not uncommon for a man to have long-term relations with a mistress called a *barragana* before he eventually married someone else. We know that Cortés thought of the child in this light because of a step he took ten years later. In the 1530s, when he finally had a son born in marriage survive to age four, he went to his lawyers and had them draw up a document naming the new son as his heir and, in the case of the child's death, any other children who might be born to Cortés's wife in the future. If, however, the boy should die and there were no surviving siblings, then the inheritance would revert to his oldest son, Martín.[6]

From the point of view of someone born into a theocratic, tribute-based, and polygynous society, Malintzin had indeed arrived: she fraternized with priests and governors, collected vassals' payments, and was, at least for the time being, the mother of the heir. She had no reason to seek to make a great change or to risk throwing away all that she had.

But in the middle of 1524 Cortés came to her with a dramatic announcement and a petition. A rebellious captain who had once been under his command—Cristóbal de Olid—had set up a competing colonial government in Honduras, and Cortés was determined to go see to the matter himself. He needed Malintzin to leave their toddler son with his cousin, the licenciado Juan de Altamirano, so that she could accompany him and hundreds of others on a trek through the swampy Mayan jungles where she had once been enslaved and march all the way to the sea. It was a trip that she of all people, given her life experience, knew would take months if not years; in fact, the travelers might not survive at all. Cortés was not mad. He did have his reasons: he believed he needed to march overland to Honduras with an extraordinary force of men and horses in order to demonstrate to the Indians throughout the land that it was he whom they should fear and in order to guarantee victory over his Spanish rival. He knew well that he would need Malintzin's translation skills and her guidance if he were to have any hope of success.

However compelling his arguments may have seemed from his own point of view, the situation must have looked quite different to Malintzin. Yet she did agree to go. What could possibly have induced her to leave her son, her regular meals, her relative security, and her currently high status to embark on this wild venture that had as good a chance of weakening Cortés's position—and thus her own—as of strengthening it? To the extent that the question has been asked at all in the past, it has generally been assumed that she loved him and made his desires hers. That possibility, however, is too far-fetched to be taken seriously. Captive Nahua concubines did not tend to entertain twenty-first-century fantasies about romantic love or companionate relationships, especially not in regard to their polygamous masters. And even if Malintzin's being in love with Cortés were not culturally improbable, there is other evidence against its having been a particularly relevant factor: if she had ever felt anything for him, his behavior in the past few years would certainly have cleared her vision. He had shown her no particular tenderness but, rather, had had more favorites come and go in the short span of time that she had known him than we can count today. We know that Malintzin was a beautiful, talented, and self-confident woman who was both practical and politically astute. There is no reason to believe that she would have failed to see the truth: "If anyone ever really loved Marina," one Mexican historian has written bluntly, "it was not don Hernán Cortés."[7]

It is conceivable that Malintzin had no choice but to consent to go—that she went under duress. She certainly knew what kind of power Cortés had at his disposal, what kind of violence he was willing to employ. This interpretation, however, does not stand up to the events of the trip itself. It is clear that she worked with her usual energy and gusto and was not simply dragged along, present in body but not in spirit. The conquerors who later referred to their experiences on the grueling trek expressed particular gratitude to her. Cortés, who always spoke of her as little as possible in his reports to the king, actually mentioned her by name on this occasion and made it clear that the Spanish owed their ability to escape from difficult circumstances to her.[8] In short, she does not appear to have acted like a coerced woman doing only what she was bid in order to avoid brutal punishment; rather, she was, as usual, a strong and memorable presence.

Why? What could have been the inspiration for her commitment to such a cause? In September and October of 1524, when Cortés was contemplating the trip, he was a widower and free to marry. Whether he had murdered Catalina or not, that lady was most certainly out of the way. Malintzin may have raised the question of marriage; we will never know. Whether or not they spoke of it explicitly, Malintzin was savvy enough to see that the contrast between Hernando Cortés, married to a former Indian slave girl, and Hernando Cortés, married to the daughter or sister or niece of a Spanish nobleman, was so stark that there could be no contest in his mind. In his continuing struggles for power in relation to other Spaniards, other factors would obviously trump her ability to communicate on his behalf with the indigenous.

There remained, however, the path soon to be taken by many another Indian mistress of a conquistador: she could marry a less powerful Spaniard, one for whom marriage to an influential Indian would be more attractive than damaging. As long as the man were powerful enough, her interests would still be protected. The timing of the sudden marriage—at the start of a major expedition that Malintzin would obviously not have favored herself—speaks volumes. She must have bargained for a husband. Sixteenth-century legal documents provide ample evidence that Indian noblewomen were well aware that they could use Spanish husbands to their advantage in legal battles over land and other matters. Today we often think of sixteenth-century wives as having been at a legal disadvantage. We unconsciously compare their position to that of their husbands. Not so sixteenth-century women. They did not compare themselves to men. They compared the position of a wife to the position of a mistress, and they saw clearly which was better. The catch for most Indians was that usually only high-ranking noblewomen could obtain Spanish husbands who were powerful enough to be useful. Even indigenous princesses sometimes found themselves forced to accept partners who were not as influential as they might have wished—for the higher a Spaniard's social standing, the less likely he was to be interested in an Indian spouse, unless she could promise to bring extraordinary resources. So Malintzin's options were quite limited, unless Cortés would help her.[9]

A marriage to one of Cortés's original captains with claims to hidalgo status was certainly the highest-level match she could hope to attain.[10] Remarkably enough, she got just that. Rather than being married off to a drunken commoner, as is usually implied, Malintzin in fact secured a relatively well-placed and useful husband. The list of captains who had been part of Cortés's original company in Tenochtitlan—thus giving them certain privileges, as well as rendering them well known to Malintzin— included Pedro de Alvarado, Gonzalo de Sandoval, Cristóbal de Olid, Juan Velázquez de León, Cristóbal de Olea, Juan de Escalante, Diego de Ordás, Francisco de Montejo, Pedro de Ircio, Alonso de Avila, Francisco de Luga, Andrés de Tapia, Luis Marín, and Juan Jaramillo. Of these, only three were present and available in 1524; the others were married, or else had died, returned to Spain, or gone off to conquer other areas. One of the three, Ordás, was not the marrying kind and eventually died without spouse or issue.[11]

That left Tapia and Jaramillo. Each was working to solidify his hidalgo status: they were of good families, not high nobles, but good enough to claim some distant connection to nobility and hoping to improve their status even further with time. Both were *vecinos* of Mexico City. Indeed, they had nearly neighboring plots of ground there. Each held a substantial encomienda in the central valley and enjoyed the friendship of Cortés. Jaramillo perhaps had a slight advantage, in that he was named Cortés's lieutenant, his second-in-command, for the duration of the expedition to Honduras. He was also the son of Alonso Jaramillo, who had been active in the conquests of Hispaniola and Venezuela. Alonso had arrived in Mexico shortly after the conquest and been appointed *regidor*, a member of the governing council, or *cabildo*. These were choice positions: ten years later, a man of doubtful noble origins would not have been so fortunate. In 1522 Cortés was not in a position to be as particular as the Crown would later be in assigning similar offices, but Alonso still had to be a man of some means and presence in order to have been selected even then. In June of 1524, Juan Jaramillo was himself considered dignified enough to act as substitute regidor for his father, probably during an illness. Compared to Jaramillo, Andrés de Tapia may have been more insecure or more ambitious or both; it may be relevant that he later married a Spanish noblewoman and changed his name to the more impressive Andrés de Tapia y Sosa. We will never know how the final selection came to be made, but Malintzin married Jaramillo.[12]

As a result, she left the days of being a vulnerable mistress behind forever and entered the ranks of well-born Spaniards with legal rights. Only in that state did she cross the border to her homeland and come face-to-face with those she had once known. And there was more. Apparently, she was able to inform the people of her homeland that the altepetl of Olutla had been given to her as an encomienda. Cortés had given it to her as her dowry.

For Malintzin to have demanded an encomienda was remarkable: only three indigenous persons in Mexico ever received them in a permanent sense. Two of these were the daughters of Moctezuma, and the other was don Juan Sánchez, a powerful nobleman from Oaxaca who seems to have become thoroughly Hispanized.[13] It is possible that the story simply is not true, that Malintzin did not, after all, have enough leverage, even with her current importance, to receive an encomienda. Indeed, no paper record of such a transaction in 1524 exists. But then, no legal documents written in Espíritu Santo at that time have survived at all.

The evidence that Malintzin received such a "wedding present" comes from testimony collected more than ten years after her death by the daughter she later bore to Jaramillo. In the 1540s, the daughter and her husband argued that they should inherit Juan Jaramillo's original encomienda of Xilotepec in the central valley (rather than the one-third share he wanted to leave them) because Malintzin had brought to the marriage as a dowry the encomienda of Olutla and Tetiquipaque, which had subsequently been stripped from her, and which should, by rights, have been handed down to her daughter. Obviously, the couple was strongly motivated to make this claim, but they had an impressive list of over twenty witnesses who all seemed to agree in this, though in the past they had often been at each other's throats on other issues. Most significantly, perhaps, they had on their side the father of Juan Jaramillo's second wife—the woman who stood to inherit two-thirds of the profits of the encomienda if their claim were not brought forward. Jaramillo's father-in-law said very specifically that he would not allow his relationship to the principals of the case to interfere with his telling the truth. He and other witnesses said that they were certain Malintzin had received Olutla and Tetiquipaque—either because they had been present at the time or because it was common knowledge. Their stories diverged slightly, reflecting their different positions within the drama, and some of them mispronounced or confused indigenous place names, but in no case did they actually contradict each other.[14]

We might wonder why the altepetl was available to be gifted, since the Spanish had carved up the area two years earlier, in 1522. One of the witnesses answered this question, though it had not been put to him. After saying that he saw Olutla given into Malintzin's hands, he added that it had previously belonged to Juan de Cuéllar but that Cortés took it away from him. This story could easily be true. Cuéllar was a lowborn trumpeter who had arrived with Narváez and would have been just the type to have landed in the Coatzacoalcos area. In 1525, for some unspecified reason, he returned to Mexico City with a document from Cortés giving him the encomienda of Ixtapaluca on Lake Chalco. Perhaps we have found the reason why Cortés suddenly rewarded a trumpeter so richly.[15]

Another witness, Alonso Valiente, who was related to Cortés and very wealthy, mentioned that Malintzin and Jaramillo left a man in Coatzacoalcos to oversee their interests while they were away in Honduras.[16] This was in fact exactly the procedure followed by encomenderos who did not remain in residence. Jaramillo, for example, had someone working for him back at Xilotepec. Presumably, the couple made their arrangements with the locals and then packed up their piece of legal paper in one of the chests that indigenous porters were expected to carry to Honduras. Malintzin's daughter could not produce any documentation in the 1540s, but then, almost none of the cavalcade's baggage ever made it to the coast.

In sum, we have more compelling evidence that the claim made by Malintzin's daughter was true than we have for numerous other more tenuous claims made by Spaniards, which we have long assumed reflected reality. It seems virtually certain that Malintzin demanded—and received—unique rights to command labor from Olutla and Tetiquipaque, the place of her birth. Whether she returned there with the intention of protecting some of the altepetl's people or punishing others we will never know. But she knew. It was her world, and she knew what she was about. In this context, she was hardly Cortés's creature.

There was still the price to be paid, however, for whatever triumph she may have experienced. There was still the trek to Honduras before her. They were about to plunge into Maya territory. Cortés had agonized about a variety of issues in connection with the trip, not least how best to maintain authority in the City of Mexico during his absence. He had at length appointed two royal officials, the treasurer, Alonso de Estrada, and the royal accountant, Rodrigo de Albornoz, to govern in his place. In Coatzacoalcos, however, letters caught up with him from others claiming that these two were mismanaging affairs badly. So he sent the royal inspector, Pedro Almíndez Chirinos, and the Crown's business agent, Gonzalo de Salazar, back to Tenochtitlan posthaste with letters ordering that they share authority with Estrada and Albornoz. Cortés's absence from the capital city in the ensuing months was to prove costly to him, and his last-minute panic about delegating his power only exacerbated the problems. In November of 1524, however, he could not foresee all of this. In Coatzacoalcos, he marshaled the two hundred Spaniards who were to accompany him, their many African slaves, and all their indigenous followers—who together totaled something approaching three thousand souls. The indigenous included men who would be expected to fight wherever necessary, as well as burden bearers, servants, mistresses, musicians, and jugglers. And they included hostage princes from the major altepetls of the central valley, whose presence on the expedition, it was believed, would keep their subjects back home on good behavior. Even Cuauhtemoc was forced to go along.

They set off overland through the swampy region where Malintzin had once been enslaved. Cortés sent supply ships along the coast, with the idea that his land and sea forces would keep in touch via messengers who would come and go in small boats along the rivers that ran down to the gulf at regular intervals. The idea, however, worked better in theory than in practice. The two groups narrowly missed each other more than once. While docked at Xicallanco, the Spaniards onboard one of the supply ships got into such a vicious brawl that the survivors were rendered relatively helpless and the indigenous were able to finish them off. (That fact, however, the locals hid for a while from the Spaniards who later came to inquire as to the fate of Cortés.) Traveling without his expected supplies, and eventually leaving behind the region that Malintzin knew well, Cortés found himself becoming more and more dependent on the Indians of the area not only for food but also for guidance; unfortunately they tended to try to elude him. The territory was nearly impossible to cross, logistically speaking. Often the cavalcade spent whole days making no real progress at all as the crow flies, due to the need to circumvent a quagmire, cross a river, or traverse a section of uncut jungle. The travelers slept in the rain and occasionally had their horses sink into marshes. If it had not been for Malintzin's extraordinary ability to function in more than one Mayan dialect and her deftness in assessing situations, they would have been lost, literally and figuratively, on more than one occasion. As it was, they lurched forward pathetically slowly, arms always at the ready, and were often hungry. Soon the least powerful members of the company—who received the least to eat—began to die.

In a place called Acalan—meaning "Land of the Boats" in Nahuatl—the company ground to a halt for about twenty days. The region was situated about fifty miles in from the Gulf Coast near the headwaters of the river that the Spanish had named the Candelaria; it was the locale where traders from the Xicallanco area interfaced with those who came down the mountains from Chiapas and Guatemala or up from the Atlantic coast via another network of rivers. The people who lived there were the Mactun Maya, and they called their country in their own language, not Acalan, but Itzamkanak. The king was not pleased to have such visitors, but Malintzin assured his emissaries in their tongue that the company was but passing through and that it was in the king's own best interest to receive them in peace. Cortés, of course, wrote to his king that he was happily welcomed as the representative of Charles V, as he wanted to make his position as Conqueror of Mexico seem secure, but other contemporary Spanish accounts give the lie to this, as does an account left by the Maya themselves. Still, Cortés would have argued in his own defense that it was only a question of "spin": the Mactun did after all grudgingly allow the foreigners to pause and rest and replenish their supplies.[17]

During their stay, an event occurred that still shakes Mexican consciousness to its core: Cortés executed Cuauhtemoc. He had him hanged and then left the head on a spike and the body hanging by the heels from a ceiba tree. At least one other Mexican nobleman died with him and perhaps also Coanacochtli, the former king of Tetzcoco with whom Cortés had once argued in front of all his noblemen.

There are several different accounts of what happened.[18] Cortés later claimed that an indigenous informer revealed a plot hatched by Cuauhtemoc: since there were far more indigenous than Spanish present in the cavalcade, the Mexican prince had purportedly suggested that they rise against their erstwhile conquerors and free themselves, then return to the central valley and launch a rebellion there as well. Others, including some Spaniards, believed it was all a misunderstanding and that Cuauhtemoc and his compatriots were merely celebrating a rumor that they had just heard (inaccurate, as it turned out) that Cortés had at last come to his senses and agreed to go home. In the joking and horseplay that ensued, some things were said in sarcasm and bitterness that perhaps should not have been uttered aloud—that they would prefer to die at once, for instance, rather than perish slowly of starvation, leaving their bodies scattered along the route to Honduras—but the comments did not really mean that they planned to pursue violence.

Cortés had each of the men involved tortured separately, so that none could hear what the others said. Presumably Malintzin found herself translating yet again in such hideous circumstances. Having obtained the kind of evidence he wanted, Cortés, with summary dispatch, ordered that Cuauhtemoc and one of his cousins be executed. Later, some accounts by people who were not present claimed he condemned others to death as well, but he himself said he was merciful to the others, having become convinced that widespread carnage was not necessary to make his point. In fact, the others probably died natural deaths along the route, as they themselves predicted they would. Had Malintzin cautioned him? Certainly it must have been she who worked to explain the bitter jokes that some Spaniards believed had been made by Cuauhtemoc and his cohort. How else could Spanish men have come to understand in such clear detail subtle comments that had been made in Nahuatl? In stories the Nahuas later recounted among themselves, some of which appeared in the Nahuatl text of the Annals of Tlatelolco, Malintzin played a very active role in the political bargaining that occurred.

Certain Spanish and indigenous sources both mention Cuauhtemoc's involvement in some kind of Christian rite before his death—either a baptism ceremony or a last confession. Bernal Díaz insisted that the intrepid translator was the intermediary between the Nahua prince and the Franciscan brothers at the very end. If so, she was the last person who spoke to him in his own tongue and who heard what he had to say. She had the power to help him to unburden himself if he chose; we cannot know if she used that power or was simply a conduit for what the condemned man might have perceived as the harangues of the churchmen. Bernal Díaz also claimed Cuauhtemoc made a raging speech before he died. "O Malintze," he supposedly said, speaking to Cortés, who, we remember, shared his translator's name in indigenous addresses, "now I understand your false promises and the kind of death you have had in store for me. For you are killing me unjustly. May God demand justice of you." If indeed the last Mexica king really said anything like this, the Spanish only knew of it through Malintzin. The story is probably apocryphal, but Malintzin—and other translators in like circumstances—had in general made enough of the sentiments of the indigenous clear to the Spanish to make it possible for Díaz to put such words as these in his Indian characters' mouths when he wrote his book in his declining years.[19]

The travelers left Acalan on the first Sunday in Lent. They had been on the road since the previous November and, unbeknownst to them, had several more months to go before they reached the sea. They were moving to the south and east, across the base of the Yucatan Peninsula. It was green, mountainous territory; the whitened remains of ancient Maya monuments rose up from the forest at intervals, but it was not these that Cortés sought. He wanted only to make it across this craggy yet lush, tropical land that did not resemble the mountains he had known in Europe at all. The combination of precipice and jungle was like nothing he had ever imagined. In his letters, he found he could not convey what the experience was like. "Not even one who is more skilled at writing than I could adequately express it, nor could one who heard of it understand it fully, unless he had himself seen it with his own eyes."[20] The people with him grew ever more desperate for food. They were reduced to taking it by force whenever they could and seizing individuals to try to make them act as guides. Forced guides, however, are usually no guides at all; the traveling host lost all sense of where they were, of how much farther they would have to go. In that state, many died.

At length, in questioning two kidnapped women, Malintzin suddenly learned that they were only two days' march from a coastal town called Nito, where there were apparently some Spaniards living. "I cannot describe to Your Majesty the great joy which I and all my company felt on hearing this news," wrote Cortés.[21] When they at length got there (it took them not two days, of course, but many days of agonizing travel, given their lumbering style of movement and state of semistarvation) they met with good news and bad. The good news was that the rebel Cristóbal de Olid had been killed by a rival faction that was sympathetic to Cortés; the rebellion was long since over, as it turned out. The bad news was that the Spaniards in Nito were starving, too; they were in desperate need of help themselves and were in no position to provide succor to others. Still, they had a ship, and in that ship, and in another that happened to come along, Cortés and some followers made their way along the coast to the Bay of Honduras and then to the main Spanish settlement of Trujillo.

It was probably already August or even September 1525, and true to style, Cortés flew into action. Through Malintzin, he parleyed with the local indigenous, promising them peace in exchange for tribute offered in the form of food and labor in Spanish fields. There may have been some skirmishes that he failed to report, but these coastal peoples already knew all about him—presumably from their trade networks—and seemed disposed to comply with his demands rather than face military reprisals. Cortés even issued new laws forbidding some of the worst practices of which the colonizers had previously been guilty—such as kidnapping Indian women and boys from their villages to be included in labor drafts. Thus the problem of starvation was resolved—at least temporarily. (Some of the Indians would eventually choose to fight, but that was to come later.) He also made contact with all the Spanish who were living in pockets along the coast, including those he had left behind in Nito, and brought some of them to Trujillo; he said he sent the sick to the Spanish towns in the Caribbean.[22]

Then the indefatigable conquistador set about producing a flood of paperwork that would support his agenda back in Spain. One shipowner named Pedro Moreno had been uncooperative, refusing to sell certain supplies to the colonizers. Cortés wrote a letter denouncing him, insisting that he was stirring up trouble with the Indians. "When he left he took from this city in his ship more than fifty indigenous, men and women, whom he put in irons and made slaves, against all right and reason, even though several *vecinos* asked him not to take them, since it damaged the settlers." One of the kidnapping victims had even been a nobleman; two others were natives who had come voluntarily to work for the Christians. There was no question that if the Spaniards continued to behave in this way, the Indians would have no reason at all to try to work peacefully with the foreigners.[23]

It might be tempting to see Cortés as attempting to instill justice for the Indians in a lawless land; Malintzin, however—and all others who were intimately acquainted with him—knew otherwise. He had no objections whatsoever to enslaving the indigenous if it could be done without stirring up trouble. That meant it must be done only with the collusion of local chiefs. When Cortés departed from Honduras, leaving a kinsman named Hernando de Saavedra as his deputy, he left careful instructions as to how the slave trade might be continued. It was not a crime, he insisted, to maintain as chattel those who had been enslaved by other Indians before the Christians ever came. Thus the Spanish might safely purchase slaves from native lords or collect them in tribute. Of course, he said, the Spanish must not simply take the chiefs' word that these were people who had long been slaves. It behooved the Spanish to speak to those who were turned over to them in private, out of the hearing of the chiefs, and ask how they had come to be enslaved. Assuming they offered a reasonable explanation, the Spanish could then proceed with a clear conscience: the Indians should be branded on their cheeks and sent aboard the waiting ships that would take them to the Caribbean for sale as laborers on plantations and in mines.[24]

So it was that many young people who had been slaves among the Maya—just as Malintzin had been not so long ago—suddenly found themselves vomiting over their shackles in the belly of a Spanish ship, sailing east toward early death. Malintzin had found a way to save herself from her own powerlessness. Surely these others would have done so, too, if they could have.

By now Cortés had received letters from the Caribbean islands telling him that chaos had erupted in Mexico City after his departure, as the multiple leaders he had appointed were squabbling among themselves. At one point he tried to leave precipitously, but his ship met with a storm not far out and he had to return. Then some of the indigenous, already frustrated with the demands of the Spanish, began to rebel, and he had to take some time to calm that situation. It was the end of April 1526 when he successfully took ship for Cuba, together with those few who worked most closely with him and whom he regarded essentially as his household. By the middle of May, he was writing letters from Havana, and by the end of the month, he reported with irrepressible excitement that he was on the coast of Mexico, near Veracruz, and would be in Mexico City within days.[25]

Malintzin and Jaramillo were almost certainly with him; his translator and his second-in-command would have counted among the privileged few. It is possible, however, that the couple tarried somewhere along the way and followed later. For on the coast of Honduras, or perhaps even onboard ship, Malintzin had given birth to another child. They named her María, after the Virgin.[26] In her exhaustion, Malintzin looked upon her tiny daughter. This was one girl-child who would never be sold into slavery.

In Mexico City, things had gone from bad to worse. There had originally been a brief period of peace. "At first the reigning officials had seemed so close you couldn't stick a finger between them," reported one observer.[27]

But it was not long before their mutual distrust reached explosive proportions and a veritable civil war ensued. In the midst of the political chaos, one faction kidnapped—or arrested, as they put it—a cousin of Cortés named Rodrigo de Paz who had been entrusted with watching over the conqueror's personal affairs. They tortured him, demanding that he tell them where his cousin had hidden the vast wealth of Moctezuma; eventually they killed him.

At about the time that Cortés reappeared—after an absence of nearly two years—the king finally was able to extend the arm of his influence across the sea and calm the seething city. He sent Luis Ponce de León to investigate, and the venerable official arrived not long after Cortés. The rigors of travel to the New World soon proved to be too much for him: he was beset by an illness and died almost immediately. The enemies of Cortés accused him of having had the royal emissary poisoned, but it seems unthinkable that so politically astute a man could ever have been so foolish. The death of one man could not put an end to royal investigations, as Cortés well knew. While they waited for word from the king on how to proceed, Cortés piously protested that he probably ought to resign; his friends insisted that he must continue to govern, which he did. It was a difficult time for him. Most of the properties that he had once claimed for himself had been seized by others in his absence. He set about trying to repossess them, but the results of his efforts would depend, of course, on whether or not the king ultimately sided with him—or punished him for having caused the confusion in the first place. "I am in purgatory," Cortés agonized in a letter to his father. "And the only reason it's not hell is that I still have hope of redress."[28]

Naturally, Cortés took whatever steps he could to bolster his position. First, he informed the still-young doña Isabel, the daughter of Moctezuma who had once been called Tecuichpotzin, of the death of her husband, Cuauhtemoc. Lest he be accused of brutalities on that score, and because he wanted to reemphasize his earlier claim that Moctezuma had of his own free will ceded his authority to Charles V, Cortés settled on Isabel and her heirs, as a gift from the Crown, a large and prosperous encomienda, carved from the territories that had once been her father's. In the accompanying documents, he detailed a particularly rich story, explaining that Moctezuma, on his deathbed, had asked Cortés to care for his daughters and that he had agreed to do so. The day after signing the documents regarding the encomienda, Cortés appointed an old friend of his, one Alonso de Grado, as official protector of the indigenous (*visitador general de indios*), for the king had recently shown a special solicitude for Mexico's natives. Then, with a poetical flourish, he married the Mexican princess to the protector of Indians.

Cortés certainly had had no intention of marrying doña Isabel himself. Had he done so, he would undoubtedly have been accused by his enemies of trying to set himself up as some sort of royal figure. It was far more to his advantage to marry into the ranks of the Spanish nobility and obtain powerful advocates at court in that way. In the same 1526 letter to his father in which he bemoaned his difficulties, he alluded to his family's efforts to betroth him to "doña Juana"—by whom he probably meant doña Juana de Zúñiga, niece of the Duke of Béjar, whom he later married. With his usual astuteness, Cortés seemed to recognize that it would probably be best to take no steps immediately, as if he were already certain of the king's decision regarding his own future; he told his father not to send doña Juana to Mexico yet, that he would see to that matter himself. From his perspective, it was clearly better to have it bruited about that the engagement was in the works—that he was an acceptable suitor to a duke's niece—than to seem to the king to take anything for granted.

Alonso de Grado died less than two years after his marriage to doña Isabel. She was still only about eighteen years old. Cortés, demonstrating that he had not learned humility from the reverses he was experiencing, and that he still held to the same high-handed style that so infuriated his peers, brought the girl into his household—in order to protect her, he said. It was soon public knowledge that she was pregnant with his child. A baby named Leonor was later born, but not before the pregnant bride had been married off to a follower of Cortés named Pedro Gallego de Andrade, who had no objections, as he got both wealth and position out of the arrangement. [29]

The wheels of trans-Atlantic communication and decision making turned slowly in the 1520s, but they turned surely. In 1529 the king launched an investigation into Cortés's conduct. The latter had known it was coming, and by the time the news became official, he was already on his way to Spain to plead his own cause. In Mexico City, the dam holding back resentments long harbored against him broke quickly. Literally dozens of lawsuits were filed against Cortés that same year, including one by

Martín López, whose ships had been crucial in the taking of Tenochtitlan; two by Jerónimo de Aguilar, who felt he had not received his just reward; and another by the aggrieved mother of his dead wife, doña Catalina. The instantaneous proliferation of suits demonstrates not only the weakness of Cortés's position at that moment but of his position in the preceding few years: his allies had been dwindling.[30]

Clearly Cortés had been in no position to make good on any promises he had made to Malintzin at the time of her marriage. Even if he had still retained his authority, there would have been little he could do from Mexico City to guarantee any distant encomienda holdings; as it was, the case was obviously hopeless. He could not even defend his own property, much less hers. If, as seems likely, Malintzin received Olutla and Tetiquipaque as a wedding present, it turned out to be an illusory gift. She may have harbored some hope for a while. In 1527, Baltasar de Osorio was sent to Tabasco with the power to sort out affairs there and make a record of whose encomienda was whose. He stripped the rights of most of the 1522 grantees—including Bernal Díaz—most of whom were no longer there anyway, as the region was not doing well. Then in 1529, Francisco de Montejo gained authority over the area. In the repeated reshuffling that occurred, Luis Marín was eventually assigned the labor of eight Coatzacoalcos villages, including Olutla and Tetiquipaque. At that point, no one said anything about Malintzin's prior claims, at least not in any document that has survived. By the time the news made its way back to Mexico City, it would have been too late for her to defend her own interests.[31]

The late 1520s were in general a wild and relatively lawless time that brought little good to women in Mexico City. Normally, in both the indigenous and Spanish worlds, longstanding family connections and widespread respect for governing figures ensured at least a modicum of security even to the weaker members of a community. Later, Mexico City would bring cultural achievements to heights unrivaled anywhere else in colonial America, and women and the indigenous would lead highly satisfactory lives there. But not yet. At present, it was a town of relative strangers who did not even agree on who exactly was in charge; brute force was often the most powerful factor in a given situation. Indigenous women often fared particularly poorly, in that the colonizers were no longer as dependant on them as they had been only a few years ago, and there was as yet no effective system of checks and balances to control the powerful.

A new *audiencia*, or "governing council," was set up at the end of the decade, according to royal dictate, to rule the colony. A viceroy was to come a few years later. The council was to consist of a president and four judges. Two of the first four judges named died en route to Mexico, but the president and two others made it across the sea and took up their posts. One of them, Diego Delgadillo, soon became known as one of the worst offenders against the rights of others. Besides arresting and torturing Spaniards whose actions displeased him, he apparently maintained a house full of indigenous women whom he claimed were being instructed in the faith, when in fact they were being prostituted. "That is no monastery, nor even an honest house," a livid neighbor insisted. A man named Juan Soldevilla was accused of beating his wife and three enslaved indigenous women. The relevant authorities did nothing. The said Juan soon murdered his wife; no one even mentioned the fate of the slaves.[32]

In the midst of this disastrous scene, however, Malintzin found that at least some of Cortés's promises to her had been made good. She had chosen her husband well, at least as regards material factors; Cortés continued to support Jaramillo's cause as well as he was able. This was something it was still in his power to do. At the first meeting of the city's cabildo after the return of the expedition from Honduras in 1526, Jaramillo was named alcalde, or "magistrate," a position often used to recognize an individual of merit.[33] Within a few years, in 1530, very possibly as a result of Cortés's visit to Spain, Jaramillo would receive the more prestigious position of cabildo regidor, a royal appointment now generally reserved for noblemen.

Jaramillo also energetically protected his encomienda of Xilotepec. It was a large community forty-two miles northwest of Mexico City. In a strategy typical of him, Cortés had assigned one-quarter of the income to a man of little social standing, who would be expected to remain in residence and oversee operations, and three-quarters to one of his favorites—in this case, Jaramillo. The man who lived in the altepetl of Xilotepec, Hernando de Santillana, was a shoemaker who had been part of the original conquest of Tenochtitlan. His young son had been killed, apparently in the noche triste, and that fact perhaps explains why he received more than a shoemaker normally would have. For now, Jaramillo entrusted everything to him and allowed him to keep his quarter share. The time was shortly coming, however, when Jaramillo would find an excuse to turn Santillana out, leaving the shoemaker writing piteous letters to the king and, later, engaging in a lengthy—and futile—lawsuit. "[I] the said Hernando de Santillana [was] always very poor, and Jaramillo very powerful, and a loyal servant of Cortés, and married to another servant of his," the bereft shoemaker complained bitterly.[34]

That Jaramillo was understood to be something of a rising star is proven, sadly perhaps, by the marriage that he was later able to contract almost immediately after Malintzin's death. Don Leonel de Cervantes, an official of the military Order of Santiago, had arrived in 1519 with Narváez and soon after returned to Spain to fetch his wife and son and five daughters, reappearing in 1524. He married each of the girls—who all carried the prestigious title of "doña"—to prominent encomenderos, creating an impressive and powerful family network. Doña Beatriz was between twelve and fifteen when Malintzin died, and Cervantes shortly accepted Jaramillo as her suitor. Her high social stature becomes apparent when we learn that she herself, in the more distant future, after Jaramillo's death, would marry the brother of the viceroy.[35]

Those events were yet to come, however. In the meantime, Jaramillo, Malintzin, and little María set up housekeeping on a plot of land near the main square of Mexico City. Jaramillo acquired the goods of a gentleman, buying a coat of mail, good clothing, wine, and olive oil. In 1528 the council awarded the couple land near the woods of Chapultepec to build another home, plant an orchard, and graze their sheep. The cabildo's minutes particularly mentioned that the land was not only for Jaramillo but also for "his wife, doña Marina," though wives were generally not named in this context. A number of the original conquistadors were given comparable plots, and within a decade their fine houses lined the aqueduct that ran from Chapultepec to the center of town, each one boasting such things as ornamental drawbridges, family escutcheons, and grilled windows. In a material sense, Malintzin had indeed done well for herself and her children—especially considering the context, the alternative fates that might otherwise have awaited them.[36]

We cannot know, of course, if she was happy. We know little about the character of the man to whom she was married. The name of Juan Jaramillo appears in numerous documents, but his signatures and the references to him by others cannot give indications as to the man's personality. There is only one written trace of who he was in this regard. After his death, a group of old men who had known him well and been with him on the eve of his first marriage were questioned about his reasons for uniting himself to Malintzin. Jaramillo's second wife, by then a widow, was attempting to prove that her husband had dishonored himself in wedding the indigenous translator, but she was not meeting with much success. Even the witnesses whom the wife had herself brought to court would not go quite so far as to say what she desired. Yet in the tone of their answers, some of them seemed to be chuckling, or at least expressing smiling sympathy. One said Jaramillo must really have loved the woman in order to do it, implying that the circumstances were not exactly what a husband-to-be would have wanted. Where was the rub? Was it that she was an Indian? What was it that some of the conquistadors still found almost humorous when they thought about the situation now, years later? Fortunately for us, one Miguel Díaz was more expansive than the others. He suddenly explained that Jaramillo's friends teased him for marrying Malintzin not so much because she was an Indian, but because she was "a mature woman who was running around translating." Here it was, then, the source of the old men's amusement. Malintzin was not the usual blushing bride, and certainly not what most men had in mind when they imagined marrying a captive Indian maiden. Instead, she was an independent entity, fully an adult, and one who had a very public role. She held her own every day in the conquistadors' world. In marrying such a woman, Jaramillo was choosing to put up with the same kind of jokes that many a man has endured who has united himself to an intellectual equal. Apparently, he was not afraid—either of the woman, or of the ribbing.[37]

Whatever her relations with Jaramillo were like, it is certain that Malintzin was not entirely reliant on him for companionship. There were other indigenous people living in the household with her. The servants would certainly have been Indians, most likely from Xilotepec. More to the point, perhaps, Malintzin had also taken a boy from an indigenous noble family under her protection. He had come to be raised by her when she still lived in Coyoacan. His name was don Diego Atempanecatl. He retained his Nahuatl name, but by the time he was grown, if not sooner, don Diego was fluent in Spanish. One might be tempted to imagine a homeless orphan uprooted by the war and befriended by the young Malintzin, but the title "don" belies the possibility of his having been left without connections, even if his parents were dead. And years later, in a Spanish court, he would testify immediately after don Pedro Moctezuma, a son of the former emperor, as if he himself were someone important. In the Nahuatl-speaking world before the conquest, the name "Atempanecatl" was often used as a title meaning something akin to "lord general" or "high administrator," and it may have been attached to particular families. Most likely, Malintzin had been asked to give what advantages she could to the scion of a particular altepetl's chiefly line. He was not Mexica, for he once spoke of having "asked the Mexica" a particular question. And he could not have come from Olutla, as he entered Malintzin's household before her connections with her natal land had been reactivated. Maybe he was Tlaxcalan, given that state's continued feelings of closeness to doña Marina. He himself spoke of her with warmth and affection even many years after her death.[38]

Perhaps it is as well that we have no single letter or statement that gives us an indication of how Malintzin experienced her life with Jaramillo, or her life in postconquest Mexico in general. For how she felt was undoubtedly more complicated than a document or two can express, and her reaction undoubtedly changed from day to day. More and more, a category of people called "Indians" was emerging, defined in opposition to the Spanish, at least in certain contexts and on certain occasions. There was not yet anything like an "us versus them" mentality, however, no dichotomy firm enough for her to have entertained serious misgivings about the betrayal of "her" side. If she was of a philosophical turn of mind and began to think about what it would mean to be an "Indian" in the world the Spanish were making, she still had no reason to doubt her choices. She knew the situation well enough to realize that she herself could never have turned the tide of history, that there would have been no stopping the foreigners' superior technology under any circumstances. Indeed, if anything, she had helped "Indians" on numerous occasions, limiting their loss of life and facilitating the expression of their desires to the Spanish. So guilt could not possibly have been part of the picture. She must surely have been glad to have saved herself and her children from being trampled underfoot. But it is still possible that she mourned other lost opportunities, or that she bemoaned some of what she saw the Spanish do, or that she feared for the future. Her health, which had been astonishingly good, began to weaken.

Her son, Martín, lived nearby in the household of Cortés's cousin by marriage, the licenciado Juan Altamirano. In 1528, when Martín was six, mother and son met to say their good-byes. Cortés was leaving for Spain, and he was taking the boy with him. He planned to have him legitimized by the pope and hoped to have him accepted by the military Order of Santiago before leaving him in the service of the king. If Martín were ever to become the heir, he would need to leave as much of his indigenous identity behind as possible; taking these steps would put him in the strongest position possible. If he never became the heir, he would still enter the ranks of Spanish high society. Thus it was that mother and son both knew Martín would remain in Spain for years, that they might well never see each other again. They would also have known, as others did, that Cortés hoped to remarry in the old country. A number of intimates later swore that Malintzin dressed in indigenous clothing to the end of her days. So she stood in an embroidered huipilli, saying farewell to this child of hers who was dressed as befitted the son of a wealthy Spaniard. At age six, he had left babyhood behind forever and was taking on the face and form that would eventually be his. At that age, the mother could just glimpse the man in the boy.[39]

Martín left. He would not learn until much later that within a matter of months, Malintzin at last succumbed to one of the European diseases that had been accosting her for nearly a decade. Her strength gone, she relinquished the life that she had held to so tenaciously for almost thirty years. By January of 1529, the people of Mexico City knew that she was dead.[40]

EIGHT

Doña María

WHEN THE LAST BREATH OF AIR SLIPPED OUT OF MALINTZIN AND SHE LAY still, her little daughter, María, was not yet three years old. She had long been old enough to talk, to ask questions, probably moving seamlessly between the Spanish and Nahuatl of her household. But whatever explanation the adults gave her for her mother's disappearance, she was not yet old enough to understand it. She would have continued to wonder, like all children that age, when her mother would return. Her psyche worked like that of other human beings: eventually the dull ache and the anger receded. She forgot the maternal language. She even began to forget what her mother had looked like when she had held her, scolded her.

Juan Jaramillo remarried quickly. His new wife, doña Beatriz de Andrada, was about fifteen years old. Her father, don Leonel de Cervantes was a *comendador* of the Order of Santiago and had managed to marry his four older daughters impressively well. That he accepted Jaramillo as a suitor proves how successful María's father was perceived to be by 1530.[1]

Jaramillo and his young wife were clearly ambitious. Soon after his marriage, Jaramillo took the step of petitioning the Crown for a coat of arms. In attempting to portray himself as a presence in the society of gentlemen, he mentioned his recent marriage to *doña* Beatriz on the first page of his narrative and omitted all reference to his connection to Malintzin. Jaramillo also entertained on a lavish scale and tried to fill his domestic establishment with the accoutrements of the high born. Beginning in 1527, African slaves began to enter the colony in numbers, not at first as agricultural workers—such labor was to be imposed on the Indians—but as status symbols for their owners. Jaramillo bought several, and María would thus have grown up with enslaved children. She might have played with them when she was small. Once past her earliest years, however, her contact with them would have been tightly circumscribed.[2]

It is difficult to know exactly how María herself was perceived. In Peru, within decades of the conquest, encomenderos would wage battles on behalf of their mestiza daughters, insisting that they be treated exactly like Spanish girls in the convents where they were deposited for their education. Eventually, their efforts on behalf of their mixed-blood children were defeated; mestizas were left to be treated as second-class citizens. In Mexico, perhaps fortunately for María, the matter was not aired in so explicit a sense. Mestizas who could definitely claim noble blood through their mothers were at first perceived as desirable marriage partners—at least if they were wealthy. María could hardly be touted as the daughter of royal stock, but her mother had been widely respected, and Jaramillo was rich. On the other hand, within her own household, she may well have been treated as an inferior on more than one account. Years later, doña Beatriz made it clear that she had never forgotten that María had Indian blood. And María grew to be an irritant to Beatriz for other reasons as well: María was a stepdaughter, and Beatriz herself proved unable to have children. Beyond that, there were even those who questioned whether María was really Jaramillo's child. Evil-disposed tongues wagged that she might have belonged to Cortés instead. It would have been nearly impossible for María to have remained untouched by the web of tensions that encircled her.[3]

In some senses, however, the child certainly had a pleasant life. She was not sent away to live with others or obviously neglected, as she might have been. She received some education: she learned to sign her name respectably, which was more than some young ladies in her world could do. As a small girl, she might well have been a pet of her stepmother, the very young doña Beatriz, and in her teens, she might even have been a welcome companion to a stepmother who was herself still only in her twenties. As later events proved, the two young women would one day be perfectly capable of conspiring together in ways that would infuriate María's husband. When she became a young lady, Malintzin's daughter was uniformly called doña María: in later years, even those who insulted her mother made no effort to deny her that title.

Doña María's life was at the very least relatively luxurious, for her father's encomienda of Xilotepec turned out to be one of the best in Mexico: while Indians elsewhere died by the hundreds and even thousands of the newly imported diseases, the population remained quite steady at Xilotepec. It was apparently a particularly healthy site, dry and cool, and elevated enough to provide clean water untainted by runoff from elsewhere. The region also boasted strong indigenous leadership. In 1533, when few Indians had even been exposed to the Roman alphabet, one of the noblemen there stunned the Audiencia by bringing a well-crafted petition he had had a literate Indian write out for him.[4]

Jaramillo went to court several times to keep the proceeds of the marvelous encomienda out of the hands of the descendants of the shoemaker Hernando de Santillana, who had lived at Xilotepec and overseen matters while Malintzin was alive. In the 1530s, virtually all the Spaniards in New Spain went to court concerning property-related disputes. They fumed and fulminated and cast aspersions on each other. Hernando Cortés, for example, raged against another doña Marina, the widow of Alonso de Estrada, the former treasurer. She had managed to acquire, he said bitterly, "enough riches to sustain ten conquistadors."[5]

Many of these cases depended on the testimony of Indians. Other translators had appeared to take the place of María's mother. They would have done so whether or not she had died: Malintzin had been of crucial importance in the early days because there was no one else available who was both bilingual and able to act as a cultural intermediary. That situation, however, was bound to change: the very source of her power would have limited her authority to a brief historical moment even if she had lived. Thousands of Nahuas were now learning Spanish, the language of power, and a few Europeans were learning Nahuatl. A number of the earliest Spanish translators married indigenous women and clearly learned what they knew from living with their wives. At least two of these left their encomienda holdings to their mestizo sons without any hesitation. Some of these sons chose to try to become Spanish, while others purposely kept their mothers' traditions alive: one named his own eldest son Xicotencatl Castañeda. Cortés, after the loss of Malintzin, had hired a linguistically talented young Italian, Tomás de Rigioles, to help him in his relations with the indigenous dependents on his Cuernavaca estate. Rigioles was rewarded with an encomienda of his own and soon became an established part of the life of the countryside.

The first generation of European translators had relied on personal circumstances and their own linguistic talent, as had Malintzin. By the 1530s, however, a new breed of interpreter had come into existence. They were Spaniards who did not speak much Nahuatl themselves but rather oversaw the work of others, usually Indians; by the next decade some of those who were involved were mestizos. The new translators were professionals who lived in the cities and worked for the courts or the Audiencia or the viceregal offices. They made the most of their specialized knowledge (or their employees' specialized knowledge), which was most welcome in the world they lived in.[6]

Indeed, translating Nahuatl was becoming a profitable endeavor, for interestingly, many of the Spaniards wanted to hear what the Indians had to say. The early years in which the newcomers desperately needed to understand the indigenous had passed. But the conquerors and their heirs were still listening. It is far too simplistic to assume that the colonists were "racist" in the modern sense—overtly condescending or dismissive of indigenous knowledge. On the contrary, there was a move afoot in Mexico to preserve the vanishing knowledge of the ancient people, a sense that they were somehow morally pure, the holders of old truths. When the University of Mexico was founded in 1553, the organizers set aside two chairs for scholars of native languages, so that they would be able to train translators. In the meantime, in the earliest colonial courtrooms, judges paid attention to indigenous testimony. Most of the Indians who spoke for or against certain Spaniards' claims were noblemen, usually Christians. But the courts did not insist on either attribute. The lawyers for Cortés in a 1531 case were perfectly willing to call an elderly Mexica man to testify who knew absolutely nothing about Spanish culture. He did not swear on the Bible but rather "took an oath according to his own law because he was not a Christian." Pedro García, speaker of Nahuatl, took another oath to "interpret well and faithfully whatever the Indian might say."[7] Apparently, the attorneys thought such an "authentic" witness would help their cause, not hurt it. Whenever possible, they had the indigenous bring pictoglyphic written records to the proceedings. The same impartial Pedro García interpreted Indian complaints *against* Cortés on other occasions:

> On the 24th of January, 1533, the Indians of the province of Cuerna-vaca brought eight paintings, and they gave them to me, inter-preter for the Royal Audiencia, and asked me to give them to the President of the Audiencia, and to explain them to you in the same way that they explained them to me, for they were complaining of the Marqués del Valle, their lord . . . that he did not treat them as vassals, but rather as slaves.[8]

Pedro García went on to explain that the symbols represented the extraor-dinary quantities of goods and services that the Indians were expected to provide on an annual basis. The court scribe took down every word, and the judges listened. Of course, some Spaniards were hostile to the assump-tion that indigenous records always revealed the truth. "They can paint as much as they want," the Audiencia judge Diego Delgadillo said scath-ingly, but he for one would not be convinced by what they wrote, inasmuch as Indians were "drunken liars and idolaters who ate human flesh." Still, despite the presence of some hostility, the services of translators remained much in demand, and they became relatively powerful figures in society. Sometimes they overstepped themselves. Pedro García, who became the official translator to the first viceroy, don Antonio de Mendoza, ended by being publicly whipped because he had accepted bribes from indigenous groups who came to beg the viceroy to act on their behalf.[9]

Having been called frequently as witnesses in cases where Spaniards contested each others' rights to land and labor, it did not take the indig-enous long to learn how to litigate for themselves. They soon threw them-selves into this new mode of resolving disputes. The various sub-altepetls of Jaramillo's Xilotepec—which did not all share a common ethnicity, some being Nahua and some Otomí—eventually asked the viceroy to intervene as they tried to work out which group would be responsible for which proportion of the required tribute due to Jaramillo and his family. The modern reader looking at the records they left to posterity is torn between feeling profoundly impressed at their feisty independence and their remarkable ability to adopt what was useful of Spanish ways, and saddened at the fact that they were always left fighting about who should pay more—while the colonizers in their parallel world were free to argue among themselves over who should receive more.[10]

The truth was double edged in many regards. When Malintzin's daughter looked about her, she would have been torn between thinking that the Indians' lot was a pitiable one, as their subjugation became more entrenched every day, and thinking that they in fact were the ones in control of a good many aspects of her life—the kitchen, the streets, the markets, the food supply. She would have heard about the continuing conquests of natives; she would have heard the Spaniards' incessant complaints about the arrogance of the Indians and their stubborn refusal to change their ways.

There is in fact no perfectly satisfactory way to describe the situation in which the indigenous people found themselves. The reality was paradoxical. The Indians were violently defeated; the Indians could never be permanently defeated. Their lives would never be the same again; for many of them, their daily activities went on quite unchanged. The Spanish language and Christian ethic became the dominant modes of the country they inhabited, but they themselves continued to think in Nahuatl and to understand their relationship to the world much as their parents had. Women were no longer the complementary equals of men but rather were deemed to be inferior and allowed fewer legal rights, yet women continued to do most of the talking in the markets and a good deal of it in the courts. Looking back, if we are blind to the Indians' losses, to their suffering, we diminish their courage in the face of adversity, but if we see them only as victims, vulnerable and compliant, we belittle them in another way, denying them their independence of mind. There is no simple truth here.[11]

María lived entirely as a Spaniard. Yet her later life reveals that she never forgot who her mother was, and was proud to speak her name. To some extent, she was an outsider in the Spanish world, and her own stepmother never let her forget it. Like others who do not quite fit into the world in which they move, she would have had to come to her own conclusions regarding a number of complex questions. Consciously or unconsciously, she would have been faced with such troubling conundrums as what it meant to be an Indian, or a mestiza.

She certainly made her own decisions where personal matters were concerned. In 1540 the viceroy, don Antonio de Mendoza, became so taken with the idea of the Seven Cities of Gold—which explorers of the northern terrain believed they had found—that he urged the men of Mexico City to sally forth. They were led by Francisco Vázquez de Coronado. A young kinsman of Juan Jaramillo's joined the expedition, but there were many men who did not. While the city folk waited for news from the northern lands of New Mexico, most of them continued with their usual rounds of going to market, gossiping, and flirting. Juan Jaramillo was apparently stunned when he suddenly learned that his fifteen-year-old daughter had an ardent suitor.[12]

Don Luis de Quesada, from the city of Granada, had arrived in 1535 in the train of Viceroy Mendoza. Indeed, his mother was a relative of the viceroy. He was only seventeen at the time of the crossing, and the viceroy took care to provide an income to the boy at first, until he was able to establish himself. Mendoza encouraged all his young dependents to marry well, including don Luis. In 1541 Luis was twenty-three, and he conceived the idea that Jaramillo's rich young daughter was the very bride he sought.[13]

Jaramillo set his face against the match. Either he simply did not like María's suitor and suspected his motives, or else he thought his daughter too young to marry (though he had not thought the same of doña Beatriz when he married her at fifteen). He forbade the courtship. Don Luis would not take no for an answer. One night, he brought several of his rollicking young friends to María's house with the avowed intention of taking her away by force. False abductions—false in the sense that the woman involved was to some extent complicit—were a tried and true practice in Spain, put to use when fathers proved intransigent. In this case, don Luis was somehow stymied in his efforts to leave the house with María. Since the dwelling was certainly not filled with numerous armed men, it seems likely that María put her foot down at the last and refused to leave without her father's consent. Don Luis, however, found a way around the difficulty: he told everyone he knew that although he had failed to get María away, he had at least managed to have an amorous interlude with her. In face of the dishonor that the story brought to his family, Jaramillo gave in, and María married her gallant. She left her uncertain youth behind her and became a Spanish lady.[14]

Almost immediately, María's new husband set off on a violent military campaign against some rebel Indians. In the Spaniards' recent conquest of Jalisco, the territory to the northwest, they had been particularly brutal. Early in 1541, the indigenous people there had seen an opportunity to rid themselves of their conquerors when the majority of the armed Spanish men living in the region had suddenly joined Coronado's expedition to New Mexico, riding away with pennants flying. The Indians fortified themselves in the highlands and began conducting raids against the weakened Spanish settlements. Two times they defeated Spanish forces sent against them. Even the famed Pedro de Alvarado—he who had been Cortés's right-hand man—was killed.[15]

Viceroy Mendoza now decided that he personally would lead an expedition against the indigenous rebels, who threatened the prevailing order of New Spain. Naturally don Luis, one of his protégés, was expected to go along; unfortunately, however, that young man could not afford to fit himself up for war. Apparently having patched things up with his father-in-law, don Luis approached Jaramillo to beg the necessary horses and weaponry, as well as slaves to accompany him so that he could travel in befitting style. Fortunately, perhaps, the war was largely over by the time don Luis got there. He undoubtedly joined with other Spaniards in rounding up captives—men, women, and children—so that they could be branded and sold as slaves.[16]

Not long after don Luis returned home, he and doña María learned that according to the terms of Juan Jaramillo's will, they were to be left with only a third of the encomienda when he died and doña Beatriz with the remaining two-thirds. In the face of this fact, posterity has concluded that Jaramillo did not love María much or perhaps even doubted she was his daughter. But disinheritance—complete or partial—was a common punishment for marrying without a father's permission. Moreover, doña Beatriz had, after all, come to Jaramillo as his bride with the understanding that she would be left rich. She had been a dutiful wife. María had not been a dutiful daughter. In 1542 María and Luis brought together witnesses who had known Malintzin personally and had them testify as to the importance of her contributions, both to the Spanish cause in general and to her husband's estate in particular. Witnesses were easy to find. Doña Beatriz's own father spoke in defense of Malintzin's just desserts, rather than his daughter's. The testimony was then carefully preserved, to be used later in quarreling with Jaramillo's will on his demise. In 1547 María and Luis went back to court to prove that they had been married according to the tenets of the Holy Mother Church: they had apparently learned that their names had come up in a mud-slinging contest that ultimately had little to do with them but that nevertheless had cast doubt on the status of their relationship. The enemies of Viceroy Mendoza—among them Hernando Cortés—were using any stories that told against the viceroy that they could find. In Spain, in a campaign against him, they cited numerous anecdotes, including the rather thrilling circumstances of doña María's near elopement, for the viceroy's own majordomo had been one of the friends whom don Luis had brought to Jaramillo's house that fateful night. Now the couple needed to assert that their marriage had been properly carried out, lest there be any doubt in the future.[17]

In 1546, when she was twenty, María gave birth to a little boy—Malintzin's grandson. They named him Pedro, after Luis's father. The child lived, much to everyone's surprise and joy, for María had lost several babies already and had learned to keep her expectations low. In the course of the years, one other child was also to live.[18]

In 1550 or 1551, Jaramillo's health began to deteriorate. There is no reason to suppose that any enmity existed between him and his daughter as he neared his end. Visitors later recalled seeing María in Jaramillo's house in the period before his death. And everyone, even don Luis, acknowledged that María and Beatriz came to some sort of an understanding in those sad days, with María agreeing to give up all claim to more than a third of the estate. Luis was quick to point out to the judges, however, that María had not consulted him when she made such a statement and that he should in no way be bound by it. Indeed, he had begun to prepare the paperwork for a lawsuit even while Jaramillo was still alive.[19]

When the old conquistador died, he left many debts. In order to pay them, the orchard near Chapultepec that the cabildo had once awarded to him and to Malintzin had to be sold. So did a number of the African slaves who had served the family for years. For them, Jaramillo's death was a disaster, for it meant they were wrested from loved ones. And the death led to other painful scenes as well.[20]

When don Luis and his wife contested the will, doña Beatriz went into orbits of rage. Jaramillo's death had freed her to speak her mind in ways she never had before, at least not publicly. She called Malintzin not doña Marina but "the Indian woman, Marina," and she pointed out that Marina had been given to the Spanish as a servant, for she had "lowly status, and was not a noble." Jaramillo, she claimed, did not owe anything to his base-born daughter: he had already paid dearly simply in marrying her mother. "He made that marriage to the great prejudice of his person and his honor, because he was a person of quality, and she was of low estate." Marina, on the other hand, "was rewarded more than she deserved in marrying . . . Jaramillo, for he lost much honor in the marriage." In that period, it was not safe for Beatriz to emphasize that her husband's first wife had been indigenous, for the surviving family of Moctezuma and certain other Nahua nobles still had power and prestige. No, the telling strike against Marina was not that she was an Indian but that she was of low estate. An hidalgo lost honor in uniting himself to such a woman.[21]

To the gratification of María, doña Beatriz found that when she went to court six months later, the witnesses she herself had gathered would not quite follow her to the point of insulting Marina. Over half of them—including all those who had been part of the conquest—referred to Malintzin as "doña Marina" even when they were asked about "the Indian woman." When pressed to say that she had come to them as a low-born slave, old conquistadors answered instead that the Indians told them "they had taken the women from other provinces in their wars" or that "it was true she was not a *señora* or a noblewoman at the time she was given to them." When asked whether the marriage had dishonored Jaramillo, they dodged the question and commented on something else. Cristóbal de Oñate said thoughtfully, "It is certainly true that he did not gain any honor in the said marriage." Only when asked if Marina, an Indian, had raised her status in marrying a Spaniard like Jaramillo could the witnesses testify exactly as Beatriz wished. And saying that she had certainly gained in marrying a Spaniard seemed to loosen their tongues: only at that point would the original conquerors add that perhaps Jaramillo had lost honor in the marriage. As if to ease his conscience, however, Bernardino Vázquez made an additional comment that was hardly what doña Beatriz was looking for: he added that people at the time were saying Jaramillo must have been very much in love.[22]

In response, Malintzin's daughter and her husband gathered over thirty witnesses whose names were among the most impressive in Mexico. They included several of the first conquerors—including Rodrigo de Castañeda and Andrés de Tapia—as well as Juan Cano, now married to Moctezuma's daughter, doña Isabel, the educated *bachiller* Alonso Pérez, the highborn

Spaniard don Luis de Avalos, one of the most famous clerics in Mexico, fray Toríbio Motolinia, and two indigenous noblemen, don Diego de Atempanecatl and don Pedro de Moctezuma. These men, like the other witnesses, resisted perjuring themselves. When don Luis and doña María went too far in their leading questions and asked if it wasn't the case, for example, that the population of Xilotepec had grown in the years that Marina was mistress there, because the Indians of the land respected her and desired to serve her, the witnesses balked and said they did not know about that.[23]

Don Diego de Atempanecatl—he who had lived with Malintzin for a while as a youth—clearly remained very much his own man. When asked if Jaramillo was a principal person in the land, he answered tersely that obviously he was. When asked if Jaramillo had conducted himself super-latively in the campaign against the Indians, he parted company from all the other witnesses and said he did not know, "as he did not know him during the war." All the witnesses on this side agreed that the Spaniards in general and Jaramillo in particular had gained immeasurably because of their connection with Malintzin. Diego de Atempanecatl put the case in her favor in other terms. While the Spaniards debated their own notions of honor, he asserted that she had always behaved with the reserve and dignity of an indigenous noblewoman. "I lived in the household of the said doña Marina, and I was always with her. I saw that she went about in the manner of an honest woman, in the Indian clothing that is customary in this land, and this fact was well-known among all those who knew her." To be "honest" in this context was to behave honorably, to do as one should, to comply with the dictates of society. In don Diego's view, Malintzin had done all that a good woman should. She had dishonored no one.[24]

Don Diego's words may have been uttered not only in the context of the scorn heaped upon Malintzin by doña Beatriz but also possibly in the face of suspicions of Malintzin in his own indigenous world. She had, after all, violated the primary rule by which noblewomen were expected to live: she had left her home and hearth. She had become a wanderer. Still, the peo-ple of her world were well acquainted with the fates of women from con-quered altepetls, and she probably needed no defending in their eyes. It is true that indigenous language sources in the middle of the century refer to her as "Malintzin," not as "doña Marina"—and by then all indigenous noblewomen were customarily given the title the Indians had adopted from the Spanish world. But the name "Malintzin" had almost certainly crystallized in the form it naturally took in the early 1520s, when she was still alive, for all the midcentury visual representations of the woman, as we have seen, show her as a powerful—and sometimes even a well-loved—noblewoman.

The angry doña Beatriz remarried a respectable thirty-four months after Jaramillo's demise.[25] In the interim, she undoubtedly had the world of eligible bachelors at her feet. She was a rich widow from an extensive and well-positioned clan, and besides that, she was only in her early thirties, her face and figure unravaged by the strains of pregnancy, childbirth, and nursing. In 1550, shortly before Jaramillo's death, the king had asked don Antonio de Mendoza to become the Viceroy of Peru, a region recently torn by civil war, and had appointed don Luis de Velasco, a very capable man, to fill Mendoza's place in Mexico. The new viceroy's younger brother, don Francisco de Velasco, accompanied him to Mexico. It was he whom doña Beatriz chose as her new husband.

In the meantime, María's young son was growing up. In 1556 or 1557, when Pedro was ten or eleven, his father took him to Spain to be educated. Like her mother before her, María had to bid her son farewell, not knowing when she would see him again. In making the trip across the Atlantic, don Luis undoubtedly also had the intention of pressing his suit concerning the Jaramillo inheritance, which was dragging through the courts at the usual snail's pace, and which certainly had doleful prospects, now that the defendant was married to the viceroy's brother.[26]

The late 1550s was an exciting time to be in Europe. In 1554 the Spanish prince Philip had married the Catholic queen Mary of England, creating an alliance between two great powers. In the spring of 1556, in Brussels, the aging Charles V had abdicated in favor of his son Philip. Charles died in 1558, leaving his son undisputed master of many realms. In the same year, Queen Mary died and was succeeded by her younger sister, the princess Elizabeth, who was a Protestant, thus ending Spain's alliance with England. In the upheaval, France took the opportunity to wage war against Philip's dominions on various fronts, but the Spanish monarch eventually emerged victorious. To cement Philip's power, coronation ceremonies were held for him in the various kingdoms he had inherited from his father. While he was in Spain, don Luis de Quesada decided to travel to Italy and attend such a ceremony himself.[27]

His trip may have had something to do with the formation of a new friendship: somewhere during the course of his travels, perhaps at court, he had come to know María's half brother Martín—Malintzin's son by Cortés—who had been sent to Spain to be educated and who certainly remembered fondly the little sister he had left behind with his mother. Indeed, she was the only person who had been part of his early childhood who still lived. Don Martín was now in military service and, during this period, traveled back and forth to France and Italy to defend Philip's interests wherever they were threatened. Don Luis could easily have traveled to Italy in his company. In any case, the two men made grave promises to each other that they would help to defend each other's interests in future.[28]

Luis left his son, Pedro, in Spain and returned to María in Mexico, bringing news of her brother to comfort her. The trip had undoubtedly been expensive, and Luis complained that their share of the Xilotepec encomienda, consisting of tribute from the Otomí community, was much smaller than it was reputed to be.[29] He had not made any significant progress in the legal case, and in about 1560, both sides called a new round of witnesses.

This time doña Beatriz and her husband don Francisco de Velasco said what had been unthinkable in earlier years, when New Spain's collective memory of the conquest was fresher: they claimed that Malintzin had never been particularly important as a translator and that there was even some reason to suspect that she had been a traitor. When asked if there hadn't been others who were capable of speaking with the Indians by the time the Spaniards returned to Tenochtitlan in 1521, witnesses who had been present at that time said that yes, there were. They all mentioned Jerónimo de Aguilar, without explaining that it was a Mayan tongue, not Nahuatl, that he spoke. And a few gave other known names: Rodrigo de Castañeda, Juan Pérez, and the Italian Tomás de Rigioles. Martín López—the shipwright of old, who had come to Cortés's rescue when he built the brigantines for the lake in 1521—wanted to please the viceroy's younger brother, but all he could bring himself to say was that doña Marina often still worked with Jerónimo de Aguilar, "but about the rest, he did not know."[30]

Two of the Spaniards trying to help prove that Marina had been unimportant after all referred to Juan Pérez as Juan Pérez Malinchi, quite unselfconsciously, as if "Malinchi" were his final surname, apparently unaware that he had been termed that by the Indians because of his association with the woman they called "Malintzin." Of course, the translators themselves were supremely conscious of doña Marina's crucial importance in the period of first contact. In 1551 Rodrigo de Castañeda had spoken strongly in her favor, and now Juan Pérez was called to the stand by doña María and her husband. He made no bones about the fact that it was her translation efforts that were essential then, not his. Other old companions remembered an incident in July or August of 1521 in which Cortés had been trying to parley through the medium of young Tomás de Rigioles, but the Indians, after a period of frustration, at last announced that they would only talk to Malintzin. Cortés had been forced to send a boat to get her where she was, eight leagues away, in Tetzcoco. Juan Pérez said he did not remember that specific incident but that it certainly could have happened, as that sort of thing happened all the time.[31]

Even the witnesses who most sought to please the viceroy's brother found they could not bring themselves to say that doña Marina had actually been a traitor. Of the list of twelve witnesses, only four were called by doña Beatriz's lawyer to answer that question, the others apparently having demurred ahead of time. One said something, then had part of his testimony scratched out, as if he had not understood the question or doubted his memory. Two said they remembered an incident in which someone had been hanged for some reason but knew nothing about why, and one said he remembered nothing at all about any problem having occurred. When asked if Cortés had not eventually begun to prefer other translators, they almost all said they did not know. When asked if Cortés had not ended up suspecting Marina's faithfulness in a personal as well as a political sense, only one could come up with any particularly relevant memories: he dredged up the old rumor that Cortés had been jealous of the time doña Marina spent with Jerónimo de Aguilar, but he did not say anything that implied that she had actually been unfaithful. In fact, he suddenly added that after the biggest squabble on that issue, Cortés learned that Aguilar had actually left Marina at the usual time and spent almost the whole night gambling with some fellows.[32]

We will never know how galling it was to María to have to defend her dead mother's memory from slander, whether she desired her husband to drop the case, or if by now her dander was up, too. In either case, something that would have been profoundly comforting to her occurred in

1562: her brother Martín arrived from Spain. Old conquerors and don Diego de Atempanecatl had been able to tell her stories about her mother, but Martín was her brother, and he still retained childhood memories of the woman who had slipped away when María was still too young to be left with anything to hold onto.

This was perhaps the last happiness she would know. In 1563 doña María died, not yet forty years old. If she was conscious toward the end, she faced the fact that, like her mother, she was dying while her son was far away in an unimaginable land across the sea; she would never know him as a man. María left money so that six Masses a week would be said at the Santa Clara monastery. It had been called La Santíssima Trinidad when it was founded in 1526, near the place where Malintzin was living with Jaramillo. More than one person has wondered if María knew of a connection—if the mother she only vaguely remembered was buried there or had often prayed there.[33]

News traveled slowly across the sea, but in due course, Pedro received word that his mother was dead. In 1565 and again the following year, he considered going home. He went so far as to apply for permission to take a black servant named Adunte, probably a slave, to the New World. He did not actually leave, however, until the summer of 1567. In 1566 there had been political trouble in Mexico, in which his uncle, Martín, was deeply involved, and he had probably been warned to stay where he was for a time. When he returned home, he learned that doña Beatriz had tried to have his family's case dismissed, on grounds that María was dead, and her heir indefinitely absent from Mexico. In 1571, when he had attained his twenty-fifth year, Pedro reopened the case in his own name. At about the same time, he married doña Melchiora de Puga, daughter of a powerful and well-educated man, an Audiencia judge, the doctor Vasco de Puga, who had been a staunch supporter of his uncle in the political troubles that had wracked the colony a few years before.[34]

In 1573, after more than two decades of legal battling over the terms of Jaramillo's will, the Council of the Indies, the highest court ruling over New Spain, gave its verdict in Madrid. "We find that . . . don Luis de Quesada and doña Maria Xaramillo and don Pedro de Quesada have not proved their case . . . We give and pronounce it as unproven. . . . We absolve don Francisco de Velasco and doña Beatriz de Andrada his wife in the case against them, . . . and we place perpetual silence on the said don

Luis de Quesada and his consorts, that they may never ask or demand anything else of them." The Quesadas' lawyer appealed, but the sentence was upheld in October of the same year.[35]

Malintzin's grandson, the mixed-blood offspring, had lost the bitter contest to a viceroy's brother. Or so it appears at first. In fact, however, there was more going on than first meets the eye. The Crown had spent at least the past three decades attempting to curb the power of the encomenderos and trying to limit the number of descendants who would have the right to inherit the privileges won by a fortunate few, the lucky first conquerors. Doña Beatriz had had no children by her second husband, either. Her share of the encomienda could easily escheat to the Crown within a few years. It was obvious that don Pedro, on the other hand, might well have many descendants. The Council of the Indies had little motivation to hand them more wealth and power than they already stood to inherit.

A few years later, doña Beatriz's name appeared in two confidential, unsigned government reports: she was mentioned as having inherited as a widow, not a daughter, and she also appeared on the list of encomenderos who had no children. "And she is no longer of an age to have any," bluntly commented the bureaucrat, little caring, apparently, that she was the respected wife of a former viceroy's brother. On both counts, then, doña Beatriz could safely be informed—without arousing too much ire or anyone else's sympathy—that she would not be allowed to pass on her share of the encomienda to anyone else. When she died, the estate did escheat to the Crown. The Council of the Indies, not doña Beatriz, had won in 1573. The verdict, after all, had little or nothing to do with Malintzin and the debate over her merits.[36]

In one important regard, Malintzin did win in the end. For Pedro and Melchiora had four children in their first decade together, and the oldest son, named Luis, continued to thrive on the wealth of Xilotepec for years to come. He heard stories about his great-grandmother. "If she had wanted to, it would have been easy for her to sell all the Spaniards to the Indians." She had given her word, however, and as a person of honor, she refrained.[37] Things had changed some in the telling; Malintzin's grandchildren did not really understand what her situation had been like. But their loyalty was heartwarming. Her children and her children's children revered her memory, as any Nahua wife would certainly have wished.

NINE

Don Martín

It had been on a day in March 1528 that Martín stood on the deck of a ship, waiting to pull away from Mexico; everyone aboard waited. Some of the sailors had deftly climbed the rigging. When the shouted command came, they untied the rolled-up sails and dropped them down, thud after thud. Then came a cracking noise as the canvases suddenly filled with wind and strained at the confining ropes and beams. The ship was moving. The other sailors flew into action; each knew his task as the boat got under way. The passengers said their last farewells to land.

Within a few hours, many of them regretted it. The rolling waves would not have surprised the Spaniards onboard the two ships that were traveling together: they had all made the crossing before at least once and had steeled themselves for the first few days of overwhelming nausea. But Malintzin's young son could not have known what to expect. Nor could the Nahuas with whom he sailed. Cortés was traveling with about forty indigenous passengers—some his servants and others a troupe of acrobats who were sure to impress the king. With him also were a number of high-ranking indigenous noblemen who had taken Christian names on top of their old appellations. There were two sons of Moctezuma—don Pedro Moctezuma and his half brother don Martín Cortés Nezahualtecolotl—

and various companions of theirs. And there were also three highborn Tlaxcalan princes—don Lorenzo Tianquiztlatohuantzin, don Valeriano Quetzalcoltzin, and don Julián Quaupiltzintli—as well as several lesser Tlaxcalan nobles. Cortés wanted the natives along to prove he had won for the monarch the loyalty of the indigenous people. And they wanted to go along for their own reasons—to gather information about the nature of the place called Spain and to petition for favors on behalf of their altepetls and family lineages. They were mostly young men in their twenties—too young to have lost their lives in the early battles, but old enough at this point to be recognized by their people as political leaders. As children, they had been raised, like all future warriors, to flit about easily in canoes. Some had probably even gone out to sea, but always hugging the coast. Crossing the ocean was an entirely different matter. Even a seasoned traveler like Diego de Ordás later complained that the voyage had been dreadful. "The sea destroyed me," he said. And the food was particularly bad, he added. "Leaving the channel of the Bahamas, the chickens were drowned in the very first storm, and so we were left with just cheese and bacon."[1]

When the native princes had recovered from their varying degrees of seasickness and regained the composure of noblemen, they would have impressed a child Martín's age. They were strong young men, accustomed to being listened to, confident and still hopeful. At least some of them still chose to dress in indigenous clothing, and they wore their fine cloaks with flair. (The king would later put a stop to that, even offering to pay for clothes that better befit Christians.) Most of the Tlaxcalans would live to return home and report on their mission, offering advice to their compatriots on how best to control the situation. Moctezuma's son don Pedro would spend his life battling in Spanish courts and ultimately would obtain significant royal favors. The other Martín—don Martín Cortés Nezahualtecolotl—would actually marry a relatively highborn Spanish woman.

At age six, Malintzin's son would have been old enough to perceive that his father, the great conqueror, was even more high strung than usual just at present. He had the upcoming confrontations in Spain to think of. And there had been a wild flurry of preparations before the trip that the man was still recovering from. He had written out extensive instructions regarding his properties to Francisco de Santa Cruz, a kinsman who had promised to see to them, with the help of local indigenous authorities.

Nor had Cortés neglected the personal. Before leaving, he ordered annual commemorations for his departed wife and for all the Spaniards who had died in the conquest. "May they be in glory." He left his three illegitimate daughters in good hands, as well as another young son named Luis who had recently been born to a Spanish woman outside wedlock. Remarkably, he had also decided to raise the orphaned son of a former enemy, Francisco de Garay, a man he had once loved to loathe. "Take care to collect Amadorcico," Cortés instructed Santa Cruz. "Look out for him, see that he is well treated and continues with his schooling, and punish him moderately if he makes mistakes; this I entrust to you, take special care." Martín, his eldest son, was the only child he brought with him.[2]

Six weeks after embarking, they drew into port at Palos de la Frontera on the Spanish coast. There was the usual sending of messages and purchasing of much-desired fresh food. While they rested, Gonzalo de Sandoval died. It had been he who had led the expedition to Coatzacoalcos, Malintzin's birthplace, as the first of the sorties from the City of Mexico. Cortés came to see him on his deathbed: here was another link with the events of 1519–21 gone. But there was no time to be lost. As soon as Sandoval had breathed his last, Cortés and his party made their way to the mouth of the Guadalquivir River and passed upward when the tide was right, dropping anchor in front of the city of Seville. From the first, the indigenous onboard could see the immensity of Europe's technological power in comparison with their own. What they had seen already in Mexico, and a few days ago in Palos, was in fact not the best the Spaniards could do; it only represented the fringes of their mighty estate. The many ships, the stone ramparts with their cannons, the bridges over wide channels, the great towers, the rushing carriages, all bespoke a world the Mexicans had never imagined before. Wherever they went in the city, they could see the great Giralda, a tower reaching to the sky with its fine arched windows, built by Muslims over many years as a minaret for the mosque that once had stood there. Next to the Giralda the Christians were still in the midst of raising a cathedral of intricate sculptures looking heavenward, carven stone suggesting something as light and beautiful as gauze. Centuries of engineers passing on and expanding their knowledge were memorialized in those buildings. Anyone could see that here was a force to be reckoned with. Not that any of the visiting Indians had continued to harbor illusions about their ability to rid Mexico of the newcomers; any thoughts of that nature had likely been driven from their minds a number of years before. But their first sight of a major European city would have been a significant moment to them—when their most dire assessments were confirmed. Little Martín, on the other hand, as a son of Cortés, was undoubtedly taut with excitement.

Cortés of necessity had to spend some time in Seville dealing with bureaucratic officials. There was the king's fifth to be paid on the treasure he brought with him and arrangements to be made for the indigenous passengers to travel to the king's court. Then he secured horses for his immediate entourage and turned his steps toward Medellín, his birthplace, for the first time in twenty-five years. He had been about nineteen when he left to go to the Caribbean; he was forty-four now. The way to the village of Medellín lay northward over the mountains, toward the plains of Extremadura, the strip of land that ran along the border of Portugal. We do not know if Cortés and his son were already aware that his father, the first Martín, had died. At the end of 1527, Cortés had sent his father a tame ocelot that the indigenous servants on one of his estates had raised from a baby. He wrote that it should be taken to the king as a present. But Martín did not live to receive the letter or the ocelot. Only Cortés's mother still waited to welcome her son back to his natal village; only she met the small, dark grandson.³

It was not long before they said good-bye to her and took to the road again. Cortés wanted to visit the Monastery of Guadalupe, one of Extremadura's most holy sanctuaries, and he had to make it his business to see the king as soon as possible. Charles V had a roving court, and it was not yet certain if he was in Toledo, and if not, where they would catch up with him. Father and son passed from village to village, each of which, like Medellín, had an ancient castle or stronghold at its heart. Not so long ago, each nobleman had done his best to protect his own land and people, and though petty nobles considered that they owed allegiance to greater nobles, there had been nothing remotely resembling a peninsula-wide kingdom. The region's strongmen had once been Christian lords, but from 711 onward, Muslims were the greatest power in the land. Only in the twelfth and thirteenth centuries had Christian forces, working together, begun to be effective in driving the Muslim lords southward. In 1248 they retook Seville. Such successes, however, did not mean that they necessarily perceived themselves as one people. Even now, King

Charles still struggled to cement together the country of Spain that his grandparents, Ferdinand and Isabella, had worked so hard to create as they defeated Granada, the last Muslim state on the peninsula. The king moved from place to place, exerting his influence everywhere he went. Since he was also Holy Roman Emperor, it would not be long before he moved on to Bologna and then Germany for several years.

Cortés reached Toledo by the end of May but found the king gone. He went on to Madrid by early July but found he had missed the monarch again. He sent a letter to him via a messenger, asking if he planned to return soon, or if he should follow him somewhere else. Cortés's opponents were clearly watching him, for that very same day, an old enemy from Mexico who was also now in Madrid, Luis de Cárdenas, sent his own letter to the king. He wrote a vitriolic epistle, almost hysterical in tone. Cortés's perfidy was so well known, Cárdenas insisted, that the very children in Mexico would soon be singing rhymes about it.[4]

Cortés eventually returned to Toledo and kept busy until the king returned there in October. To gain general support, he gave out gifts—some called them bribes—with impressive liberality. He showed off his Mexican treasures, introduced the indigenous princes, and had the fascinating acrobats perform. In good time, Charles granted him an audience. Cortés knelt to kiss his feet, then offered him a long document that presented his side of the story of the conquest. He spoke eloquently in his own defense. His supporters and his enemies both watched eagerly.

Charles, though not yet thirty, was already a wise man. On his father's side, he had been born into the Duchy of Burgundy in the Low Countries, and as duke, he was recognized, in effect, as the monarch of that region. When he was seventeen, he inherited, in addition, the rulership of Spain through his mother, Juana, Ferdinand and Isabella's daughter. When he was nineteen, his paternal grandfather, Maximilian, died, and he was elected Holy Roman Emperor, which was the title given to the high king of several conglomerate Germanic states. That honor was not hereditary. Charles had expended all his wealth in purchasing the necessary votes from the various monarchs involved. He had done it, not out of misplaced vanity, but out of a clear-sighted conviction that he needed to do so in order to prevent the French king from winning the seat and becoming a frightening world power. Early in his career, Charles experienced rebellions in his far-flung territories, the most serious one of all in Spain itself.

The details had not been known to Cortés at the time, but while he was conquering Tenochtitlan, the army of the twenty-year-old Charles V was putting down the Comuneros Rebellion on Spanish soil. Unlike a number of other monarchs of his era who panicked when faced with such events, Charles did not become defensive in the wake of the uprising; he did not dole out brutal punishments. Instead he issued a general amnesty, having learned he could continue to wield his immense powers only if the various countries under his rulership remained happy with him. He became a good listener and acutely sensitive to the likely ramifications of various steps he might take.

In this case, he might side with the many enemies of Cortés, confiscating his wealth and bringing the man low, so as not to encourage a presumptuous and perhaps even dangerous arrogance. Cortés's enemies insisted that the man might even rebel against the king someday and certainly would not abide by royal policy in the distant colonial fiefdom that he would doubtlessly set up for himself if given the chance. But if Charles sided against the charismatic conquistador, he would be left with the various factions in Mexico fighting viciously against each other, and he would render other explorers of the New World suddenly doubtful if their ventures were worth their time. He took another course. In the spring of 1529, after months of deliberation, he made his announcement. "You, don Hernando Cortés . . . have rendered many great and distinguished services to the Catholic Kings, our parents and grandparents, and to Us, and each day you do so, and we hope and are certain, that your loyalty and faithfulness will continue from hereon in." Indeed, the king had in mind some specific future services: he would shortly hit up Cortés for a significant loan, which he was sure his obedient subject would be only too delighted to give. Charles knighted Cortés and gave him a heritable title. He would be the Marqués del Valle de Oaxaca—the Marquis of the Valley of Oaxaca. As an encomendero, he would have twenty-three thousand indigenous vassals, and he would have the right to build his palace on the Plaza Mayor, where the castle of Moctezuma had once stood. As a child, Cortés could never have imagined such a glorious future for himself.[5]

Yet in fact, Cortés seems to have been quite disappointed. He wanted to be viceroy, the official who would govern in the king's place in Mexico. And he would not be viceroy. Charles had listened to his advisors to that extent: it was important that some other official, whose first loyalty was to Charles himself, be sent to govern. The other petitioners who had accompanied Cortés had, of course, received even less, and they too had spent a great deal in the course of their journey. Diego de Ordás expressed the anger of the cohort from Mexico. "Those who came with [Cortés] are leaving with him, as clean [empty-handed] of special favors as they are of money."[6]

At some point during the course of the negotiations—as the petitioners persisted in calling their audiences with the king and his council—Cortés fell gravely ill, perhaps for the first time in his life. He had spent years waiting for the moment when he would be vindicated before the eyes of all his countrymen and richly rewarded by a grateful monarch. Whether at the eleventh or the thirteenth hour—we do not know which it was— the pressure was suddenly too much for him, and his son had to watch as his father gave way before it. He was sick enough to die, the doctors said. King Charles gave him the signal honor of striding down the palace corridors with his most trusted aides at his side and coming to visit him for a few moments. Cortés recovered.

On March 14, the last day before he left for Barcelona, King Charles issued definitive orders regarding the Indians who had come with the famed conquistador, now marqués. They were all to be given Christian clothing. The noblemen from Mexico City and the most important Tlaxcalan prince, don Lorenzo, were to be given blue velvet coats and doublets of yellow damask. Then they were to be sent to Seville and put up in good houses at the king's expense until they could take ship. The Indians did indeed travel southward almost immediately and were lodged in two well-to-do households in Seville. But there they were forced to wait for months on end—and there they began to die. The twenty-two-year-old don Lorenzo of Tlaxcala was among the first to go. Several others soon followed. Perhaps those who could do so hid the symptoms of their illnesses, for the proffered cures made them worse. In their well-intentioned zeal, the officials of the king paid a local barber for sixteen bleedings. Still, the travelers did not give up hope, and the majority lived to return to Mexico, some in August and some in December.[7]

In the meantime, as soon as the emperor had departed, Cortés announced that he was on his way to get married and to pick up his aging mother, who wanted to accompany him to his New World. As soon as he could, he would meet the rest of his party in Seville and would sail with them. He left on March 29. Martín did not go with his father. He was left in the care of Queen Isabel, the Portuguese princess whom Charles had married, to become a page and a loyal servant to her two-year-old son, Philip. Martín joined the ranks of other sons of counts and dukes left there for the same purpose. They would grow up with their future king, united to him not only by political bonds, but also by ties of affection.

It must have been a difficult good-bye. It would have been impossible for any seven-year-old child not to feel adulation for such a father, even if he were occasionally cruel, as is more than possible. And Cortés later wrote in a private letter how much he loved the boy. Still, they had reason to hope that they would meet again in life, either in Spain or in Mexico, as the future might dictate. Cortés told his son that he had sent a representative to Rome, to apply for a papal bull legitimizing him and two of his siblings—Catalina, his oldest child, who had a Cuban mother, and Luis, whose mother was a Spanish gentlewoman. The man would do the necessary paperwork and pay the requisite fees. Given the recent decision of Charles V, it was almost certain that the request would be granted.

We can never know how well young Martín steeled himself for the separation. The process must have been made more difficult when Cortés's departure from Spain unexpectedly became a long, drawn-out affair. Dramatic news soon came to his friends in Toledo: he had in fact not yet gotten married and was not to sail anytime soon after all. He had received reports from Mexico, and it seemed that the investigation of his conduct that had been launched just as he left was not going well. Thus he had decided to follow the king to Barcelona and appeal for more support. After further parleying, the king did indeed give Cortés an even more impressive-sounding document and a few more small favors, including a grant of two hunting preserves. He did not budge to any significant degree: the importunate conqueror would have to consider himself satisfied. It would, however, be helpful to Cortés to have these new documents dated within days of the king's departure from the country, thus proving that the monarch had not changed his mind at the last minute, whatever others might say.[8]

Someone in the church hierarchy must have taken the news of the king's support to Toledo, where it made its way to the offices of the military Order of Santiago. Or Cortés himself may have paid a messenger. For twelve days later a remarkable hearing occurred there, granting little Martín honors that were reserved for "persons of quality." It is possible that the order's officials had merely received word of the papal bull rendering the child legitimate—which had been issued in the middle of April—and they considered that sufficient in this case. Diego de Ordás apparently took the boy to the hearing on July 19, which had been requested by Cortés before he left. The proud father had been granted admission to this exclusive order in 1525, and he wanted the same honor for Martín. He wanted him to be able to ride to battle wearing the habit and bearing the shield that everyone in his world would recognize as giving him special status. On that hot July day, a silent Martín stood at attention in a somber room built of stone, full of self-important men. At first, given who the child's mother was, the proceedings seem to the modern ear to have been something of a farce: four witnesses took an oath as to the "purity of blood" of Cortés's parents: his family, they all swore, was untainted with the blood of Moors, Jews, converted Jews, or serfs. But this was no farce. Ordás and Herrera then swore that Martín's mother, Malintzin, was of high birth among her own people, of noble stock, and married to an honorable Spaniard named Juan Jaramillo. This was good enough, it turned out, at least for a mother. Impure blood, at this point, did not connote the blood of darker people but, rather, the blood of declared enemies and of commoners. Even twenty years later, we remember, doña Beatriz across the ocean in Mexico refrained from condemning Malintzin for having been an Indian; in her efforts to demean her, she would only insist that she had been of low estate. Eventually, all Indians would be defined as a racial Other, but that had not happened yet. Martín became a knight of the prestigious Order of Santiago.[9]

At about that same time, Martín's father married doña Juana de Zúñiga, niece of the Duke of Béjar, who was godfather to the heir apparent, Prince Philip. Cortés promised to bring his bride and her family wealth and honor over time; she brought a dowry of ten thousand ducats for his immediate use. He needed the funds to pay the many debts he had amassed in Spain and to give the king the requisite "loan." After the ceremony, they spent some time in Extremadura, whence they both hailed. They returned at least briefly to Toledo. (In August Diego de Ordás complained to a friend that he had not seen them yet, implying that he expected to, and in October, the empress granted the conquistador another audience.) In the spring of 1530, apparently having waited for the winter storms to pass, Cortés really did sail away with his mother and his new bride. Martín was left alone.

From then on he lived sometimes in Madrid and sometimes in Toledo, for the household of the queen moved about, depending on the king's whereabouts and on political necessities, as Isabel acted as regent during Charles's many absences. The prince's companions slept and ate together in great halls. They studied and celebrated Mass together, read aloud to each other, and put on musical entertainments. Sometimes they were cruel to each other. One of the boys who arrived a few years after Martín had a strong Catalan accent. Even his extremely high birth and his powerful father could not protect him. "Two days ago the prince and six other children took part in a prank," complained his noble mother. Perhaps not surprisingly, Martín became known for being quiet and reserved. Cortés had arranged for a cousin to oversee the child's education and pay for tutors. Diego Pérez de Vargas, a longtime member of the royal household, became Martín's teacher. He would have schooled the child in reading, writing, and arithmetic and, as he grew older, in Latin and the classical authors as well. There would have been training in horseback riding and sword fighting, too. Prince Philip's most loyal men were to be soldiers, by definition.[10]

Cortés constantly sent Martín messages and money, but he was still alone. He received word that his mother had died, that his grandmother had died shortly after reaching Mexico, and that his new stepmother had given birth to a son and then a daughter, who both died. Doña Juana tried again, however, and in 1532 gave birth to a baby named Martín. A second Martín. This son, born to a Spanish mother, was the one who would now inherit the *marquesado*. This was the one who, by virtue of his identical name, would almost erase the existence of his older brother. Down through the centuries the two have been confused by historians, archivists, and the general public alike. Many have thought that Malintzin's son inherited the estate, but he did not. He became instead a shadowy Martín, displaced by the "real" Martín—the heir and then the new marqués. Mexican intellectuals "in the know" have written about this in a bitter and ironic tone, but few others have ever noticed the eclipse of the mestizo son.[11]

The mestizo "don Martín" as he came to be called, by virtue of his father, presumably had expected the birth of the new and more important younger brother. At that age, it was perhaps the least of his concerns. Before he could have learned of it, he was already failing to thrive. He could not seem to fight the infections that assailed him. He had scrofula:

the lymph nodes in his neck swelled, eventually creating abscesses and then hideous oozing ulcers. Cortés was informed, and he experienced some panic. He wrote to his cousin:

> With your letter of October 1532 you sent me a letter from [the tutor] Diego Pérez de Vargas and an account of don Martín's illness, and you said that you would go to see him and would write me the truth of the matter and in the packet that those letters arrived in, others came from Seville dated the following January, but in those three months there was nothing more from you. Telling me about the illness you could well believe would give me pain, and perhaps you didn't want to write me about it. Indeed I tell you that I don't love him any less than the other one whom god has given me with the Marquesa, and thus I always want to know about him.[12]

Then, in typical style, the father expressed some rage that the child had obviously been misdiagnosed: no child of his could suffer from so inelegant a disease as scrofula. "I think that it is the greatest falsehood in the world." Surely it was something else. Probably the boy would have remained healthy if he had just been taken to the countryside, Cortés insisted. He would send another five hundred pesos to the Count of Miranda, who had promised to look out for the boy. "Write to me bluntly about his health, for having sent me the account I mentioned, you haven't [since] alleviated my anxiety, nor have I received any other letter from the count or Diego Pérez or anyone I have written to."

Martín lived. In the future, he was often unwell, but he mastered his ailments and remained determined—perhaps all the more determined—to be a courageous knight. In the spring of 1539, when he was seventeen years old, the beautiful and well-loved Queen Isabel died in childbirth. The seventy sons of noblemen who had served her as pages officially became members of the household of the twelve-year-old heir apparent, Prince Philip. First, however, they carried the queen's coffin from Toledo to the royal tombs at Granada, where Isabella and Ferdinand rested. It took them fifteen days to make their way through the stark, dry lands of Andalusia.[13] Soon after, Martín received the news that his father was returning to Spain. And with him were coming his younger half brothers, Luis and the new Martín. He was not, it seemed, alone in this world after all.

Cortés was returning to Spain not only because he wanted to deposit his boys in the mother country to receive their education, but also because he was finding himself unable to defend his extensive holdings in Mexico against a relatively hostile colonial administration. He and the viceroy don Antonio de Mendoza had little sympathy with each other; each felt the other to be something of a usurper. "It may be said that it is more difficult to defend my wealth from the officials than it was to win it from the infidels," Cortés complained to the king. He was now in his fifties, though, and had learned some humility. He reminded himself brusquely of his former sins: "I give thanks to God for everything; he is being repaid in this way for the many offenses I have given him."[14]

What Malintzin's son thought of the adolescent Luis we will never know, but he seems to have found a place in his heart for the eight-year-old brother who shared his name. Both little brothers joined Martín in Prince Philip's service, and he became their liaison to their new social world. Soon, in 1541, Hernando Cortés and his children joined Charles V on an expedition against the North African city of Algiers. Ferdinand and Isabella had defeated the last Muslim state in Spain years before, in 1492, but Christian Spaniards continued to distrust the Muslims who now lived to the south, across the Strait of Gibraltar in Africa. This was, after all, the era of the Ottoman ruler, Suleiman the Magnificent, whose territory reached from the border of Austria around the Mediterranean all the way to what is now Morocco. In 1535, to make a point, Charles had attacked the city of Tunis and had managed to win and hold it. He failed miserably in the case of Algiers. A terrible storm destroyed his fleet before it could land, and the emperor was forced to order a withdrawal. Many ships sank; the Cortés brothers and their father were fortunate to make it back to Spain alive.[15]

It was not long, however, before Malintzin's son experienced genuine warfare. He was nineteen now, and no longer a page in the prince's service, but a knight. Throughout the 1540s and 1550s, he fought to defend the interests of Charles V. He traveled as a soldier throughout Europe, to places that today are marked as parts of France, Germany, and Italy, and was wounded several times. He entered into an informal relationship with a woman whose name has not come down to us and had a child by her. The boy was called Hernando Cortés, after his grandfather, but the name usually was spelled in the more modern style, as "Fernando."[16]

Meanwhile, the original Hernando Cortés had stayed on in Spain for another six years. He was treated with respect, but Emperor Charles, in those periods when he was in the country, paid no attention to him. For Cortés's problems were by now simply his own; they were no longer synonymous with those of New Spain, as they had been in the chaotic 1520s. And Charles had weighty matters pressing at him from all sides. At last Cortés decided to return to Mexico. He was ill and apparently wanted to die in the New World. But before he could sail from Seville, in December of 1547, he breathed his last.

His last will and testament should put an end to any lingering belief that there had been a great love between him and doña Marina. It was Leonor, the mother of his oldest child, the daughter called Catalina, who was still particularly dear to him. Leonor was probably Cortés's first love; certainly he had been with her during the years in Cuba. After the conquest she had come to Mexico and, like Malintzin, married one of Cortés's friends. Whether she was indigenous or a Spanish commoner is impossible to say. In any case, she was mentioned in various capacities in his will, and her daughter, Catalina, was left with a sizeable estate. Cortés made no mention of Malintzin or of any of the other mothers of his various illegitimate children.

The legitimate Martín received almost everything, of course, though he was charged with the responsibility of caring for his other siblings out of the proceeds of the estate. His full-blood legitimate sisters were to receive substantial dowries, and his illegitimate half sisters minor ones. (Cortés took care to name the amounts, not leaving matters of that sort to his son's discretion.) Don Martín, Malintzin's son, and don Luis, the son of a Spanish gentlewoman, were each to receive one thousand ducats annually. It was a generous amount, but it rendered them dependent on their little brother. To drive the point home, Cortés spoke to the two older sons very explicitly in his will about their duty to the family: "I command the said don Martín and don Luis my sons to serve, respect and obey the said successor of my estate in all things licit and honest that he asks them to do, as the principal stock and head [of the lineage] from which they proceed. For no reason may they disobey or fail to respect him; they are to support and serve him in all that is not against the [law of] God or against the Holy Catholic Faith or against the King." If they failed to obey him, Martín the successor was directed to cut them off. The day before he died,

Cortés himself suddenly added a codicil disinheriting don Luis, probably because he was insisting on marrying a woman who was the niece of an old enemy. He said nothing further about the presumably more obedient don Martín.[17]

Cortés's tone indicates that he was well aware that he was leaving the estate in the hands of a potentially problematic personality. Martín the heir, now to be called the marqués, was only fifteen when his father died. Immediately upon his eighteenth birthday, his mother found it necessary to sue him because she realized that only a reiterated legal agreement would induce him to remember to take care of her and to do what his father had asked him to do on behalf of his sisters. Her relatives and lawyers in Spain met with Martín and he signed a document promising to give his mother an allowance, to maintain her brother (who was a Dominican friar in Mexico), and to pay his sisters' dowries. Unfortunately, that document did not save his mother from having to sue him again later when it came time for the girls to marry, as the young marqués always seemed to have spent more than he had available to him.[18]

López de Gómara, the chaplain who had been in Cortés's service, had in the meantime finished a biography of the illustrious conquistador that the legitimate Martín had commissioned after his father's death. Naturally, the book was dedicated to the son and heir. Someone had apparently induced the author to include a little homily addressed to the dedicatee:

> Your inheritance obligates you to emulate the deeds of your father, Hernán Cortés, and to spend well what he left you. It is no less praiseworthy or virtuous, or perhaps laborious, to retain one's wealth than to increase it. Thus one's honor is sustained; and it was to conserve and perpetuate honor that entails were invented, for it is certain that estates diminish with many divisions thereof, and that with their diminution nobility and glory are lessened and even brought to an end.

In the spirit of aggrandizing the lineage, the book mentioned the older don Martín only once, calling him, "a son whom [Cortés] had by an Indian woman," even though the story of the famous doña Marina had been included earlier. The book appeared in 1552; perhaps the older Martín did not mind when, in 1553, the office of the Crown had it banned—probably because it made too much of the accomplishments of a single hero and too little of the work of thousands that had gone into the making of the empire, thus implicitly belittling the role of the nation and the monarch.

In 1554 Prince Philip traveled to England, along with four thousand troops and nearly all his courtiers—including the new Marqués del Valle and, very probably, don Martín. Charles V saw an opportunity for a fruitful alliance with that country and had arranged that his son should wed Queen Mary, the daughter of Henry VIII. Her mother had been Catherine of Aragon, Ferdinand and Isabella's younger daughter, who had been displaced by Anne Boleyn as Henry broke away from the pope and the Roman Catholic Church and formed the Anglican Church, which was to be answerable only to him. Mary had suffered years of being considered a bastard before finally being restored to the line of succession not long before her father's death. Now that she was queen, she wanted to reimpose Catholicism on her country, for she earnestly believed it was the one true faith; it had sustained her in her darkest period. There had been Protestant rebellions almost immediately upon her succession, and Mary had responded with vicious punishments. Her charismatic younger sister, Princess Elizabeth, Anne Boleyn's daughter, was naturally a focal point for the discontented and therefore stood in grave danger of her life. She languished in the Tower, and many believed it would not be long before enough evidence of treason was found to execute her, for torture made men talk.

Philip arrived with his enormous entourage to impress the English people with the power and grandeur of their new ally—and to fight them, if need be. He was well aware that the best thing he could do, however, was to make friends and not enemies. To the joy of his father, the usually rather obstreperous Philip surprised everyone by behaving with extraordinary courtesy and gentility. He apparently even convinced Mary to release the red-haired and witty Elizabeth, who resembled her father and was beloved by the people. No one could then have foreseen that when Philip and Elizabeth were both old, he would send the Spanish Armada against her and live to regret it. That was decades in the future. In the meantime, he did his best to accomplish the task he had been sent to pursue.[19]

The royal court was to be publicly entertained. In December, for example, the visiting Spaniards held a great tournament in the fields near Westminster, and Philip himself participated, along with several of his courtiers, including the Marqués del Valle. The prizes were to be given out by Queen Mary herself. The marqués did not compete in an actual contest of the pike or sword but, rather, entered the competition for the "best appointed armor and apparel." He must have prided himself on his good looks and state-of-the-art weaponry, for according to the rules of the game, he was to enter the arena as gallantly fitted out as possible, but without wearing any gold or silver, real or counterfeit, not even embroidered into his tunic. He came in third. A higher-born Spanish knight received the jeweled brooch from the hand of the queen.[20]

The next few years were a heady time for Philip and his entourage. In 1556 the ailing Charles abdicated in favor of his son. In 1557 the French, threatened by the new political alignment that came with Philip's English marriage and then his accession, attacked his territory at several points. Philip summoned troops from all his various realms and, together, they attained a resounding victory at St. Quentin in France, one that ensured that the French would leave them in peace for years to come. Malintzin's son, don Martín, was proud to say he had been there, when Spain's dominance in Europe was established—at least for the time being. The following year, Charles died, and Philip was recognized everywhere.

In the midst of these stirring events, don Martín experienced some strong emotion in his private life as well. Don Luis de Quesada came from Mexico, bringing news of Martín's little sister, María, the only other child his mother had ever had. Perhaps feeling less alone in the world with this old connection rekindled, don Martín for the first time allowed himself to express his frustration regarding the spoiled marqués. He was, he admitted, growing disgusted with his dependence on his arrogant younger brother. Now that he had an ally in Mexico, he made his move. In 1557, while in Spain for a few months, he initiated a lawsuit against his brother the marqués, saying that he no longer wanted to be in personal communication with him and asking that he be given ownership outright of some mines that his father had transferred to his three sons before he died, in an arrangement quite distinct from that of the will. In exchange for this he would gladly give up his right to the thousand ducats annually—which he rarely received in any case. He gave don Luis power of attorney to act for him in Mexico City.[21]

All three of the Cortés brothers seem to have quarreled passionately at this juncture. Luis sued both his older brothers regarding the property in

Mexico and then turned around and pestered King Philip—who was, after all, their old playmate—to intervene. In May of 1558, Philip responded by ordering an investigation, and in 1561 he stipulated a compromise between the three brothers that favored the marqués, commanding that Luis accept it and cease to place "petitions or demands." He signed the document as he always did, "I, the King."[22]

Something brought the two Martíns together again in this period. Perhaps they were shamed by the king's having become involved in their private quarrels, or perhaps they experienced a genuine rapprochement. The marqués was approaching his thirtieth birthday and may have begun to behave with more sensitivity. And there were other potentially catalyzing events—the two brothers' marriages and the birth of their first legitimate children, whom they would have seen on a daily basis, rather than only occasionally, as in the case of any previous children, born out of wedlock. The marqués married doña Ana Ramírez de Arellano, a cousin on his mother's side, and she bore a son almost immediately, named Fernando Cortés, like don Martín's illegitimate son. Don Martín married doña Bernardina de Porras. She was the daughter of a man who did not have the right to style himself a "don," but he was probably well-to-do, as his wife was a "doña." Bernardina was from Logroño, far to the north, not a place don Martín had many reasons to visit—except that, as one historian has pointed out, it was directly on the path to the shrine at Santiago de Compostela, to which all initiates of the Order of Santiago made a pilgrimage at least once in their lives. Bernardina soon gave birth to a daughter named Ana, and Martín's older illegitimate son, Fernando, came to live with them, in an arrangement that was quite typical in Spain.[23]

In 1562 the three Cortés brothers decided to travel together to Mexico, bearing with them the remains of their father, who had asked to be buried there. The wife of the marqués traveled with them, though she left her young son and heir in Spain for safekeeping; she bore another son en route. Doña Bernardina, on the other hand, was to come later with the children when don Martín sent for her. It was a fortunate decision, for the crossing was a terrible one. The ship was virtually wrecked and barely managed to limp into port at Campeche, on the Yucatan Peninsula. From there the brothers made their way to Mexico City, the home they had not seen since they were six and eight. The marqués was welcomed on a grand scale.

He quickly wore out his welcome, however. Within months he was taking sides in local arguments with deep roots and in less than a year was writing opinionated letters to Philip about how to handle the affairs of the colony. He and his companions frequently participated in drunken carousing, and he sowed dissension when he had a rather public affair with doña Marina Vázquez de Coronado, the daughter of the man who had led the conquest of New Mexico, and the wife of one of his own good friends. The name was too much for people: they began to circulate lampoons and riddles. "A good man won this land by Marina, as I am a witness, and now the one I speak of will lose it by another woman of the same name." The marqués's brothers lived in his household and were financially dependent on him. Don Luis was closely associated with the marqués in all his activities. Don Martín, however, was known for being withdrawn and silent.[24]

Martín had been reunited with his sister, María, but the meeting was not entirely joyous. The tiny girl he remembered was gone, and in her place was not a young and vibrant woman, but an aging lady, weakened, apparently, by the many pregnancies that had come to nothing. She died within months of Martín's arrival in Mexico City. Alone now—his sister dead, his wife and children still in Spain, and his brother the marqués behaving as badly as ever—don Martín considered returning to Europe. It would mean going back to the military life, however, and he was in his forties now. He eventually grew ill and began to go to confession frequently, thinking that he might be near death.[25]

Don Martín had instructed his wife to come to him, but the preparations for her departure were complicated. She was living in her hometown of Logroño, and there were many there who wanted her to use her connections to make it possible for them to travel to New Spain. It was apparently useful to be married to an old playmate of the king's: Philip issued orders that don Martín's wife be allowed to travel not only with the two children, but also with six dependents, more than were strictly necessary, or even at all usual for someone of her station. Doña Bernardina eventually brought three young men and three young women. The girls were not from particularly good families—one was the daughter of a barber, and another used her mother's last name. But they had every chance of increasing their status in Mexico, where Spanish wives were much in demand. It was not until the summer of 1565 that doña Bernardina had completed all her preparations and was able to cross the ocean to New Spain.[26]

She arrived to find that the political situation in Mexico City had grown extremely tense. For some time, discontent had been growing among the encomenderos. More than twenty years before, in 1542, Charles V had promulgated the New Laws of the Indies, with the twin intentions of protecting the Indians and limiting the power of the conquistadors' families. He forbade indigenous slavery, for example, and announced that encomienda rights would not be indefinitely hereditary. The colonists' wrath was such that the viceroy had wisely refrained from implementing the new legal strictures, and over time the laws had been modified to better fit reality. The issue had hardly gone away, however: the indigenous population was dwindling as disease cut down young and old, while the Spanish population was rapidly rising. And King Philip was as determined as his father to prevent the families of the lucky first arrivals from becoming a distant class of all-powerful lords. Thus recent legal decisions had left encomienda-holding families angry. Rights to Indian labor would apparently not be extended beyond the current holders. It was not yet certain if this policy would really be rigidly upheld or only applied if a man died without direct biological heirs or committed some delinquency. In either case, the encomenderos were on edge.

The most belligerent of the conquistadors' agitated sons looked to the Marqués del Valle to lead them in their political battle, ignoring the fact that his own holdings had been awarded to his father's family in perpetuity and that he had grown up with Philip as a personal friend. Then in 1564, the viceroy don Luis de Velasco, doña Beatriz's brother-in-law, died suddenly, probably of a heart attack. His younger brother, don Francisco, led the funeral procession in his honor. The Audiencia was left to govern in the viceroy's stead until a replacement arrived from Spain. In the confusion—one might almost say power vacuum—the marqués seemed to enjoy the heady feeling that the angry political talk gave him, and to some extent he encouraged the ringleaders in their posturing. At one point he asked his older brother, don Martín, if he thought the rebellious comments had gone a bit far, and Malintzin's diplomatic son suggested that the marqués had better begin to say he was sure that Philip would address their grievances soon. One evening the marqués became convinced that one of the many enemies he had made in other contexts was going to bring men to attack him in exchange for some of the political comments that he had allowed to pass; he asked his brother to stay with him in his apartments that night for protection.[27]

In July of 1566, in the midst of some celebrations in honor of the twins just born to the marqués's wife, Malintzin's son was suddenly arrested by order of the royal officials of the Audiencia. Later that day, he learned that the marqués himself as well as their brother, don Luis, had also been taken into custody. There had purportedly been a plot afoot on the part of the city's young gentlemen to take over the Audiencia chambers by force, publicly renounce allegiance to the king and his representatives, and set the marqués up to rule in Mexico. Naturally, the Audiencia members assumed that all three of Cortés's sons were implicated. Over the ensuing weeks, they were each interrogated. Don Martín was closely questioned about his own and his younger brother's activities. He said he had known about the angry talk but did not believe it amounted to anything more than the swaggering of boys, and as a loyal servant of the Crown, he thought it best to ignore such nonsense. When don Martín demanded that he be accused of something specific, or else released, he was accused of having known about the conspiracy for many months and having done nothing.

Within weeks, Gil González and Alonso de Avila, two brothers, were executed as the central figures of the conspiracy. They insisted that all their talk had meant nothing, but whether that was true or not, it was too late now to make such pleas. The young men seemed stunned when it became clear that they really were to die, that their rank and privilege could afford them no help in this situation.

In the wake of the executions of the Avila brothers, the authorities turned to questioning the marqués and his brothers again. The Audiencia judges equivocated in the case of the two Martíns, but they condemned Luis to die. He had earned as much enmity as the marqués with his arrogant and wild behavior, but he did not have his brother's wealth and influence back in Spain to shield him now. Then suddenly there came a reprieve.

A new viceroy, don Gastón de Peralta, the Marqués de Falces, had finally arrived, and he decreed that all executions should halt until he had thoroughly familiarized himself with all that had occurred. Peralta met with the informers and accusers and concluded that they and the members of the Audiencia had exaggerated the situation. He sent the Marqués del Valle home to Spain so that Philip himself could be his judge, and he sent don Luis with him, commuting his death sentence to ten years in the galleys. There was the possibility that Philip would waive even that for his old childhood companion. Don Martín's case was to be investigated further; eventually he was released to house arrest. The viceroy undoubtedly hoped that in his case, the whole matter would soon be forgotten.[28]

That was not to be. Don Martín's wife had to stand by as he was arrested again on November 15, 1567. The original informers had begun to fear for their futures and even their lives after the new viceroy concluded they were troublemakers, and the Audiencia judges for their part resented the viceroy's interference in their affairs. So they caused the word to be spread in Spain that the Marqués de Falces was covering up a serious plot for his own reasons. In 1567 a rebellion against royal authority really did occur in Cuzco, Peru. Philip thus had reason to be suspicious of events in Mexico and sent a tribunal of two special prosecutors to investigate the viceroy himself as well as the purported conspiracy. They were Alonso Muñoz and Luis Carillo.

The newly arrived pair's first act was to arrest one of the original accusers, a nephew of doña Beatriz, who had retracted the year before under the influence of the calm and reasonable viceroy. They tortured him, demanding to know which of his stories was true. Eventually he gave them what they wanted: he declared that he had been speaking the truth in his original accusations, not in his retraction. He gave them many names, including that of Malintzin's son, don Martín Cortés, knight of the Order of Santiago.

The tribunal immediately announced that don Martín would be tortured. He was to receive "the rigorous torment of water and rope." For over a month his lawyer tried to stave off the inevitable by making various requests and legal motions. Several supporters testified that torture might kill don Martín, among them his dead sister's stepfather—don Francisco de Velasco. Eventually, however, the attorney was unable to delay matters any further. On January 7, 1568, guards came to don Martín's cell and announced that the day had come. According to law, he was required to speak aloud, saying that he had heard the pronouncement and accepted it. Late that night, don Martín was escorted to the basement of the royal government's chambers and shown the rack. He was asked to reveal the names of other conspirators. Judges all over Europe had found that merely showing an accused man the rack generally had a desirable effect. Don Martín simply said that he had already spoken the truth and had no more to say.[29]

The guards removed the prisoner's clothing and tied his naked body to the two ends of the rack. They turned the levers, stretching him beyond endurance, and dislocated the bones of his arms and legs. The judges, who were present during the procedure, again asked don Martín for the names of other conspirators. The scribe there in the room reported that he said he had already spoken the truth and had no more to say. The guards turned the ropes of the rack again, with the same results.

Now by order of the judges, the guards lowered don Martín's head below his body, held his nose, inserted a horn down his throat, and poured water in slowly, in order to produce a drowning sensation that went on, and on, and on. Then they questioned him again. They had to wait before he could speak. Still he had nothing more to say. Two more times they poured the water. Each time, he said he had told the truth and had nothing more to add.

Don Martín probably knew that the first man this pair had arrested had been all but dead by the time his aunt, doña Beatriz, María's stepmother, had been able to use her influence as a former viceroy's sister-in-law and secure his release.[30] But there was no one to secure don Martín's release. These two would stop at nothing; they might well kill him in their fervor. He probably also knew that all the others who had been tortured in this whole affair had talked, every one of them. If they had nothing to say, they still talked. It was the nature of torture; it made people say anything, anything they thought the all-powerful men in the cell might possibly want to hear.

The guards poured the water down his throat a fourth time. And now don Martín faced his crisis, the battle with his own soul. He could talk. He could.

But he was not just another spoiled son of a conquistador. He was the son of Hernando Cortés, conqueror of Mexico, and of doña Marina, a prisoner of two peoples who had survived her whole life with her dignity intact. He had reason to be proud of who he was.

His mettle had already been tested. He had known violence, had fought on medieval Europe's battlefields, felt the wounds inflicted by steel, had helped to gather prisoners and see the piles of rotting dead bodies buried.

And he had always been alone. As Malintzin's son, he had always been an outsider, even before his younger brother was born. He had never expected the world to be kind to him. He was not stunned when humanity turned its face away and he was left in darkness.

If any had ever looked past him, belittled him, made him feel insignificant, they would learn now who he was. Honor came to a man by birth, but it also came from courage. His honor was all he had left at this moment, and he would keep it, in the eyes of all. All of New Spain was watching him, don Martín Cortés, the son of Hernando Cortés and doña Marina.

He whispered, "I have told the truth, and in the holy name of god who suffered for me I will say nothing more from this moment until I die."

Despite himself, he did speak after that, after the fifth pouring—but it was only to say he did not know anything else. And the sixth time, he found the strength to say again that he had told the truth and had nothing more to add. The judges gave the signal to stop.

It was three o'clock in the morning when they ceased. Daylight came, and soon the whole city knew what had happened. Word spread quickly whenever armed pikemen stood guard at the royal offices to prevent people from coming near while another *caballero* was tortured. People spoke in hushed tones of the son of Cortés. To some, he was undoubtedly the image of the silent, stoic Indian, who suffered now at the hands of others just as Cuauhtemoc had once suffered at the hands of Cortés. To others, he was simply a brave man, a man of honor. Nor were the Spanish the only ones who spoke of what had happened. In whispered Nahuatl, Indians told each other that the *tecpan*, the "royal office," had been closed down again by armed men, and they knew why it was so.[31]

That morning, January 8, two more aristocratic brothers were executed. These two confessed to having in truth planned a rebellion, though they never gathered enough support to carry it out. But on the gallows, before hundreds of observers, with the fates of their everlasting souls at stake, they said that the others currently imprisoned were innocent. Within a few days, don Martín's lawyer brought this event to the attention of the judges. The prisoner was suddenly sentenced to perpetual exile from the colonies and to paying one thousand ducats and half the cost of his confinement. He appealed. His lawyer and friends pled on his behalf, and for the first time in this affair, they mentioned his mother, asking for mercy for her sake. Someone brought in two old men who had fought with Cortés, now in their seventies, to speak for him. He was released to house arrest in order to recuperate and prepare for his voyage, and the fine was reduced to five hundred ducats in total.

In the meantime, King Philip had received word that Mexico City had become the scene of a bloodbath. He sent two more special judges to New Spain with all possible haste and secrecy and had them arrest the two-member tribunal. One of them, the licenciado Vasco de Puga, later gave his daughter his blessing when she married don Martín's nephew, don Pedro de Quesada, who had arrived from Spain in the midst of this disaster.

Don Martín and his family probably reached Spain just about the time that Vasco de Puga and his daughter arrived in Mexico. Martín rejoined the military and, early in 1569, rode across Andalusia toward Granada. The Muslims remaining there, long discontented, had recently been told that they must cease to speak or write Arabic and that the women no longer had the right to veil their faces from men's gazes. In response they had risen in rebellion on Christmas of 1568. The battles in that war were horrendous, both sides cruel in the extreme. When it was over, thousands of Muslim survivors were put to the sword, and at least fifty thousand others were expelled from the region and forcibly transferred to parts of Castile where they would form small minorities. In the violent uprooting, more than one-fourth of them would end up dying of hunger, disease, and exposure. Don Juan of Austria, under whose immediate command don Martín fought, long remembered his last sight of the people he banished: "At the time they set out there was so much rain, wind and snow that mothers were forced to abandon [some of] their children by the wayside. . . . It cannot be denied that the saddest sight one can imagine is the depopulation of a kingdom." But Malintzin's son was not there that day to see it and be haunted by its memory: he had been killed in the fighting not long before.[32]

There is no simple moral to this tale. Real lives always encompass more than one truth. "The truth" about Malintzin and her two children is as multifaceted as the truth about all the other people with indigenous blood who, without ever having asked for it or wanted it, were born into the age of conquest. Did Malintzin, doña María, and don Martín attempt to protect themselves by entering the Spanish world and lose as a result of their choices, becoming victims of Old World disease and of the personal and political machinations of Europeans who did not value them as they deserved to be valued? Perhaps.

But other arguments can be made equally well, perhaps better. Malintzin came from a long line of survivors, people who wrested their lives from the land in good years and bad, and who did not show their feelings when taken prisoner in the perennial wars over resources among indigenous states. In the most difficult of circumstances Malintzin herself showed the same spirit of life over death, the same kind of pride, and she succeeded in placing her children and her children's children in stronger positions than they seemed to have been fated.

María's son, Pedro, was not Malintzin's only surviving grandchild, nor was he the only one who grew to love the light of Mexican days. For Martín's son, Fernando, after years of military service under his father's commander, don Juan of Austria, chose to return to the New World. He went first to the kingdom of Quito and married a woman from there. In 1588, when Philip was sending his armada against Queen Elizabeth's people, the English gave the Spanish colonists a reason to remember why their king risked so much in attempting to reduce the Anglos to submission: English privateers attacked the port city of Guayaquil, terrorizing the populace just as they had done in so many places in the Caribbean. Fernando Cortés took a prominent role in the city's defense and was thanked by the viceroy in Lima. His confidence in his welcome thus restored, he traveled to Mexico with his family and received a government position in Veracruz, another city subject to the depredations of the English. His father had told him about his grandmother, and he wrote of her proudly. Indeed, he demanded special favors based on his descent from her—and got them, too. In his narrative about doña Marina's life, the expedition to Honduras loomed larger than it probably deserved to, but then, we must remember that Fernando got his information from his father, Martín, and it was that trip that had taken Martín's mother away from him for over a year and a half when he was a little boy. Fernando succinctly explained why his grandmother had had to go: "It is well known that without her no such expedition would have been successful."[33]

Today, one family's oral tradition has it that Fernando's son went on to become an official in Coyoacan, founding a lineage there that survives to the present. Thus they proudly claim descent from Malintzin.[34] Fernando Cortés certainly did have children, as did María's son, Pedro. Whether in Coyoacan or elsewhere, it seems certain that Malintzin's indomitable blood has not died out in Mexico.

Legend has it that la Llorona, the Wailing Woman, whose cries are sometimes heard in the wind, is actually doña Marina weeping for her lost children. But doña Marina did not lose her children: thanks largely to her efforts, they survived their youth, won places for themselves in the world of the conquerors, and lived to have children of their own. Those children honored their grandmother and taught their children to do the same. If the shade of Malintzin still walks on earth and weeps, perhaps it is because posterity has begrudged a captive Indian woman who survived her days as best she could even that small consolation.

Appendix

Chalcacihuacuicatl: "Chalca Woman's Song"

There seems to have existed in the Nahua world a subgenre of song that centered on the persona of the concubine. There is evidence that this version of such a song—or a version close to it—was used as a political protest by the Chalca people after they had been conquered by the Mexica and wanted their chiefly lines to be reinstated. The life of the concubine taken in war is likened to the life of a conquered altepetl. The sexual imagery and the evocation of the women's sphere through references to spinning, weaving, and marriage are typical enough in the Nahua world for us to assume that such metaphors appeared in other common versions of concubine songs as well. I believe it is safe to assume that Malintzin would have been familiar with this kind of imagery, though almost certainly not with this exact iteration of the song.

Here, the character who sings veers between trying to make the best of her life with her new lord and expressing agonizing pain and regret. In the end, she is an old woman, lamenting her life, yet asking for peace. Such mixed reactions were undoubtedly typical of women in her situation.

Readers should remember that in Nahuatl, the words are very beautiful. Because translation of Nahuatl songs is very difficult (as each stanza can be interpreted on several levels, and as many of the phrases and metaphors are unfamiliar even to the most advanced scholars), I have only felt safe in rendering the English quite literally. Normally, a good translator takes care to adjust the phrasing so that readers can catch a glimpse of the humor or beauty or elegance of a text. It should not be assumed that the Nahuatl language is in any way primitive simply because I do not make such alterations in the English in this case.

For a full discussion of all these issues and others, please see my article from 2006 in *The Americas* 62, no. 3 (January): 349–89.[1]

Intlatlalil chalca ic quimopapaquiltilico in tlatohuani in Axayacatzin ca noço yehuatzin oquimmopehuili in ma çan cihuatzitzintin. (This is a composition of the Chalca, with which they came to entertain King Axayacatl because he had conquered them as if they were just women.)[2]

[A] [Drumbeat] Toco tico tocoti, toco tico tocoti, toco tico tocoti

X[an]moquetzacan [oo] annicutzitzinhuan [aye] tonhuian tonhuian tixochitemozque [he] tonhuian tonhuian tixochitehtequizque nican mania nican mania tlachinolxochitly [oo] chimalli xochitly teihicolti huel tetlamachti yaoxochitla [oohuiya]	Stand up [or, Stop!], you who are my little sisters! Let's go, let's go, we will look for flowers. Let's go, let's go, we will pick some flowers. They were here, they were here, scorched flowers, shield-flowers.[3] It is enticing, it is enjoyable, in the flower garden of war.
Yectli [aya] [i]n xochitly [yehuaya] ma nocpacxochiuh ma ic ninapana nepapan i(n) noxochiuh [aya] nichalcatl nicihuatl [ahuayao ohuaya]	Good are the flowers. Let them be my wreath. In these my various flowers let me wrap myself. I am a Chalca woman.
Nicnehnequi xochitl nicnehneco [i]n cuicatl [aytzin] in totzahuayan in toyeyeyan [o ohuaye] noconeheuhtica ycuic in tlatohuani Axayacaton nicxochimalina nicxochilacatzohua [o oahuayao ohuiya]	I long for the flowers, I long for the songs. In our spinning place, our customary place [our womanly sphere], I am intoning the songs of the king, little Axayacatl. I twirl them together [into a strand] like flowers; I twist them forth as a flower.

[A(y)] iuhquin tlacuilolli yectli [ya(y)] incuic iuquin huelic xochitl ahuiaca noyol quimati in tlpc [ahuayyao ohuiya]	Their songs are like paintings, they are good, like fragrant [pleasant] flowers. My heart imbibes the sweet smell of the earth.
Tle(n)mach ypan nicmati motlatoltzin noyecoltzin taxayacaton tla noconahuilti [aylili aylililili hii olotzin ololo oyyaye ayyo Et^a]	What in the world am I to think of what you say, my lover [sexual partner],[4] you, little Axayacatl? What if I were to pleasure him . . . [5]
Çan nictocuilehuilia çan niquiquixhuia [hooo yeee] tla noconahuilti Et^a	I just sing Tocuilan style, I whistle to him.[6] What if I were to pleasure him . . .

Xolo xolotzin titlahtohuani taxayacaton [ohuiya] nel toquichtli iz maçonel titlayhtolli; cuix nel ahoc tiquahquahuitiuh [ayye] xoconquetzan nonexcon cenca niman xocontoquio	Boy, little servant boy, you who are king, little Axayacatl, are you truly a man? Though it may be you are someone spoken of [well known, chosen], is it true you no longer go to cut firewood?[7] Ay, go stoke the pot and light a big fire![8]
Xiqualcui o xiqualcui yn ompa ca o xinechualmaca o in conetzintli te' xontlatehteca tihuan tonhuehuetztozque [tzono] tompaquiz tompaquiz paquiz [tzono] nictlatlamachihuaz [oo]	Come and bring it, come bring what is there! Come give it to me! O child! You! Lay out the things [the mats]. You and I will lie together.[9] You will be happy, you will be happy, will be happy.[10] And I will do it peacefully, gently.
Macamo maca o macamo tla ximayahui xolotzin titlatohuani axayacaton [yya] aço ninicuilo y(n) cuecuetzoca ye nomaton [o ayee] ye nocuel ye nocuel tictzitzquiznequi in nochichihualtzin ach in noyollotzin [huiya]	Let it not be, please don't stick your hand in my skirts,[11] little boy, you who are king, little Axayacatl. Maybe I am painted, my little hand is itching. Again and again you want to seize my breast, even[12] my heart.
In ye ahcaço monehuian ticmitlacalhuiz[13] nonehcuilol [huiya tzono] tiquitztoz xiuhquecholxochitico [ohuaye] nihtic nimitzonaquiz onca motenchalohtzin nimitzmacochihuiz	Now perhaps you yourself will ruin my body-painting.[14] You will lie watching what comes to be a green quechol bird flower. I will put you inside me. Your *tenchalohtli* lies there.[15] I will rock you in my arms.[16]

In quetzalizquixochitl in ye tlauhquecholcacaloxochitl in çan moxochitquachpetlapan ti[ya] onoc ye oncan ytic [y yyoyyo] aocmo [huiyao aylili]	It is a quetzal popcorn flower, a flamingo raven flower.[17] You lie on your flower-mantled mat. It lies there inside . . . No longer.
Teocuitlapetlatl ipan ti[ya] onoc quetzaloztocalco tlacuilocalitic [yyoyyo] aocmo [huiyao aylili]	You lie on your golden reed mat. It lies in the [precious] feathered cavern house, inside the painted house . . . No longer.
Anquiço ye ichan ye nontlayocoya tinonantzin ahço huel nitzahua ahço huel nihquitia ça nenca niconetl [tzo] nicihuapilli ynic nihtolo yn noquichhuacan [yao]	. . . this is his home.[18] I am distraught. O mother, maybe I can spin. Maybe I even used to be able to weave[19]—but it was all for naught. As a noble girl-child, I was spoken of in connection with my [future] marriage.[20]
Tetlatlahuelcauh teyollocococan in tlpc in quenmanon nontlahtlayocoya ninotlahuelnequi onnexiuhtlatilco nichualihtoa cue conetl manoce nimiqui [yiao]	It is infuriating. It is heartrending, here on earth. Sometimes I worry and fret. I consume myself in rage. In my desperation, I suddenly say, hey, child, I would as soon die.

Ya cue nonantzin nontlaocolmiqui o ye nican ye noquichuacan ahuel niquitotia in malacatl ahuel nocontlaça in notzotzopaz noca timoqueloa noconetzin [yao ohuiya]	Hey mother, I am dying of sadness here in my life with a man. I can't make the spindle dance. I can't throw my weaver's stick. You cheat me, my child.
Auh quen nel noconchihuaz cuix yhui chimalli yca nemanalo ixtlahuatl itic ninoma'mantaz [a ayia ooo] noca timoqueloa noconetzin [ohuiya]	What in the world can I do? Am I to go along sacrificing myself, just as people are offered on their shields in the fields [of war]?[21] You cheat me, my child.
Xolotzin noconetzin titlahtohuani Taxayacaton çan timonencahua nohuic timomahmanaya tonmoquichyttohua [o ohuaye] cuix nonmati yaopan niquimiximati ye moyaohuan noconetzin çan timonencahua nohuic [ohuiya]	Little boy, my child, you who are king, little Axayacatl, you just ignore me [are negligent toward me]. You used to sacrifice yourself. You say you are manly [you consider yourself a man]. Do I [a woman] know my way in war? I know your enemies, my child. And you just ignore me.
Ma teh ticihuatini ahço nel ahticyecoz in iuhqui chahuayotl yn ixochitzin yn icuicatzin noconetzin [yiao]	I wish you yourself had been a woman. Perhaps then you would not sample [use sexually] she who is like the blossom and song of concubinage, my child.
A oquichpilli, not° titla'tohuani Taxayacaton onoço tonpeuh ye no tiqualani xolotzin ye no niauh in nochan noconetzin	Ah manly nobleman, my lord, you who are king, little Axayacatl. Instead you've taken off. You're angry, little boy. My child, I'm about to go home, too.

[C] *(continued)*

Anca ço ca nican tinechnahualan yectli ticchiuh ye motlatoltzin iz in axcan tlahuanquetl, maço teh titlahuanquetl ahço no netlacamachon tochan [yyao ohuiya]	Perhaps thus you took me with sorcery. You spoke the right words. Behold now the drunkard, maybe you yourself are drunk. Are there social rules in our home?[22]
Cuix noço tinechcouh tinechmocohui noconetzin cuix tlapa'patlaco nahuihuan ye notlahua(n) çaço tictlacanequi ye no tiqualani xolotzin ye noniauh in nochan noconetzin [yao ohuiya]	Did you buy me anywhere? Did you buy me for yourself, my child? Did my aunts and uncles come to trade? Yet you do it heedlessly [impetuously, without restraint] and you get angry, little boy. I'm going home, my child.

[D] Tocotico tititi tocotico tititi tocotico tititi

Tiniuctzin ticihuatlamacazqui ma xontlachia yn omach moman cuicatl in Cohuatepec in quauh tenampan y(n) Topan moteca Panohuayan [ohuaya yiaho]	You who are my little sister, woman priest, please look! Many songs were offered in Cohuatepec, at the wooden [or eagle] circling wall, where they came down upon us at Panohuayan.
Ço nocihuayo ninaytia noyollotzin mococohua ach quen nel noconchihuaz yhuan noquichtiz o maçoc cenca ye incue ye [ye] inhuipil in toquichhuan in toyecolhuan [yyaho ohuiya]	I make [live] my womanhood. My heart suffers. I don't know what in the world I am to do. I will become a man like [together with] him— howsoever it was that the skirts and blouses of our men, our lovers, were many and full [literally "more," "plentiful"].
Xiqualquixti nonextamal in titlatohuani Axayacaton tla ce nimitzmanili neoc in noconeuh neoc noconeuh xoconahuilti xictocuilehuili [ololotzin ololo ayye ayyo]	Hand me my softened maize, you who are king, little Axayacatl. Let me just pat one [tortilla] out for you. *Neoc*,[23] my child, *neoc*, my child. Pleasure him. Sing to him Tocuilan style.
Aço tiquauhtli tocelotl in timittohua noconetzin [ohuiya] aço moyaohuan inhuic ticuecuenoti meoc in noconeuh xoconahuilti Et[a]	Do you call yourself an eagle, an ocelot, my child? Do you boast before your enemies? *Neoc*, my child. Pleasure him . . .

Ayatle nocue, ayatle nohuipil nicihuatzintli yehua ya nican quimanaco yectli ye incuic nican quimanaco chimalli xochitl quenmach tontlaca ye nichalcacihuatl nayoquan [ohuiya]	I, a woman, don't yet have a skirt, a blouse [I have not yet attained true womanhood].[24] He's the one who came here to offer their beautiful songs; he came here to offer shield-flowers [war]. What is to become of us?[25] I'm a Chalca woman and I'm Ayocuan.
Niquimelehuia nocihuapohuan in acolhuaque niquimelehuia yn nocihuapohuan tepaneca quenmach tontlaca ye nichalcacihuatl nayoquan Et[a]	I crave my fellow women, the Acolhuaque. I crave my fellow women, the Tepaneca. What is to become of us? I'm a Chalca woman and I'm Ayocuan.
Ca pinauhticate in chahuahuilo noconetzin [yhuia] cuix no iuh tinech(ch)ihuaz i(n) no iuh toconchiuh in quauhtlatohuaton maçaço yhuian [a] ximocuetomaca(n) ximomaxahuican Antlatilolca in amiyaque [ayayya] xihuallachiacan nican chalco [ahauyya ohuiya]	They are ashamed to be made concubines, my child. Are you going to do to me what you did to the poor little Cuauhtlatoa? Peacefully take off your skirts, spread your legs, you the Tlatelolca, you who stink. Come take a look here in Chalco!
Ma ninopotoni tinonantzin ma xine[ch]xahua [oo] quen nechittaz in noyecol ymixpan(in)on tonquiçatiuh ahcaço mihicoltiz ye huexotzinco xayacamachan [ohiuya]	Let me have my plumes, mother! Paint me up! What will my lover think of me? You pass before them [her lover and his men] as you leave. Won't he be greedy, rapacious in Huexotzinco, in Xayacamachan?

Quen ami in cuicatl ehualo in cuicoya o in quauhquecholli ancaço mihicoltiz ye huexotzinco xayacamahchan [ohuiya]	How is the song sung, how did people used to sing? He is an eagle *quecholli*.[26] Won't he be greedy, rapacious in Huexotzinco, in Xayacamachan?
In tetzmolocan nicihuatl ninomaoxihuia ninocxioxihuia noconcuico ye nochcue ye nochhuipil niccecentlamitaz [aytzin ay aytzin] Et[a]	In Tetzmolocan I, a woman, anoint my hands and feet with oil. I came to get my maguey skirt and blouse, and I'm going to go use them up.
Niquimelehui xaltepetlapan ye huexotzinca tzo incuetlaxtlamalin tzo incuetlaxtetecuecuex niccecentlamittaz [aytzin ay aytzin yyao] Et[a]	I desire the Xaltepetlapan Huexotzinca, their leather ropes, their leather thongs. I'm going to go use them up.

Yn quen oc çan in tlamati nechmitlania in conetl in tlatohuani in Axayacaton cue e tleon in ma ic i(n) tepal nech[ch]ahuatlalia [oohuaye] noca titlaomepiaz noconetzin a'ço iuh quinequi moyollo maçohui huian mociahuan [yyao ohuia]	He jests [or deceives, or knows] a bit more. He demands me, the child, the king, little Axayacatl. Hey! What comes of it that it seems he makes me live as a concubine in the home of [dependent upon] others? Because of me, you will have twice the kingdom [or family] to keep, my child. Maybe that's the way your heart wants it. Though it should be so . . . [27]
Cuix a'moyollocopa noconetzin in toconcalaquia in chahuayotl inic mochan [ahayayoho] ahço iuh quinequi moyollo Et[a]	Is it not wholeheartedly, my child, that you bring in concubinage, since it is your home? Maybe that's the way your heart wants it.
Quenmach in tine(ch)chiuh no yecoltzin [ayye] maca oc ic ximochichihuan huel ahtitlacatl tlein ticnenelo ye noyollotzin ticxochimalina ye motlatol [yyao ohuia]	What in the world have you done to me, my lover? Don't adorn yourself thus any longer—you are really a bad man. What have you confused [disordered]? It is my heart. You flower-twist your words.
Notzahuayan nimitzittoa in nihquitian nimitzilnamiqui xolotzin tlein ticnenelo ye no yollotzin	In my spinning place, I speak of you. In my weaving place, I remember you. Little boy, what have you confused? It is my heart.

Nahuilylama namonan nicahualylama nichpochylama ypan nochihuao nichalcotlacatl [aha aili] nimitzahuiltico noxochinenetzin no xochicamopalnenetzin [yyaho ohuia]	I am an old courtesan. I am your [plural] mother. I become a rejected old woman, an old maiden lady. I am a Chalcan person. I have come to pleasure you, my flower doll, my purple flower doll.
Ye no quelehuia in tlatoani in Axayacaton xiqualitta noxochitlacuilolmaton xiqualitta noxochitlacuilolchichihualtzin [oohuia]	Little king Axayacatl also wants it. Come see my flowery painted hands, come see my flowery painted breasts.
Maca ço can onnenhuetztiuh ye moyollotzin taxayacaton iz ca ye momatzin ma nomatitech xinechonantiuh [aayyahayiaho] xonahuiacan Et[a]	Don't go let your heart take a needless tumble somewhere, little Axayacatl. Here is your hand. Go along holding me by my hand. Be content.
Moxochipetlapan moyeyeyan xolotzin yhuian xoncocochi xonyayamani noconetzin titlatohuani taxayaca [yao ohuaya]	On your flowery reed mat, in your sitting place, little boy, peacefully go to sleep. Relax, my child, you who are King Axayacatl.

Abbreviations

Archives

AGI   Archivo General de Indias (Seville)
AGN   Archivo General de la Nación (Mexico City)
LC   Library of Congress, Manuscripts Division (Washington DC)

Published Collections of Spanish Documents

AM   J. F. Ramírez, ed. *Archivo mexicano: Documentos para la historia de México.* 2 vols. Mexico City: V. García Torres, 1852–53.

DHC   Mariano Cuevas, ed. *Cartas y otros documentos de Hernán Cortés novísimamente descubiertos en el Archivo General de Indias.* Seville: F. Díaz, 1915.

DHM   Joaquín García Icazbalceta, ed. *Colección de documentos para la historia de México.* 2 vols. Mexico City: Francisco Díaz de León, 1858 and 1866.

DIE   M. de Navarrete, ed. *Colección de documentos inéditos para la historia de España.* 113 vols. Madrid: Real Academia de la Historia, 1842–95.

DII   Joaquín Pacheco, Francisco de Cárdenas, and Luis Torres de Mendoza, eds. *Colección de documentos inéditos relativos al descubrimiento, conquista y colonización de las posesiones españoles en América y Oceania.* 42 vols. Madrid: Manuel Bernaldo de Quirós, 1864–84.

DIU   Real Academia de la Historia. *Colección de documentos inéditos relativos al descubrimiento, conquista y organización de las antiguas posesiones españoles de Ultramar.* 25 vols. Madrid: Tip. "Sucesores de Rivadeneyra," 1884–1932.

ENE   Francisco Paso y Troncoso, ed. *Epistolario de Nueva España, 1505–1818.* 16 vols. Mexico City: Biblioteca Histórica Mexicana, 1939–42.

Published Collections of Nahuatl Documents

FC   Charles Dibble and Arthur J. O. Anderson, eds. *The Florentine Codex: General History of the Things of New Spain, by Bernardino de Sahagún.* 13 vols. Santa Fe, NM and Salt Lake City: School of American Research and University of Utah Press, 1950–82.

WPH   James Lockhart, ed. *We People Here: Nahuatl Accounts of the Conquest of Mexico.* Los Angeles: University of California Press, 1993.

Editions of Spanish Chronicles

BD   Bernal Díaz. *The Conquest of New Spain.* Edited and translated by J. M. Cohen. New York: Penguin Books, 1963. (This book is printed by a North American publisher primarily for an English-speaking audience, and I selected the leading English editions of all chronicles for consistency's sake. However, because Cohen omitted large segments of the text, there are numerous places in the book where I cite a Mexican edition instead.)

DD   Fray Diego Durán. *The History of the Indies of New Spain.* Edited and translated by Doris Heyden. Norman: University of Oklahoma Press, 1994.

FLG   Francisco López de Gómara. *Cortés: The Life of the Conqueror by His Secretary* (from *Historia de la conquista de México*). Edited and translated by Lesley Byrd Simpson. Los Angeles: University of California Press, 1965.

HC   Hernán Cortés. *Letters from Mexico.* Edited and translated by Anthony Pagden. Introduction by J. H. Elliott. New Haven, CT: Yale University Press, 1986.

Frequently Cited Anthologies

CAE   Eloise Quiñones Keber, ed. *Chipping Away on Earth: Studies in Prehispanic and Colonial Mexico in Honor of Arthur J. O. Anderson and Charles Dibble.* Lancaster, CA: Labyrinthos, 1994.

IWEM   Susan Schroeder, Stephanie Wood, and Robert Haskett, eds. *Indian Women of Early Mexico.* Norman: University of Oklahoma Press, 1997.

Notes

Introduction

1. "Chalca Woman's Song" (see appendix). This version seems to have been a single example of a common subgenre of song, which would not have been limited to the Chalca.
2. Haniel Long, *Malinche, Doña Marina* (Santa Fe, NM: Writers' Editions, 1939), 39.
3. Her image has been studied extensively. The best and most complete work is Sandra Messinger Cypess, *La Malinche in Mexican Literature* (Austin: University of Texas Press, 1991).
4. Jean Franco, *Critical Passions* (Durham, NC: Duke University Press, 1999), 66.
5. Ricardo Herren, *Doña Marina, la Malinche* (Mexico: Planeta, 1992). Of the many purported biographies of Malinche, Herren's is the best, the least fanciful.
6. Octavio Paz, *The Labyrinth of Solitude*, trans. Lysender Kemp (New York: Grove Press, 1961), 86.
7. This incident, like several others, was brought to my attention by Anna Lanyon in her charming travel narrative, *Malinche's Conquest* (St. Leonards, Australia: Allen Unwin, 1999), 205.
8. Ross Hassig, *Time, History, and Belief in Aztec and Colonial Mexico* (Austin: University of Texas Press, 2001), 53.
9. Diego Muñoz Camargo, *Historia de Tlaxcala*, ed. Luis Reyes García (Tlaxcala: Universidad Autónoma de Tlaxcala, 1998), 183.
10. For the many ways in which this work is embedded in the work of others, see the bibliographic essay at the end of the volume.

One

1. *FC,* 6:172. I have used Dibble and Anderson's edition of the Florentine Codex throughout, excepting only Book Twelve, retaining their use of "thou," although "you" would be more accurate, because it does help to convey a high tone or ceremonial voice. Wherever I have changed their translations, I make a note of it: here, for example, I have changed their translation of *ticiauiz* from "thou art to drudge" to "thou art to labor," as I believe it was only their own perception that feminine labor was drudgery. The Florentine Codex, of course, tells us what the Mexica believed, not what all Nahuas believed. It was *not* written by Malintzin's

people in Coatzacoalcos. However, the sense of the destinies to which male and female babies were born seems to have cut across Mesoamerican cultural boundaries. Thus I suggest that the midwife made a prayer to this effect; she might well have put the matter some other way. On the cleanliness practiced by Nahua healers, see Bernard Ortiz de Montellano, *Aztec Medicine, Health, and Nutrition* (New Brunswick, NJ: Rutgers University Press, 1990).

2. Through his father, Charles inherited the Burgundian duchy and was thus, in effect, head of state of the Low Countries. Isabella died when he was four, and Ferdinand when he was seventeen. At that point, he became King Charles I of Spain. When he was nineteen, his paternal grandfather, Maximilian, died, leaving open the seat of Holy Roman Emperor. The latter was an elected position: several small Germanic states chose their leader, who was also endorsed by the pope. When Charles was elected, he thus also became Emperor Charles V. Throughout this work, I will use the labels interchangeably, unless only one position is relevant to a particular situation. For more on Charles's position at birth, see Bethany Aram, *Juana the Mad: Sovereignty and Dynasty in Renaissance Europe* (Baltimore, MD: Johns Hopkins University Press, 2005).

3. The best synthesis of real-life practices, gleaned from postconquest mundane literature, as opposed to prescriptive and/or elicited texts, is James Lockhart, *The Nahuas after the Conquest: A Social and Cultural History of the Indians of Central Mexico, Sixteenth through Eighteenth Centuries* (Stanford, CA: Stanford University Press, 1992). On naming practices, including the sample nicknames I mention, see pages 118–22. See also Rebecca Horn, "Gender and Social Identity: Nahua Naming Patterns in Post-Conquest Central Mexico," in *IWEM*, 107. The Florentine Codex comes close to admitting that some adjustments were made to avoid particularly evil day signs; *FC*, 6:197. In sixteenth-century Tabasco, very near to the area where Malintzin was born, Nahua names did not include a numerical coefficient, as they did in the Aztec capital. A child's formal name would be, for example, "Reed" and not "One Reed." See France V. Scholes and Ralph L. Roys, *The Maya Chontal Indians of Acalan-Tixchel: A Contribution to the History and Ethnography of the Yucatan Peninsula* (Norman: University of Oklahoma, [1948] 1968), 61–63.

4. Ethnohistorical studies in the tradition of James Lockhart (see note 3, chapter 1) have made it possible to understand the Nahua mindset in ways that the prescriptive codices never could. Most such studies have explored the altepetl of the central valley; we do not have the records necessary to do a postconquest regional study of Coatzacoalcos that might shed light backward. What I have therefore included here are only the most basic cultural elements that seem to have been held in common by all Nahuas.

5. The question of Malintzin's birthplace has been to some extent a vexed one, but in my opinion, it need not be. It was certainly in the region of Coatzacoalcos. In three separate legal proceedings that occurred within about a decade of her death, each with widely differing objectives, numerous witnesses who knew her well swore to her having been born there. Diego de Ordás made the statement in Spain in a hearing regarding her son's entry into the military Order of

Santiago. ("Expediente de Martín Cortés, niño de siete años, hijo de Hernando Cortés y de la india doña Marina," Toledo, 19 July 1529, printed in *Boletín de la Real Academia de la Historia* 21 (1892):199–202. The original is in the Archivo Histórico Nacional, Madrid, Ordenes Militares, 34, E. 2167.) Cortés's lawyers summoned numerous witnesses on his behalf to ratify his version of events when the Crown was having him investigated, and among the hundreds of facts that some of them were able to corroborate was the way in which he procured his translator and her place of origin (see Robert S. Chamberlain, "The First Three Voyages to Yucatan and New Spain, According to the Residencia of Hernán Cortés," *Hispanic American Studies* 7 [1949]: 30; and, for an example of the testimony, "Descargos dados por García de Llerena en nombre de Hernando Cortés a los cargos hechos a éste," October 1529–May 1534, in *DII*, 28:131.) Her daughter also referred to Coatzacoalcos in a long, drawn-out case over her inheritance (AGI, Patronato 56, N. 3, R. 4, "Méritos y servicios: Marina, 1542") In that case, the daughter was trying to prove that she had a right to an inheritance. She could have lied about certain matters, but she had no motivation at all to lie about her mother's birthplace. She also found more than twenty witnesses, who had been part of opposing factions in other regards, to back up her various claims, and several of them said they knew where her mother was from. See chapter 7 for a thorough discussion of the case and the ways in which we can and cannot trust the evidence it offers. Even the chroniclers, famous for their discrepancies, virtually all support the idea that she was from Coatzacoalcos. Only the name of her own altepetl is at all subject to doubt. The legal documents above give a version of the name "Olutla," as does the *probanza* of her son's son, Fernando Cortés (AGI, Patronato 17, R. 13, "Enumeración de los servicios de su abuelo y de doña Marina, su abuela," 1592); the daughter and her witnesses also pair it with Tetiquipaque. Bernal Díaz confused matters by saying that her village was "Painalla" in Coatzacoalcos. All other Spanish chroniclers who mention the matter refer to Coatzacoalcos as the region, except for Francisco López de Gómara and those who copied him, who refer to Jalisco. Since he was presumably working from notes from Cortés, this is at first disturbing, except that he adds that it was in a place called "Uiluta," and since Olutla is sometimes represented as "Oluta" or "Huilota," he is clearly giving the same name. For a slave to have been brought from Jalisco in that era would have been virtually impossible; he must have copied some notes incorrectly. The Nahua informants for Book Twelve of the Florentine Codex mentioned Teticpac, as did Cristóbal del Castillo, a mestizo writing in Nahuatl at the end of the century; this could easily have been a singular version of the Tetiquipaque mentioned elsewhere. Diego Muñoz Camargo, a Tlaxcalan mestizo raised by people who knew Malintzin well, confuses many of the elements of her life, but he says with certainty that they knew her to speak "the language of the Mexica" (Nahuatl), "that of Cozumel" (Maya), and "that of Olotla" (Popoluca). Interestingly, the sixteenth-century scholar Francisco Cervantes de Salazar debates aloud the various stories of Marina's origins and comes to the conclusion that serious scholars today have reached—that she was from a family of nobles in the Coatzacoalcos region, connected with Olutla and Tetiquipaque. See his *Crónica de la Nueva España* (Madrid: Hispanic Society of America, 1914), 1:164–65. That Olutla and Tetiquipaque were separate places, rather than variable delineations from a common reference point (like one person's calpolli and altepetl), is made clear in that both were later listed as being given in encomienda to Luis Marín. See Robert Himmerich y Valencia, *The Encomenderos of New Spain, 1521–1555* (Austin: University of Texas Press, 1991), 189. For more on Olutla and Tetiquipaque, see note 10, chapter 1.

6. Stephanie Wood, *Transcending Conquest: Nahua Views of Spanish Colonial Mexico* (Norman: University of Oklahoma Press, 2003), 143. Much has been written on the nature of Mesoamerican militarism. See especially Ross Hassig, *Aztec Warfare: Imperial Expansion and Political Control* (Norman: University of Oklahoma Press, 1988). Pedro Carrasco has recently argued eloquently that the political alliances that formed were in fact stable enough for the Mexica government to merit the term "empire." In one light, that is definitely true, and yet we must not imagine a bureaucracy as complex and effective as that of Rome, for example. See his book, *The Tenochca Empire of Ancient Mexico: The Triple Alliance of Tenochtitlan, Tetzcoco, and Tlacopan* (Norman: University of Oklahoma Press, 1999).

7. Frances Karttunen was the first to comment in depth on Malintzin's linguistic abilities and what they demonstrate about her background in "Rethinking Malinche," in *IWEM*. It is also worth noting that Diego de Ordás (see note 3, chapter 1) stated that he had been to Coatzacoalcos (and he had been, twice) and that he had seen doña Marina received as a peer by noble families there. Of course, it was his avowed agenda to demonstrate that her son should be received as a noble, and so what he said is suspect, but the specific way in which he put it rings true. If he were only interested in making the case, not in telling the truth, he could simply have insisted that he knew her to be a princess, as Bernal Díaz did.

8. Historians and anthropologists studying the Aztecs have engaged in a debate about whether or not the long-distance trade economy was purely politically driven, in that the Mexica often demanded tribute in goods that an area did not have, so as to force them to engage in exchange. See Frank Salomon, "Potchteca and Mindalá: A Comparison of Long Distance Traders in Ecuador and Mesoamerica," *Journal of the Steward Anthropological Society* 9 (1977): 231–48; Pedro Carrasco, "Markets and Merchants in the Aztec Economy," *Journal of the Steward Anthropological Society* 12 (1980): 249–69; and Ross Hassig, *Trade, Tribute, and Transportation: The Sixteenth-Century Political Economy of the Valley of Mexico* (Norman: University of Oklahoma Press, 1985), 117–26. An excellent discussion of the mindset of the merchants is Inga Clendinnen, *Aztecs* (New York: Cambridge University Press, 1991), 132–40.

9. Anne Chapman, "Port of Trade Enclaves in Aztec and Maya Civilizations," in *Trade and Market in the Early Empires,* ed. Karl Polyani, Conrad Arensberg, and Harry Pearson (Glencoe, IL: Free Press, 1957); Frances Berdan, "The Economics of Aztec Luxury Trade and Tribute," in *The Aztec Templo Mayor*, ed. Elizabeth

Hill Boone (Washington, DC: Dumbarton Oaks, 1983); Johanna Broda, "The Provenience of the Offerings: Tribute and Cosmovision," in Boone, *The Aztec Templo Mayor.*

10. S. Jeffrey K. Wilkerson, "Nahua Presence on the Mesoamerican Gulf Coast," in *CAE,* discusses the long-term nature of the "corridor of migration" along the Gulf Coast. For an excellent linguistic map of the region see Peter Gerhard, *The Southeast Frontier of New Spain* (Norman: University of Oklahoma Press, 1993). In the 1920s and 1930s, Olutla still existed as a self-contained linguistic island of about three thousand Popoluca speakers about forty miles west of Coatzacoalcos, exactly where Bernal Díaz, who once lived in the area, placed it. A linguist who studied the people there said they had to have been in that place since ancient times, rather than having been relocated more recently, as their variant of the language was distinctly different from the Popoluca spoken by others not many miles away. See George M. Foster, "The Geographical, Linguistic and Cultural Position of the Popoluca of Veracruz," *American Anthropologist* 45 (1943): 531–46. In 1990 there were only 102 speakers remaining. For a thorough discussion, see Felix Báez-Jorge and Felix Darío Báez Galuán, "The Popoluca," in *Native Peoples of the Gulf Coast of Mexico,* ed. Alan R. Sandstrom and E. Hugo García Valencía (Tucson: University of Arizona Press, 2005), 140–42. For more on Olutla Popoluca as a language, see Sören Wichmann, *The Relationship among the Mixe-Zoquean Languages of Mexico* (Salt Lake City: University of Utah Press, 1995). Foster found a 1580 document that listed three Popoluca-speaking villages in the area (including Olutla) and several Nahuatl-speaking ones. Interestingly, Tetiquipaque was not mentioned, but a place called Xaltipan was. And Malintzin's grandson, writing in the 1590s, had also been given to understand that the place paired with Olutla was called Xaltipan (see chapter 5). Tetiquipaque no longer exists, but Jaltipan does, so a resettlement probably occurred during the population holocaust of the sixteenth century (see chapter 5). We cannot know with certainty why a Popoluca settlement and a Nahuatl-speaking one were quite consistently linked together, but the pattern fits perfectly with what is known about Mesoamerican politics in general. Dependent villages were intermingled with tribute receivers almost everywhere. See Carrasco, *The Tenochca Empire,* for a thorough discussion of the phenomenon.

11. FLG, 56–57. "She was the daughter of wealthy parents, who were related to the lord of that country." This statement contrasts strongly with Bernal Díaz's rather wild claim that she was a king's daughter. Its reasonableness and specificity make it ring true.

12. There is an extensive literature on complementarity between the sexes within the Nahua world. See Louise Burkhart, "Mexica Women on the Home Front: Housework and Religion in Aztec Mexico," in *IWEM;* Karen Bruhns and Karen Stothert, *Women in Ancient America* (Norman: University of Oklahoma Press, 1999); Clendinnen, *Aztecs;* Rosemary Joyce, *Gender and Power in Prehispanic Mesoamerica* (Austin: University of Texas Press, 2000); Susan Kellogg, "The Woman's Room: Some Aspects of Gender Relations in Tenochtitlan in the Late Pre-Hispanic Period," *Ethnohistory* 42 (1995): 563–76; Sharisse McCafferty and

Geoffrey McCafferty, "Powerful Women and the Myth of Male Dominance in Aztec Society," *Archaeological Review from Cambridge* 7 (1988): 45–59; Thelma Sullivan, "Tlazolteotl-Ixcuina: The Great Spinner and Weaver," in *The Art and Iconography of Late Post-Classic Central Mexico,* ed. Elizabeth Hill Boone (Washington, DC: Dumbarton Oaks, 1983). Most of these studies have been based on formal texts, but currently some younger scholars are using mundane literature to study real women's lives, and they are proving that in the sixteenth century, at least, women were active participants in their marriages and social relations. See Lisa Sousa, "Women in Native Societies and Cultures of Colonial Mexico" (PhD diss., University of California–Los Angeles, 1998). Sousa argues that there was a "high degree of cultural conformity" among the Nahuas, Mixtecs, and Zapotecs as regards gender. We thus have every reason to believe that what is known about gendered ideals and practices in Tenochtitlan can also largely be applied to the Nahuas in such places as Coatzacoalcos.

13. The best study of the subject is Patricia Anawalt, *Indian Clothing before Cortés: Mesoamerican Costumes from the Codices* (Norman: University of Oklahoma Press, 1981).

14. Fray Alonso de Molina, *Vocabulario en lengua mexicana y castellana* (Mexico City: Porrúa [1571] 1993), 90v.

15. To follow the debate on the nature of laborers' relationship to the land, see first Frederick Hicks, "Dependent Labor in Prehispanic Mexico," in *Estudios de Cultura Náhuatl* 11 (1975): 243–66; then Pedro Carrasco, "The Provenience of Zorita's Data on the Social Organization of Ancient Mexico," in *CAE*; finally Lockhart, *The Nahuas,* 96–102.

16. Fray Toríbio de Benavente Motolinia, *Memoriales o libro de las cosas de la Nueva España* (Mexico City: Porrúa, 1971), 366–72, is the best source on the legalistic practices employed in Tetzcoco; Diego Durán and the Florentine Codex, among others, also refer to people selling themselves or their children into slavery. The attack on the woman who chose to be a mistress is in *FC,* 4:95. My translation differs slightly from that of Dibble and Anderson, so I quote: "Auh in ie oquichiuh . . . ic tehuic, ic temecapal mochiuhtinemi: auh çan no ihui aontleiecoa, aontlaeltia, in itecuacan in ompa teltacauh." For the "Chalca Woman's Song," see appendix.

17. Analyzing fray Diego Durán's narrative (DD), which is essentially a recitation of wars, reveals the subtleties of what it meant for a city to be taken, depending on the overall political context. Compare the conquest of Xochimilco on pages 109–10 with the conquest of the Huaxtecs on pages 165–66, for example. We cannot assume that the text is accurate as regards dates, numbers of people, etc., but we can be sure that it unintentionally reveals widespread concerns and unconscious assumptions regarding warfare. In one instance, the queen of Tlatelolco is actually made to assert that some captives simply become slaves rather than sacrifice victims; she begs her husband to avoid war with Tenochtitlan for the sake of the children: "They will become perpetual slaves if we are conquered" (DD, 254). She might have meant tenants, figurative slaves, but in another source Moctezuma's descendant Tezozomoc actually states what is implicit in

most texts—that prisoners who were not sacrificed became slaves. Hernando Alvarado Tezozomoc, *Crónica mexicana* (Mexico City: Porrúa, 1975), 360.

18. Motolinia, *Memoriales,* 313, 322–23. Motolinia did not speak Nahuatl and could easily have gotten the words wrong, but someone had clearly tried to explain to him subtle distinctions between women he would simply have called *mancebas,* or "concubines." For an excellent analysis of the specific kinds of political alliances made in marriage, see Pedro Carrasco, "Royal Marriages in Ancient Mexico," in *Explorations in Ethnohistory: The Indians of Central Mexico in the Sixteenth Century,* ed. H. R. Harvey and H. Premm (Albuquerque: University of New Mexico Press, 1984).

19. "Chalca Woman's Song" (see appendix).

20. They could have traveled overland, but in that location, almost all travelers followed the waterways. She could not have been much younger than eight, for in that case, she would not have retained perfect fluency in her natal language, and she would not have been much more than twelve, as all sources agree she was taken as a child. It is also true that the slave dealers would have been less interested in very young children who still needed supervisory care, or in full-grown women who were already mothers.

21. BD, 267 and HC, "Second Letter," 95–96.

22. Besides references in Francisco López de Gómara and Bernal Díaz, Andrés de Tapia mentions this, writing in the 1540s, independently of the latter two (as their texts were not yet written), as does Francisco Cervantes de Salazar, purportedly interviewing locals and writing shortly after 1558.

23. Karttunen in "Rethinking Malinche" (*IWEM,* 311) suggests she may have been "constitutionally unfit" for the life of a noble girl. Jeanette Peterson reminds us what she stood for, regardless of her own behavior: "Of noble stock, but not of the royal line, Malinche would surely have qualified as a 'woman of discord,'" "Lengua o Diosa? The Early Imaging of Malinche," in *CAE.* For statements that recalcitrant concubines could be sold, see *FC,* 4:95.

24. Julie Greer Johnson, *Women in Colonial Spanish American Literature* (Westport, CT: Greenwood Press, 1983), 16–17; and Cypess, *La Malinche,* 28–31. The tale of Amadís was a thirteenth-century story, but Garci Rodríguez de Montalvo had published an edition of the work in 1508 in Zaragoza; the work was known to a number of the men who went to the New World. Modern readers must understand that Bernal Díaz and other writers of his era conceived of the project of history writing differently than we do today. See Ruth Morse, *Truth and Convention in the Middle Ages: Rhetoric, Representation, and Reality* (New York: Cambridge University Press, 1991).

25. *FC,* 9:17–18, "açocihuatl, açooquichpiltontli, in ompa quimonnamacaia." Scholars who have looked at this phenomenon include Hassig, *Trade,* 116; Chapman, "Port of Trade Enclaves," 125–26; Carrasco, "Markets and Merchants," 261–62; and Frances Berdan, "Economic Alternatives under Imperial Rule: The Eastern Aztec Empire," in *Economies and Polities of the Aztec Realm,* ed. Mary G. Hodge and Michael E. Smith (Albany: State University of New York Press, 1994), 297–98. For the shift in women's work, see Elizabeth Brumfiel, "Weaving and Cooking:

Women's Production in Aztec Mexico," in *Engendering Archaeology: Women and Prehistory,* ed. J. M. Gero and M. W. Conkey (Cambridge: Cambridge University Press, 1991), 232–33.

26. *FC*, 11:29–30.

27. Archaeologists have not found enduring architecture, but the area is still geographically fascinating and deserves a visit. Scholars believe that Nahuatl was the dominant language—though it clearly was not that of the majority—because there are two separate stories of Moctezuma having either a fortress or a brother monarch there, though he had neither, and because the percentage of Nahuatl personal names among all names recorded in sixteenth-century documents at different points on the isthmus seems to correlate perfectly with how powerful Nahuas were generally understood to be at each location. Languages besides Nahuatl that would have been common at Xicallanco, given its location, include Chontal, Yucatecan, and Tzeltal Maya. Other languages that might have been heard include Popoluca and Tzotzil Maya. Scholars who have culled and analyzed all the references to the place include Chapman, "Ports of Trade," 129–42; Gerhard, *Southeast Frontier*, 48–49; and especially Scholes and Roys, *Maya Chontal Indians*, 27–35, 318.

28. Chroniclers describe the area, and Scholes and Roys in *Maya Chontal Indians* discuss past excavations, pages 20 and 37. They also discuss a fascinating 1541 document representing the name of the king's lineage as "Cipac" or "Acpac." "Tabasco" or "Tapasco" could easily represent a Spanish effort to record such a morpheme, indicating, as was typical, that the place and the lord were named for each other. The area is well worth a visit: day trips are possible from Villahermosa.

29. Scholes and Roys, *Maya Chontal Indians*, 28–30, 56–59. Scholes and Roys postulate that a good number of the slaves brought to the Tabasco region may have been put to work in the cacao fields. Their book is a stupendous achievement: they spent many years gathering every relevant document pertaining to the region and they interpreted them with care and precision. Still, this is one element of which I am not convinced. We will probably never know with certainty.

30. Anawalt, *Indian Clothing,* 182–84. For an introduction to the literature on Maya women, readers might begin with Traci Ardren, ed., *Ancient Maya Women* (Lanham, MD: Rowman & Littlefield, 2002), and Lowell S. Gustafson and Amelia M. Trevelyan, eds., *Ancient Maya Gender Identity and Relations* (Westport, CT: Bergin & Garvey, 2002).

31. This paragraph is largely based on Yucatecan sources, but the most basic elements of that culture were almost certainly shared by the Chontal, for whom we unfortunately have fewer surviving artifacts. In fact, it is thought that the Chontal elites absorbed much of what they encountered in their travels among Nahuas and Yucatecan Mayas. See Gabrielle Vail and Andrea Stone, "Representations of Women in Postclassic and Colonial Maya Literature and Art," in Ardren, *Ancient Maya Women*. On the likelihood of the pilgrimages to Cozumel, see Scholes and Roys, *Maya Chontal Indians*, 57.

32. On the labor-intensive stages of cloth production, see Marilyn Beaudry-Corbett and Sharisse McCafferty, "Spindle Whorls: Household Specialization at Ceren," in Ardren, *Ancient Maya Women*; Joyce, *Gender and Power*, 186–87; as well as, for the Nahua world, Frederick Hicks, "Cloth in the Political Economy of the Aztec State," in Hodge and Smith, *Economies and Polities*. Codices referring to the ages at which young Nahua girls learned to weave include not only the Florentine, but also the Mendoza and fray Juan Bautista's Huehuetlahtolli.

33. Yucatec Maya women's skeletons and the materials found in their graves, including the shells, have been studied by Traci Ardren, "Death Became Her: Images of Female Power from Yaxuna Burials," in Ardren, *Ancient Maya Women*.

34. Birgitta Leander, *Herencia cultural del mundo Náhuatl a través de la lengua*. (Mexico: Secretaría de Educación Pública, 1972), 63–64. "Nonantzin ihcuac nimiquiz/ mitlecuilpan xinechtoca/ ihcuac tiaz tetlaxcalchihuaz/ ompa nopampa xichoca./ Ihuan tla acah mitztlatlaniz,/ nonantzin, tleca tichoca/ xiquilhuiz ca xoxohui in cahuitl/ ihuan in nechchoctia ica cecenca popoca." This was collected by a linguist in the twentieth century, in the way that an old nursery rhyme like "Ring around the Rosy" might be collected. Thus we cannot be absolutely certain of the song's age. The tone, themes, and grammatical endings are very much in keeping with what we know of the classical period, but clearly it was reformulated in the colonial period, in that the version we have is rhymed in a style popular in the sixteenth and seventeenth centuries but nonexistent as far as we know among the preconquest Nahuas. On old themes being turned into rhyming couplets in the colonial period, see Lockhart, *The Nahuas*, 399–401.

35. On menarche and abortion-inducing drugs, see Bruhns and Stothert, *Women in Ancient America*, 137, 158.

36. Bernal Díaz recounts the first three Spanish expeditions' interactions with Champoton and Putunchan in *Historia verdadera*. I have read between the lines of what he reported to infer what the indigenous concluded at each stage. He does, however, explicitly state that the governor of Putunchan had already heard from his counterpart at Champoton by the time the Spanish got there. Fray Juan Díaz provides an important corrective to the exaggerations of Díaz; see his account in *The Conquistadors: First Person Accounts of the Conquest of Mexico*, ed. Patricia de Fuentes (Norman: University of Oklahoma Press, 1993). For more on this subject, see note 1, chapter 2.

Two

1. Most of the Spanish chroniclers wrote many years after the events, and they always wrote with a specific agenda. Their accounts are rarely in full agreement. It is necessary to sift carefully before deciding what can be taken as fact. We have, for example, three detailed accounts of Juan de Grijalva's 1518 visit to Putunchan—one by fray Juan Díaz, who was the expedition's appointed chaplain, another by Bernal Díaz de Castillo, who said he participated, and a third by Gonzalo Fernández de Oviedo, who was not there, but who clearly had seen the

ship's log. Fray Juan wrote a report to the king not long after his return, while Bernal Díaz wrote when he was an old man. At that distance in time, he was freer to change the story: for example, he exaggerated the damage the Spanish had done at Champoton, wanting to show that they had actively avenged the battle the previous expedition had lost there, when in fact they apparently actually attacked a different town on the coast most aggressively. If he were really there, the details at Putunchan had clearly faded from his mind: he wrote that there was a moment of tension, but that the interpreters resolved the situation; he did not remember that it had been a two-day process. He thought that they spent the night *after* the nobleman visited their captain, not before. Fray Juan says explicitly that they left immediately, despite an invitation to stay, because of the winds. Fray Juan was attempting to show that more could have been accomplished if Juan de Grijalva had proceeded differently, but he did not lie about basic ship-log events, as is evident when comparing his account to that of Oviedo. See Bernal Díaz, "The Chronicle of Juan Díaz," in Fuentes, *The Conquistadors*; and Gonzalo Fernández de Oviedo, *Historia general y natural de las Indias*, ed. Juan Perez de Tudela Bueso (Madrid: Atlas, 1959), 2:132–34. I continue this sifting process throughout this chapter, but without continuing commentary of this nature except where most necessary.

2. FLG, 50. Gómara claims that Cortés asked them very directly what they had been thinking. I interpret their comment based on knowledge of their political and economic position within the Mesoamerican world and the actions they chose to take.

3. BD, 68. I believe—as do a number of scholars—that Díaz may not really have been on the previous expedition, given the errors in his account (see note 1, chapter 2). He clearly, however, at the very least spent considerable time talking to companions who had been part of it.

4. BD, 70.

5. We have several accounts of the battle: besides Bernal Díaz and Francisco de Gómara above, we have Hernando Cortés, "The First Letter," in HC, as well as Andrés de Tapia in Fuentes, *The Conquistadors*. It is necessary to compare accounts thoughtfully. Writing within weeks of the event, Cortés said 220 Indians were killed. Years later, his secretary Gómara wrote that it must have been more like 300, and Bernal Díaz raised the number to 800. This is typical: the Spaniards seem to have become more and more invincible in their own eyes the further they were from the period of conquest. For a thoughtful and thorough analysis of the military capabilities of both sides in this battle and the others that ensued, see Ross Hassig, *Mexico and the Spanish Conquest* (London: Longman, 1994).

6. The chronicles give varying estimates of the number of women handed over, ranging from eight to twenty, with the latter being most common. In a court case, eyewitnesses under oath either avoided giving a number or recalled that it was twenty, which is certainly culturally plausible. AGI, Justicia 168, "Auto entre partes de México," 1564, fol. 1060v.

7. Karttunen, "Rethinking Malinche," in *IWEM*, 301–2.

8. Ricardo Herren draws together what is known about the relationship between Cortés and Puertocarrero in *Doña Marina, la Malinche*, 26–27, 72. There are of course numerous full-scale studies of Cortés. A classic that still makes a "good read" is Salvador de Madariaga, *Hernán Cortés, Conqueror of Mexico* (New York: Macmillan, 1941). From the same era, but much more skeptical, and in my view accurate, is Henry Wagner, *The Rise of Hernando Cortés* (New York: The Cortes Society, 1944). Wagner promised to write a sequel, which he would entitle, "The Fall of Hernando Cortés," but he never did. Recently, two monumental studies have appeared that draw on far more documentation than did the older works: José Luis Martínez, *Hernán Cortés* (Mexico City: UNAM, 1990); and Juan Miralles, *Hernán Cortés, inventor de México* (Mexico City: Tusquets Editores, 2001). Miralles is clearly responding to the older ideas embodied in Madariaga's work in his title.

9. All the chroniclers mention the crucially important Jerónimo de Aguilar. See, for the earliest account, HC, 13–17. His role was also discussed in various legal cases. In 1520 his brother learned that he was still alive from messengers Cortés had sent home, and gathered witnesses to prepare an *información* about his life. (AGI, Patronato 150, N. 2, R. 1). Aguilar was from Ecija, in Andalusia, and had gone with others in 1509 to settle Darién in Panama. As far as we know, he did not write about his experiences living with Indians, but other captives did. See chapter 3, note 10.

10. That Columbus's thinking at the time was understood to be far more complex than is often assumed today—that the debate was not only about the feasibility of sailing west to travel east, but also about the likelihood of finding inhabited lands in the southern hemisphere—has been ably proven by Nicolas Wey-Gómez in *The Machine of the World: Place, Colonialism, and Columbus's Invention of the American Tropics* (Boston: MIT Press, 2006).

11. Louise Burkhart, *Before Guadalupe: The Virgin Mary in Early Colonial Nahuatl Literature* (Albany, NY: Institute for Mesoamerican Studies, 2001), 3, 117, translating Pedro de Gante, *Doctrina cristiana en lengua mexicana* (1553).

12. Jonathan Spence, *The Memory Palace of Matteo Ricci* (New York: Penguin Books, 1983), 244–45

13. Cortés, in his first letter, and Bernal Díaz both comment on how quickly the Indians made their appearance. The Florentine Codex, Book Twelve, tells us that Moctezuma had had the place watched. Thus both sides reconfirm each other's accounts. The Florentine says that the messengers back to the capital passed through Xicallanco. That makes no sense, geographically speaking. But news from the Maya world would have come through Xicallanco. The elderly informant(s) speaking in the 1550s apparently had their details confused.

14. Book Twelve of the Florentine Codex in *WPH*, 70. All citations to Book Twelve are to Lockhart's edition rather than to the Dibble and Anderson edition cited elsewhere, as it provides a superior translation. DD, 499. For more on the Indians' clear-sighted and pragmatic response to Spanish material culture, see Wood, *Transcending Conquest*, 46–59.

15. DD, 495, 505.

16. FLG, 56.

17. In 1551 Malintzin's daughter would end up fighting for her inheritance against opponents who called her mother "that Indian woman, Marina." However, her opponent's own witnesses continuously slipped and referred to "doña Marina," as they had obviously been accustomed to doing. AGI, Justicia 168, "Auto entre partes," pt. 10. See chapter 8 for a full discussion.

18. This period on the coast is not covered in Cortés's letters to the Crown except very briefly. Bernal Díaz indirectly provides a running commentary on Gómara's account; between the two, we can determine the basic elements of what happened. I have only accepted details as true where they seem guaranteed to be accurate—such as the need to wait for low tide before trying to impress the people by exercising the horses. BD, 91.

19. Ibid., 102. J. H. Elliott provides a superb analysis of the legalistic maneuvering of Cortés in his introduction to *Letters from Mexico* (HC).

20. BD, 107.

21. Ibid., 119. It is only through Díaz that we learn of this; Cortés is careful not to mention this part of the story.

22. DD, 493. This is a recurring motif in the text. On the students' possible inspiration for the omens they described, see Felipe Fernández-Armesto, "Aztec Auguries and Memories of the Conquest of Mexico," *Renaissance Studies* 6 (1992). It is also true that most of the students were presumably Tlatelolcan and thus very willing to scapegoat the political leader of their own erstwhile conquerors, the Tenochca. For a more complete treatment of this topic, I refer readers to my article, "Burying the White Gods: New Perspectives on the Conquest of Mexico," *American Historical Review* 108, no. 3 (2003): 658–87.

23. *WPH*, 18. I note that certain sources written in Spanish but purportedly based on interviews with Nahuas demonstrate the same bipartite treatment—a recitation of myths suddenly becomes detailed and realistic description of battles.

24. Fray Toríbio de Benavente Motolinia, *Historia de los indios de la Nueva España* (Madrid: Alianza Editorial, 1988), 108. Susan Gillespie has done the most detailed study of the transformation of the Quetzalcoatl story in *The Aztec Kings: The Construction of Rulership in Mexica History* (Tucson: University of Arizona Press, 1989), 185–98. Hassig also deals with the topic in *Time, History, and Belief.* For a study of the ancient feathered serpent motif throughout Mesoamerica, see Enrique Florescano, *The Myth of Quetzalcoatl* (Baltimore, MD: Johns Hopkins University Press, 1999).

25. The version most popular among the fathers held it that Quetzalcoatl had been the apostle St. Thomas. For treatment of the church's wrestling with the question of Indian souls, see Jacques Lafaye, *Quetzalcoatl and Guadalupe: The Formation of Mexican National Consciousness, 1531–1813* (Chicago: University of Chicago Press, 1976).

26. John Bierhorst, ed. and trans., "Annals of Cuauhtitlan" in *History and Mythology of the Aztecs: The Codex Chimalpopoca* (Tucson: University of Arizona Press, 1992), 29, 41. I refer scholars to John Bierhorst, ed., *Codex Chimalpopoca: The Text in Nahuatl* (Tucson: University of Arizona Press, 1992), 7–13. The style

suddenly differs markedly. It is as if the story has been inserted into some traditional annals of Tula.

27. In the negotiations after the surrender, for example, an enraged priest responds to the Spanish demands for gold and jewels by shouting, "Let the *teotl,* the Captain, pay heed!" The defeated Cuauhtemoc calms him by making a speech in which he reminds him that they have lost and uses the word "tecuhtli" to refer to Cortés. See *WPH,* 252.

28. DD, 499–500. Anja Utgenannt, University of Cologne, stresses that Malintzin would likely have had an important role in this regard. See her "Gods, Christians and Enemies: The Representation of the Conquerors in a Nahuatl Account" (paper presented at El Cambio Cultural en el México del siglo XVI, University of Vienna, June 2002).

29. Louise Burkhart has done a detailed study of the impossibility of directly translating the word "teotl" as "god," though the Spanish did their best. See *The Slippery Earth: Nahua-Christian Moral Dialogue in Sixteenth-Century Mexico* (Tucson: University of Arizona Press, 1989), 36–42. Examples of ambiguous usage of the word in reference to the Spanish abound—in which cases the Spanish tended to assume it meant simply "god." In the Florentine Codex, for example, Sahagún's students wrote that when Moctezuma was in hopes of establishing a tributary relationship with the Spanish by giving them annual gifts, he ordered his men, "Xicmotlatlauhtilican in totecuio in teotl." This translates best as "Address our political lord, the *teul,* in a courtly manner," but it was rendered in the Spanish gloss as "Worship the god in my name." *WPH,* 68–69.

30. BD, 112, 117.

31. A printed version of this document, taken from earlier printed sources, is available in José Luis Martínez, *Documentos cortesianos* (Mexico City: Fondo de Cultura Económica, 1990), 1:265–71. I have unfortunately only been able to locate a fragment of the original in the AGI, Patronato 180, R. 4, "Instrucciones de Carlos V a Hernando Cortés," 26 June 1523, fols. 1–3.

32. The clearest presentation of these ideas is Jared Diamond, *Guns, Germs and Steel: The Fates of Human Societies* (New York: Norton, 1997). This book won a Pulitzer prize, but historians are sharply divided as to whether its argument is compelling. I, for one, am completely convinced by the evidence as to where the remains of ancient protein-rich plant seeds have been found: I urge skeptical colleagues to pursue Diamond's references for themselves if they remain unconvinced. Subsidiary—but still important—aspects of the argument include the presence of animals appropriate for domestication in the Old World and the lengthy east–west axis in the Old World that allowed for the relatively easy diffusion of crops, animals, and resulting technologies; these elements seem more clear cut to people and have aroused less ire. Some historians have rejected the argument as a whole under the misapprehension that Diamond is arguing that all human behavior is dictated by the environment. Historians, who have studied so many specific examples of human achievement, know that to be false. But what Diamond is actually saying is that although villages in the Fertile Crescent responded to their environment in a multiplicity of ways, as did those of Papua

New Guinea, for example, those few who chose to turn their gathering into farming would eventually become successful in the one place, while those few who insisted on it would fail to feed their people adequately in the other.

33. The literature on the importance of the corn complex in the development of Mesoamerican civilization is vast. For a clear and insightful summary, see Janine Gasco and Michael E. Smith, "Origins and Development of Mesoamerican Civilization," in *The Legacy of Mesoamerica: History and Culture of a Native American Civilization*, ed. Robert Carmack, Janine Gasco, and Gary H. Gossen (Upper Saddle River, NJ: Prentice Hall, 1996).

Three

1. There has been some confusion as to why the Spanish heard the expected vocative "Malintzine" as "Malinche." The brilliant seventeenth-century scholar of Nahuatl, Horacio Carochi, elucidates this point, noting the unusual vocative form. See *Grammar of the Mexican Language*, ed. James Lockhart (Stanford, CA: Stanford University Press, [1645] 2001), 44–45. Repeated examples of the vocative form "Malintze" are found in the Annals of Tlatelolco. See Ernst Mengin, ed., *Unos anales históricos de la nación mexicana* (Copenhagen: E. Munksgaard, 1945), 55–56. "Malintzine" also appears in certain contexts in that work.

2. James Lockhart first noted the use of these words in several contexts in stories written in the 1550s and later referring to the period soon after contact. See *WPH*, ix, 13.

3. Bernal Díaz tells us that Cortés and Juan Pérez de Arteaga were both addressed as "Malinche" (BD, 172), as does Camargo, *Historia de Tlaxcala*, 184. Importantly, the label's being applied to Cortés is also confirmed in documents from the 1520s in the charges brought against him in his *residencia*: "Cargos que resultan contra Hernando Cortés," 8 May 1529, in *DII*, 27:40. The phenomenon is also highlighted in a probanza submitted by Isabel Pérez de Arteaga, Juan's daughter, in which witnesses who could not yet have read that Bernal Díaz gave testimony. The manuscript is in the collection of the Jay I. Kislak Foundation, Miami Lake, Florida, and cited in Karttunen, "Rethinking Malinche," in *IWEM*, 296. Witnesses unself-consciously refer to "Juan Pérez Malinchi" in AGI, Justicia 18, "Auto entre partes de México," 1564, fol. 1062v. Karttunen discusses the likelihood that all of them were perceived as representatives of or conduits for another entity (293–94). Bernal Díaz tried to explain the phenomenon by saying that the Indians were referring to Cortés as "Malintzin's captain" (*Malintzin ycapitan*) and then shortening the phrase to the first word (BD, 172). But they would not have shortened a possessive that way, and the explanation cannot apply to Arteaga. Nor would they have been familiar with the word *capitán* just at first.

4. Many of these admonitions and sacred formulae as uttered in Tenochca practice were recorded in the Florentine Codex. Direct and oblique references in other sources indicate that comparable memorized speeches for use on specific occasions existed in most Nahua cultures. To this day, certain rites of passages

and various holy days are marked by traditional speeches in Nahuatl-speaking Mexican villages. Midwives and elderly mothers always participated actively in family celebrations. It is possible that only male priests participated in high religious events, at least among the Tenochca, but Betty Ann Brown has argued convincingly that even here there is evidence that women sometimes spoke aloud. "Seen but Not Heard: Women in Aztec Ritual—the Sahagún Texts," in *Text and Image in Pre-Columbian Art: Essays on the Interrelationship of the Verbal and Visual Arts*, ed. Janet Catherine Berlot (Oxford: British Archaeological Reports Press, 1983), 123–28.

5. The story of the Lady of Tula and Huexotzincatzin, the son of the king of Tetzcoco, appears in several places, most notably in Juan de Torquemada, *Monarquía Indiana* (Mexico City: Porrúa, [1723] 1975), 1:189–90. Readers should understand that Torquemada can hardly be considered a primary source; there is no evidence to indicate that events occurred just as he describes and in fact every reason to suppose that Huexotzincatzin was actually removed to make way for a political rival. However, the existence of stories like this one does prove that women could be poet-singers. See also Miguel León-Portilla, *Fifteen Poets of the Aztec World* (Norman: University of Oklahoma Press, 1992), 175–77.

6. AGI, Justicia 168, "Auto entre partes," fol. 986v. HC, "Third Letter," 246.

7. Margarita Zamora, "'If Cahonaboa Learns to Speak': Amerindian Voice in the Discourse of Discovery," *Colonial Latin American Review* 8, no. 2 (1999): 191–206. Matthew Restall devotes a chapter to white men's imaginings in this regard: "The Lost Words of La Malinche: The Myth of (Mis)Communication," in *Seven Myths of the Spanish Conquest* (New York: Oxford University Press, 2003). He points out that the colonial "myth of communication" has given way in more modern times to the myth of miscommunication—that is, to a belief that the indigenous could not possibly have understood what was going on at all.

8. Jean Franco discusses Gómara's use of the word and its meaning in *Critical Passions*, 69.

9. "The Chronicle of Fray Francisco de Aguilar," in Fuentes, *The Conquistador*, 137.

10. The accounts of Cortés and Bernal Díaz both indicate that Aguilar made an extreme effort to catch up with the Spanish when he heard that they were in the area. A particularly fascinating and accessible account of a Spaniard's experience in captivity is Alvar Núñez Cabeza de Vaca, *The Narrative of Cabeza de Vaca*, ed. Rolena Adorno and Patrick Charles Pautz (Lincoln: University of Nebraska Press, 2003). The same authors and press have also published a three-volume set that includes extensive contextual materials: *Alvar Núñez Cabeza de Vaca: His Account, His Life, and the Expedition of Pánfilo de Narváez* (1999).

11. Part of the evidence for these statements is indirect: Jerónimo de Aguilar later evinced bitterness against both Malintzin and Cortés, and he did not accompany them on the trip to Honduras when they set out in 1524. But there is also direct evidence. In the 1550s Malintzin's daughter had to fight for her inheritance against opponents who insisted that her mother's role as a translator had not been very important and that other people, especially Aguilar, had been crucial.

But the opponents' own witnesses undercut their assertions in the stories they told. One of them actually said that Cortés had become so irritated with Aguilar, and Malintzin so adept in Spanish, that he began to leave him out more and more often even in these early days. AGI, Justicia 168, "Auto entre partes," fols. 1062–63. See chapter 8 for a full discussion of this case.

12. HC, "Second Letter," 56.

13. Ibid., 57–59. Cortés could indeed be fabricating his account, but in general it fits exactly with what we would expect and has the ring of truth, with the exception of certain twists he obviously includes to protect the heroic reputation of his men—such as the Indians' having needed five thousand men to surround and kill two horses. The accounts of Francisco de Aguilar, Andrés de Tapia, and Bernal Díaz also support him regarding the Tlaxcalan campaign, and there are other parts of the narrative, as we shall see, where they subtly or even explicitly undermine him.

14. BD, 144–45.

15. HC, "Second Letter," 60.

16. BD, 149.

17. HC, "Second Letter," 61.

18. Ibid., 62.

19. Ibid., 66.

20. BD, 156.

21. On what is known of preconquest Tlaxcalan political structures, see Charles Gibson, *Tlaxcala in the Sixteenth Century* (Stanford, CA: Stanford University Press, 1952), 1–27; and Lockhart, *The Nahuas*, 20–23. The land formation is remarkable in the "four corners" area that eventually became the city of Tlaxcala: particularly prominent rounded hills exist within a few kilometers of each other. Even today the view is striking.

22. Several scholars have commented on the indigenous images of Malintzin: Gordon Brotherston, "La Malintzin en los codices," in *La Malinche, sus padres y sus hijos,* ed. Margo Glantz (Mexico: UNAM, 1994), and *Painted Books from Mexico* (London: The British Museum Press, 1995), 33–44; Karttunen, "Rethinking Malintzin," in *IWEM*; Jeanette Favrot Peterson, "Lengua o Diosa? The Early Imaging of Malinche," in *CAE*; Restall, *Seven Myths*, 86; Wood, *Transcending Conquest*, 33–34.

23. On the Huamantla Codex, see John Glass and Donald Robertson, "A Census of Native Middle American Pictorial Manuscripts," in *Handbook of Middle American Indians: Guide to Ethnohistorical Sources,* ed. Howard F. Cline (Austin: University of Texas Press, 1975), 14:133–34; and Brotherston, *Painted Books*, 36. There are nine existing fragments of the whole. Scholars do not know if the piece dates from midcentury or later. If later, it still comes from a relatively isolated location less subject to the influences of Spanish artists than certain urban locations were, and so it is treated here as an early text.

24. Brotherston comments on this *mapa* in both his relevant works as does Wood (see note 22, chapter 3). The original is in the American Museum of Natural History.

25. The most detailed study of the different versions of the lienzo is Travis Barton Kranz, "The Tlaxcalan Conquest Pictorials: The Role of Images in Influencing Colonial Policy in Sixteenth-Century Mexico" (PhD diss., University of California–Los Angeles, 2001). Kranz places each version in its proper political context.

26. The original—usually referred as the "Texas fragment"—is housed in the Nettie Lee Benson Collection of the University of Texas at Austin.

27. Kranz in "The Tlaxcalan Conquest Pictorials" points out that the goods in this scene have traditionally been interpreted purely as tribute and posits that they were in fact gifts, in that this codex represents negotiations between equals. I would only add that the two categories were not mutually exclusive: exchanges of goods were always embedded in complicated and shifting power relationships. In the same way, a royal daughter might be given away "voluntarily" by an altepetl who would otherwise lose a war, and she might find herself more a hostage than a bride.

28. Much ink has been spilled over the question of whether the women offered were mere slaves or princesses who went with some retainers. The confusion began early on. Diego Muñoz Camargo, the famous mestizo historian of Tlaxcala, insisted—probably based on wishful thinking—that the native lords would only have given up slave girls immediately after the defeat but then a few pages later acknowledges that several highborn ladies were married to Spaniards. Muñoz Camargo, *Historia de Tlaxcala*, 190–91. An indigenous historian who wrote in Spanish, Fernando de Alva Ixtlilxochitl, mentioned that the noble daughters went with "mothers" and servants to be their retainers, and some have taken this statement literally. See his *Obras históricas*, ed. Edmundo O'Gorman (Mexico City: UNAM, 1997), 214. The Tlaxcalan lords, however, would never have sent their wives with the Spanish. If someone told Ixtlilxochitl that "mothers" went along, and if they spoke the truth, they meant old palace servant women, usually former concubines, who were often called by that term. These, however, would never have been considered important enough to merit inclusion in the painted record of events. The common women in the third category in the painting would simply indicate that a given number of anonymous slaves were transferred to the Spanish for their use.

29. In a note to his edition of Muñoz Camargo's *Historia de Tlaxcala*, 191, Reyes aptly points out that the name that actually appears, "Tecuilhuatzin," could not be correct. The writer had to have meant "Tlecuilhuatzin" or perhaps even "Tecuhcihuatzin," which means literally "female noblewoman of the chiefly line" and would certainly have been the title of the leading princess offered to the Spanish. Doña Luisa, as she was called in Spanish, has been written about on several occasions, most recently in Mercedes Meade de Angulo, *Doña Luisa Teohquilhuastzin, hija de Xicoténcatl, señor de Tizatlán* (Tlaxcala: Gobierno del Estado de Tlaxcala, 1994). For Bernal Díaz's memory as to which Spanish men received the women, see BD, 178.

30. Pedro Carrasco, "Indian-Spanish Marriages in the First Century of the Colony," in *IWEM*, 95. Juan Pérez legitimized his mestizo children, but after his death

they still had to fight to defend their inheritance against a Spanish woman whom he had legally married.

31. A lienzo with one large scene and eighty-seven smaller scenes hung in the municipal building in Tlaxcala until the nineteenth century but was removed by the French during their occupation and never saw the light again. Fortunately, two copies were made before it disappeared—one freehand copy in the late eighteenth century that is now in the national museum in Mexico, and another nineteenth-century tracing that has since disappeared but was first used to produce lithographs that were published. They form the basis of the best edition available today: Josefina García Quintana and Carlos Martínez Marín, eds., *El lienzo de Tlaxcala* (Mexico: Cartón y Papel de México, 1983). The plate referred to in this paragraph is number 7.

32. See H. B. Nicholson, "A Royal Headband of the Tlaxcalteca," *Revista Mexicana de Estudios Antropológicos* 21 (1967): 71–106. Kranz in "The Tlaxcalan Conquest Pictorials" points out that the red-and-white symbol for Tlaxcala might well be a postconquest invention: those colors were most likely the insignia for the Xicotencatl lineage alone before the conquest (211–12). In plate 19 of *El lienzo* Marina appears with an unidentified woman who is almost certainly doña Luisa, as the scene comes just after the noche triste; the latter's having survived was crucial to the Spaniards' ability to return to Tlaxcala and ask for more help.

33. Brotherston in *Painted Books* and Kranz in "Tlaxcalan Conquest Pictorials" both develop this point.

34. Don Fernando de Alva Ixtlilxochitl, writing in Spanish, inserted "por lengua de Marina" with great frequency when alluding to interactions between Cortés and the indigenous. Chimalpahin annotated Gómara (Susan Schroeder, personal communication).

35. Bierhorst, *History and Mythology,* 126–27, and *Codex Chimalpopoca,* 77. This text is a set of annals from Cuauhtitlan, but it is clear that the author drew on a variety of sources. The mountain called Matlalcueye was still known by its original name among Indians in seventeenth-century Tlaxcala. See Don Juan Buenaventura Zapata y Mendoza, *Historia cronológica de la noble ciudad de Tlaxcala*, ed. Luis Reyes García and Andrea Martínez Baracs (Tlaxcala: Universidad Autónoma de Tlaxcala, 1995).

36. Karttunen, "Rethinking Malinche," in *IWEM*, 293–95; and Max Harris, "Moctezuma's Daughter: The Role of la Malinche in Mesoamerican Dance," *Journal of American Folklore* 109 (1996): 149–77. Susan Gillespie, *The Aztec Kings*, treats the theme of legitimizing female consorts in depth.

37. For the material in the Annals of Tlatelolco, see the facsimile edition Mengin, *Unos anales históricos,* 53–56. On that set of annals probably dating to the 1540s, see WPH, 38–42. In the pictorial fragment, the woman could be Tecuichpotzin, or some other altepetl's leading noblewoman who had been given the same Christian name. The other clues in the picture are somewhat ambiguous. See Glass and Robertson, "A Census of Native Middle American Pictorial Manuscripts," 14:183, fig. 51. "Doña Isabel" also appears in a wartime lament as a woman who

has been seized from Cuauhtemoc and is now "at the side of Cortés," implicitly as a captive wife; in that context, she does not have Malintzin's usual role of speaker and honored consort. Indeed, the character of Malintzin is given a separate role in the words of the same song. See John Bierhorst, ed., *Cantares Mexicanos: Songs of the Aztecs* (Stanford, CA: Stanford University Press, 1985), 322, 424.

38. See Carochi, *Grammar of the Mexican Language*, as cited in note 1, chapter 3, for an example of the two names being interchangeable. Teresa Rojas, ed., *Padrones de Tlaxcala del siglo XVI* (Mexico City: Centro de Investigaciones y Estudios Superiores en Antropología Social, 1987), 160.

39. Burkhart, *Before Guadalupe,* 4.

40. "Doctrina, evangelios y epístolas en nahuatl," late sixteenth century, found and translated by Burkhart, *Before Guadalupe*, 33.

41. For the first, see "Atequilizcuicatl," in Bierhorst, *Cantares Mexicanos*, 329. For a discussion of the translation, see chapter 5. For the second see "Tlaxcatecayotl," in Bierhorst, *Cantares Mexicanos*, 318. The line is as follows: "çan conilhuia in capitan ya o tonã ye malintzin y[n] xacaltecoz acachinanco." A more accurate translation than Bierhorst's appears in James Lockhart, "Care, Ingenuity, and Irresponsibility: The Bierhorst Edition of the Cantares Mexicanos," *Reviews in Anthropology* 16 (1991): 129. As Lockhart has pointed out to me, the *tonã* could easily have been an early effort to represent the title "doña." (The *d* sound was often replaced with *t* before Nahuas became more familiar with Spanish.) Doña Isabel, for example, was called *toya yxapeltzin* and *doyan yxapeltzin* in the same text. On the other hand, inserting *ye* between title and name would have been unusual. In the *Cantares,* the Virgin is usually referred to as Santa María or Malía or as *tonantzin*, but they do also use the simpler *tonan* on several occasions (Bierhorst, *Cantares Mexicanos*, 148, 220, 404). So it is possible either that the reference to the figurative character of Malintzin did refer to "our mother," or else that it dated from a time before the use of the term "doña" was exactly clear to the indigenous. Of course, by the time the songs were written down in the second half of the sixteenth century, the men doing the writing, who worked closely with priests, were well aware of exactly who they meant when they referred to the Virgin Mary or to doña Marina or to a particularly important female progenitor. *They* were not blurring identities or mixing metaphors. But they may have been recording an older oral tradition that did so.

42. HC, "Second Letter," 69.

43. Ibid., 73.

44. "The Chronicle of Andrés de Tapia," in Fuentes, *The Conquistadors*, 36.

45. Gómara simply repeated Cortés's story, but Bernal Díaz, of course, embellished it dramatically. Marina "burst into the room" to tell the Spanish what she had learned. Ross Hassig offers a masterful deconstruction of this legend in "The Maid of the Myth: La Malinche and the History of Mexico," *Indiana Journal of Hispanic Literatures* 12 (1998): 101–33.

46. BD, 214. On the tales of Amadís, see chapter 1, note 24.

47. BD, 215.

Four

1. HC, "Second Letter," 84–85. Numerous scholars have analyzed the scene on the causeway. Two of the best treatments are Restall, *Seven Myths*, 95–99, and Inga Clendinnen, "'Fierce and Unnatural Cruelty': Cortés and the Conquest of Mexico," *Representations* 33 (1991): 65–100.
2. Frances Karttunen was the first to note this discrepancy in speaking styles in her assessment of the scene in the Florentine Codex in "Rethinking Malinche," in *IWEM*.
3. J. H. Elliott, "Cortés, Velázquez, and Charles V," introduction to HC, xviii–xxviii. Elliott's essay on this topic is a tour de force, building, as he himself says, on the work of a previous generation of scholars.
4. HC, "Second Letter," 85–86. Cortés's letter was published in Europe not long after its appearance, but his story only made its way into book form with the appearance of Francisco López de Gómara's *Historia de la conquista de México,* which appeared in Zaragoza in 1552.
5. Restall, *Seven Myths*, 97–98. The quotation from the Florentine is in *WPH*, 116.
6. HC, "Second Letter," 86.
7. BD, 224.
8. Florentine Codex in *WPH*, 94; BD, 222; DD, 503–6.
9. Florentine Codex in *WPH*, 106.
10. Clendinnen, "'Fierce and Unnatural Cruelty,'" and Hassig, *Mexico and the Spanish Conquest*, 77.
11. FLG, 134; BD, 205.
12. The exact words were: "pensando que los cristianos se irán de aquí." Interrogation of Francisco Serrantes by Lucas Vázquez de Ayllón, San Juan de Ulúa, 23 April 1520, in Camilo Polavieja, ed., *Hernán Cortés: Copias de documentos existents en el archivo de Indias en su Palacio de Castilleja de la Cuesta sobre la conquista de Méjico* (Seville, 1889), 127–31.
13. HC, "Second Letter," 103–4.
14. Ibid., 105.
15. Francis Brooks wrote a pathbreaking article on this topic, "Motecuzoma Xocoyotl, Hernán Cortés, and Bernal Díaz del Castillo: The Construction of an Arrest," *Hispanic American Historical Review* 75 (1995). The quotation of Gómara is in FLG, 187.
16. HC, "Second Letter," 107; BD, 276.
17. "The Chronicle of Fray Francisco de Aguilar," in Fuentes, *The Conquistadors*, 148; "The Chronicle of Andrés de Tapia," in Fuentes, *The Conquistadors*, 39, 44. Motolinia is the priest who omits the discussion of the topic in *Historia de los indios.* Witnesses in the 1529 residencia against Pedro de Alvarado detail events surrounding the later abduction of Cacamatzin of Tetzcoco and obfuscate the situation regarding Moctezuma himself. See Ignacio López Rayón, ed., *Proceso de residencia instruido contra Pedro de Alvarado y Nuño de Guzmán* (Mexico:

Valdes y Redondas, 1847). The residencia against Cortés is useless in this regard, in that it focuses on his political battles with other Spaniards.

18. See Book Twelve of the Florentine Codex and the Annals of Tlatelolco in *WPH*, 120 and 257, respectively. Diego Durán comments on varying indigenous interpretations of the events in DD, 530–31. For a scholarly treatment of the great variety of sixteenth-century indigenous pictorials, see Juan José Batalla Rosado, "Prisión y muerte de Motecuhzoma, según el relato de los codices mesoamericanos," *Revista Española de Antropología Americana* 26 (1996): 101–20.

19. Frances Karttunen and James Lockhart, *The Art of Nahuatl Speech: The Bancroft Dialogues* (Los Angeles: UCLA Latin American Center Publications, 1987), 143. A set of polite speeches were written down in Tetzcoco in the second half of the sixteenth century and later most probably edited by Jesuits working with Horacio Carochi. In this utterance, a young boy is speaking to an elderly noblewoman. Donald Chipman has summarized the story of Tecuichpotzin's life in "Isabel Moctezuma: Pioneer of Mestizaje," in *Struggle and Survival in Colonial America,* ed. David Sweet and Gary Nash (Berkeley: University of California Press, 1981). Chipman now has a more complete study, *Moctezuma's Children: Aztec Royalty under Spanish Rule, 1520–1700* (Austin: University of Texas Press, 2005). The chroniclers mention Moctezuma's having wanted to marry a well-born daughter to Cortés. See BD, 276.

20. HC, "Second Letter," 94–95. Francisco Serrantes also made extravagant claims for the area in his 1520 statement published in Polavieja, *Hernán Cortés.*

21. Hernando Cortés, Bernal Díaz, and Andrés de Tapia all mention hearing of this through Moctezuma's informants. It is the latter who mentions the pictorial record. Only Cortés pretended that he learned of it first on his own, from Spanish messengers.

22. The paperwork produced by Diego Velázquez was voluminous. The original statement by the witness who visited the ship is in AGI, Patronato 180, R. 1, "Petición de Gonzalo Guzman ante Diego Velázquez," Santiago de Cuba, 7 October 1519. Velázquez put his "spin" on events as described here in his letter to the royal representative licenciado Rodrigo de Figueroa, Santiago de Cuba, 17 November 1519, reproduced in *DHM*, 1:401.

23. Journal of Albrecht Dürer, quoted in Benjamin Keen, *The Aztec Image in Western Thought* (New Brunswick, NJ: Rutgers University Press, 1971), 69. Others, such as Peter Martyr, were equally impressed. The letter from Seville is quoted in what is still the best work on the early dissemination of news about Mexico: Marshall Saville, "The Earliest Notices Concerning the Conquest of Mexico by Cortés in 1519," in *Indian Notes and Monographs* 9, no. 1 (New York: Heye Foundation, 1920), 38.

24. "La tardanza se podría seguir daño e detrimentos a la dicha villa e vecinos de ella por falta de los dichos bastimientos e provisiones." Memorial presentado al Real Consejo por Martín Cortés, en nombre de su hijo, March 1520, in *DHC*, 4.

25. Contrast HC, "Second Letter," 119, with FLG, 188–89. The discrepancy is notable, for Gómara was generally a rather sycophantic and certainly a credulous biographer.

26. Brooks in "Construction of an Arrest" makes a strong case for this point. It is he who notes that Diego Durán's informant mentioned eighty days.

27. DD, 530–31. Compare the "Chronicle of Francisco de Aguilar" in Fuentes, *The Conquistadors.*

28. Francisco Serrantes in Polavieja, *Hernán Cortés.*

29. Numerous historians have detailed the power struggle that occurred between Cortés and Narváez, drawing from the chronicles of Cortés, Andrés de Tapia, and Bernal Díaz, as well as sworn statements made by Cortés's followers after they were later ejected from Mexico City and the 1529 investigations into the conduct of Cortés and Pedro de Alvarado. In the following paragraphs I include only what I consider to be incontrovertible, after careful assessment of the sources, and I reject much that is normally accepted at face value. Cortés's men, for example, insisted that Moctezuma and Narváez had secret and very detailed communications concerning Cortés's tenuous legal position, and that Narváez was thus a prime instigator of the noche triste. But for this to have been the case, a translator who was even more adept than Malintzin would have had to be present in Narváez's camp, and other events indicate that this was clearly not the case. When they made their sworn statements, Cortés's men were eager to believe that there had been such communications, for they wanted to have someone other than themselves to blame for the disaster that had since occurred, and they wanted to be sure that no one would blame them for fighting Narváez.

30. AGI, Patronato 180, R. 2, Jerónimo de Aguilar, witness in "Petición de los oficiales de Sus Altezas contra Diego Velázquez e Pánfilo de Narbáes," 4 September 1520, fol. 15v. HC, "Second Letter," 128. In matters like this one, we can take our sources' statements as reflective of the truth. However, both these statements were made before a final Spanish victory had occurred, and so both speakers hid the reality that "the messengers" were Tlaxcalan Indians rather than Spaniards. Common sense tells us that it must have been so, and the commonsense view is corroborated by later Spanish accounts, such as that of Bernal Díaz.

31. HC, "Second Letter," 128–29.

32. Ibid., 130–31.

33. The later investigation into Pedro de Alvarado's conduct, though full of inconsistencies and obviously false statements given by Spaniards who wished to justify their own behavior, does provide an overview of the events and certainly conveys the mounting tensions experienced by the Spanish. We see a range of witnesses in López Rayón, *Proceso de residencia.* The Florentine Codex offers some corroboration, in that it is clear that resentments on the part of the indigenous were indeed percolating, and "witch hunts" against those who worked for the Spanish did begin to occur. See *WPH*, 142.

34. Florentine Codex in *WPH*, 132–34.

35. Ibid., 142.

36. HC, "Second Letter," 134–35.

37. Florentine Codex in *WPH*, 138–39. I am necessarily suspicious that the Nahuas may have included the story of this speech because it was very important to the Spanish who supervised their work on the codex to believe that Moctezuma had

made it. On the other hand, the details they give—the time of day, the exact spokesperson he used, etc.—render it believable. He probably did say something to this effect at some point.

38. Annals of Tlatelolco in *WPH*, 259.

39. Ibid., 265.

40. "Texcoca Accounts of Conquest Episodes," in *Codex Chimalpahin*, ed. Arthur J. O. Anderson and Susan Schroeder (Norman: University of Oklahoma Press, 1997), 2:187, 193. Other less direct evidence that Malintzin was associated with this school of thought is found in the Annals of Cuauhtitlan. There, a skull rack lord bears her name, and the skull rack lords were known for having prophesied to Moctezuma that he could not resist the strangers without inviting destruction. See Bierhorst, *History and Mythology*, 124–27.

41. AGI, Patronato 56, N. 3, R. 4, "Méritos y Servicios, Marina, 1542," Francisco Maldonado, fol. 34r; Comendador Leonel de Cervantes, fol. 41. Their words were: "Ella por sí tenía mucha sabieza e manera con los naturales, para hacerles entender queran los españoles gran cosa e bastantes para aunque se xuntase todo el mundo contra ellos, no eran parte para les dañar," and "La dicha doña marina hablaba con los yndios sin estar el marques presente e les hazia venir de paz." In another case, other witnesses said similar things: AGI, Justicia 168, "Auto entre partes," fols. 964v–966.

42. Juan de Mansilla mentioned the captain's having had sex with "doña Francisca" right before the flight in the 1529 residencia against Cortés. See *AM*, 1:264. Of course, many men were adding random accusations at that point, but the details he mentioned make the story ring true. Bernal Díaz mentioned the behavior of Narváez's men as "crazed and uncontrolled" in their great rage at having been led into this situation, in BD, 293.

43. AGI, Patronato 56, N. 3, R. 4, "Méritos y Servicios, Marina, 1542," Gonzalo Rodríguez de Ocaño, fol. 19v; Anton Brabo, fol. 33; Diego Hernandez, fol. 38. Jerónimo de Aguilar, like many others, attacked Cortés in the 1529 residencia against him; he was the only one who seemed to feel that Cortés's many sins tarred Marina as well. On the innuendos concerning his interest in Malintzin, see Justicia 168, "Auto entre partes," fols. 1065, 1082.

44. Numerous Spanish documents refer to the events of that night. Two collections of statements prepared under Cortés's supervision not long afterward are published in G. R. G. Conway, ed., *La noche triste, documentos: Segura de la frontera en Nueva España, año de MDXX* (Mexico City: Antigua Librería Robredo, 1943). The quotation of the indigenous is from the Florentine Codex in *WPH*, 156.

45. BD, 299. Fray Juan Díaz made a disgusted comment about this subject in the residencia against Pedro de Alvarado. "Nobody at that moment had any care other than saving himself." See López Rayón, *Proceso de residencia*, 127. The comments about the drowned women appear in Cristóbal del Castillo, *Historia de la venida de los mexicanos e historia de la conquista,* ed., Federico Navarrette Linares (Mexico City: Instituto Nacional de Antropología e Historia, 1991), 183–84. I quote: "huel no miequintin iz cihua oncan omicque in inmecahuan,

in cihuapilhuan españoles huel moch quaqualtin qualnezque ixtilmatique cihua oncan omicque huel mochtin ic tenque, huel ic tzoneuh in Tolteca acalotli."

46. BD, 302. The story about the captain's asking for Martín López may be apocryphal, in that it was mentioned by López himself in his request for the granting of a coat of arms; he did have several witnesses, however, and it is certainly true that Cortés was dependent on the shipbuilder's skills. See Porrua Muñoz, "Martín López," *Revista de Indias* (1948), cited in Hugh Thomas, *Conquest: Montezuma, Cortés, and the Fall of Old Mexico* (New York: Simon & Schuster, 1993), 735. López later had to take Cortés to court to receive what he saw as his due. The documents of that case are housed at the Library of Congress, Manuscripts Division.

Five

1. The Florentine Codex in *WPH*, 176–82.
2. The literature on the importance of disease in the conquest of the New World is extensive. The subject was ignored for generations, until the middle of the twentieth century, when such scholars as Woodrow Borah and Sherburne Cooke first forced the reading public to focus attention on the population holocaust that occurred. A classic text emerging as a result of that period, which all students should read, is Alfred Crosby, *The Columbian Exchange: Biological and Cultural Consequences of 1492* (Westport, CT: Greenwood Press, 1972). Recently, Noble David Cook drew together myriad studies of particular regions in the Americas to create one overarching compendium, *Born to Die: Disease and New World Conquest, 1492–1650* (Cambridge: Cambridge University Press, 1998). Some historians persist in arguing that accounts of the spread of disease are exaggerated, but in my opinion, such historians are simply wrong. A better informed but still critical approach has been taken by Suzanne Austin Alchon in *A Pest in the Land: New World Epidemics in a Global Perspective* (Albuquerque: University of New Mexico Press, 2003). Alchon points out, as do scientists, that epidemics have wrought havoc in human populations for many centuries and in many places. The New World was not unique in this regard, though the "virgin soil" population was larger than elsewhere, because of the people's previous isolation from Old World diseases. Studying world history shows us that on its own, drastic population loss is never enough to decimate people and their cultures beyond repair. It was other aspects of the European presence in the New World that began to erode the lifestyles of the Native Americans in a permanent sense. Approaching the same theme from another angle, Diamond reminds us in *Guns, Germs, and Steel* that germs were part and parcel of the Old World technological complex that had been evolving for millennia and should not be isolated as a factor in the conquest. Furthermore, we must remember that the Spaniards' allies were hit as hard by the microbes as were their enemies: it is illogical to assume that the Mexica were somehow incapacitated by disease but that the Tlaxcalans, for example, were not. For all these reasons, it is clear that we must take disease into account without letting it overwhelm the narrative.

3. Zapata y Mendoza, *Historia cronológica*, 132–33. Don Juan Zapata's annals, composed in the seventeenth century, were far more detailed than most and drew from a variety of Nahuatl sources. His is the only set of extant Tlaxcala annals to mention building the ships. Other shorter annals mention only the pox. It should be noted that the entries for 1521 do mention the Spanish, and more particularly, the final defeat of the Mexica.

4. HC, "Second Letter," 140–41. The Florentine Codex also describes the efforts the Mexica warriors made to keep up the attack on their retreating enemy.

5. The later Tlaxcalan annalists do not mention their forebears' divided opinions. If they knew about it—which is doubtful—they surely felt that the least said on that subject, the better, as they were anxious to defend the political rights they had won as loyal allies. We know that the Tlaxcalans took some time to reach consensus from the Spaniards themselves. The gist of their argument we can deduce from the context and their actions.

6. HC, "Second Letter," 154–58, "Third Letter," 181.

7. HC, "Second Letter," 131, "Third Letter," 218.

8. Two of the newly arrived ships had been sent from the Caribbean to aid Narváez, and four more were part of an independently organized venture from Jamaica. Francisco de Aguilar in Fuentes, *The Conquistadors*, 157. HC, "Third Letter," 182. See also HC, 147–48, 164–65, 191–92.

9. A version of the story is in the Annals of Tlatelolco. HC, "Third Letter," 207, 221, 247.

10. Florentine Codex in *WPH*, 186. The Annals of Tlatelolco tell a story in many respects similar to that of the Florentine. In the following pages I quote almost entirely from the Florentine merely because of the greater beauty of the language and greater detail.

11. Florentine Codex in *WPH*, 216. Inga Clendinnen has commented on the scorn the Mexica warriors seemed to feel for the Spanish with their terror of sacrifice and other characteristics that struck them as pathetic. See her "'Fierce and Unnatural Cruelty,'" 65–100.

12. Florentine Codex in *WPH*, 218.

13. Ibid., 146.

14. Ibid., 224. Hassig has analyzed the arms capabilities of both sides in depth in *Mexico and the Spanish Conquest*, 121–33.

15. HC, "Third Letter," 257.

16. Florentine Codex in *WPH*, 230.

17. Ibid., 80, 90, 96, 110.

18. The stories of arrows with wills of their own come from an extant document from Tlaxcala, not Tenochtitlan, but this trope was widespread. See an ancient fragment included in Zapata y Mendoza, *Historia cronológica,* 84–85, and Paul Kirchoff, Lina Odena Guemes, and Luis Reyes García, eds., *Historia tolteca chichimeca* (Mexico City: INAH, 1976), 174.

19. Florentine Codex in *WPH*, 74, 86, 98, 116.

20. HC, "Third Letter," 246.

21. Ibid., 259, 263–64. See also Florentine Codex in *WPH*, 244 and the Annals

of Tlatelolco in *WPH*, 269. On the Spaniards' reaction to the Mexica warriors' unwillingness to sue for peace, see Clendinnen, "'Fierce and Unnatural Cruelty.'"

22. Florentine in *WPH*, 246–49. The Spanish chroniclers also refer to the starved and wretched state of the city's people, and to their exodus.

23. BD, 409.

24. Florentine in *WPH*, 252–54. It is not simply common sense that tells us the Mexica considered Malintzin integral to any successful negotiations with the Spanish. We have more direct evidence. In a later court case, Spanish witnesses said that in the period of crisis, the Indians would deal with no other translator. See AGI, Justicia 168, "Auto entre partes," fol. 986v.

25. Brotherston, "La Malintzin en los codices," 17; and Davíd Carrasco, *City of Sacrifice: The Aztec Empire and the Role of Violence in Civilization* (Boston: Beacon Press, 1999), 222. We cannot be sure that the innuendo is there, but it is definitely true that in modern Nahuatl-speaking villages, references to a woman's skirt are considered very suggestive.

26. Malintzin's role in the "Manuscrito del Aperreamiento" (Savaging-Dog Manuscript), as it has come to be called, is analyzed by Brotherston in *Painted Books*, 35.

27. *Atequilizcuicatl* or "Water-Pouring Song" in Bierhorst, *Cantares Mexicanos,* 326–41. I do not agree with Bierhorst's translation in numerous places, and there are certain segments of the song that I do not believe we can translate at all; however, Bierhorst does largely convey the gist of the piece. He misses the parallels with the Florentine Codex, even including mention of the comet omen, which appears nowhere else; this theme deserves to be developed elsewhere. The lines concerning Malintzin are as follows: "Yye hualtzatzia in Malia teucçihuatl quihualihtoa in Malia, Mexicah, ma hualcalaqui in amopololtzin ma ontlamemelo teteuctin." Here, the lords are being instructed to give the orders to others, but in several other places it is they themselves who must do the work. The example I have directly quoted is as follows: "onateca in Mexico in tépilhuã." "In Mexico, princes pour out water."

28. Florentine Codex in *WPH*, 222.

Six

1. Licenciado Alonso Suazo al Padre Fray Luis de Figueroa, 21 November 1521, in *DHM*, 1:358–67.

2. Other indigenous were well aware of what was occurring. See the Annals of Tlatelolco in *WPH*, 271–73. This was a text produced in the 1540s at the earliest, but it may have been based on some sort of statement made in the 1520s. What it says on the subject of the torture inflicted is corroborated in other sources, both Spanish and indigenous.

3. "Registro del Oro, Joyas y Otras Cosas que ha de ir a España en el navio Santa María de la Rábida, año de 1522"; "Traslado de lo que hasta el presente ha pertenecido a Su Magestad, del quinto y otros derechos, año de 1522"; "Memoria

de los Plumajes e Joyas que se envían a España para dar y repartir a las iglesias e monasterios siguientes"; and "Memoria de Piezas, Joyas y Plumajes enviados para Su Majestad desde la Nueva España, y Que Quedaron en los Azores en poder de Alonso Dávila," in AGI, Patronato 180, R. 83–R. 90. That the enslavement of random groups of indigenous continued is made manifest in the letter of Contador Rodrigo de Albornoz to Emperor Charles V, 15 December 1525, in *DHM*, vol. 1.

4. Florentine Codex in *WPH*, 248. López Rayón, *Proceso de residencia*, 70. AGI, Patronato 180, R. 4, "Instrucciones de Carlos V a Hernando Cortés sobre Tratamiento de los Indios, Valladolid, 26 junio 1523."

5. Annals of Tlatelolco in *WPH*, 273.

6. "Unsigned Nahuatl Materials and a Letter by Juan de San Antonio of Tetzcoco," in Anderson and Schroeder, *Codex Chimalpahin*, 2:196–97.

7. Ibid., 196–97. The story of the royal lines of Tetzcoco is gleaned from many Spanish chronicles and indigenous annals. The sources contradict each other as to details; one source's hero is another source's villain, and the Spanish often did not understand the import of what they had been told and mangled the narrative. But the fratricidal rivalries and their origins come through clearly enough. I am currently involved in a separate study of this subject.

8. Ibid., 198–99. They could have been referring to a young Italian boy, Tomás de Rigioles, who was learning Nahuatl at the time, but in the more usual scenario, local indigenous boys began to learn Spanish.

9. Ibid., 194–95.

10. Fernando Benítez, *The Century after Cortés* (Chicago: University of Chicago Press, 1965), 2. See also pp. 7–11. Cortés's son by his second wife later sued the municipality, insisting that his father had claimed the palace that bordered the square that was by then known as the Zócalo, and that the space was thus rightfully his.

11. Annals of Tlatelolco in *WPH*, 272–73.

12. For indigenous perceptions of Coyoacan contrasted with those of Spaniards, see Rebecca Horn, *Post-Conquest Coyoacan: Nahua Spanish Relations in Central Mexico, 1519–1650* (Stanford, CA: Stanford University Press, 1997), 4–11. The author analyzes a detail of the "Map of the Valley of Mexico Attributed to Alonso de Santa Cruz" (ca. 1550) housed by the University of Uppsala, Sweden.

13. Many of the proceedings of the 1529 residencia taken against Cortés, consisting of hundreds of pages, were published in *AM*. Aguilar's testimony appears in 2:198–99 and should be read in the context of other witnesses' statements. For the response, see "Descargos dados por García de Llerena en nombre de Hernando Cortés a los cargos hechos a éste," in *DII*, 27:238–39. Sharisse and Geoffrey McCafferty analyze the information about women marketers provided in the Florentine Codex in "Powerful Women and the Myth of Male Dominance," *Archaeological Review from Cambridge* 7 (1988): 48.

14. AGI, Justicia 168, "Auto entre partes," fols. 1065, 1082. Such cases are full of random, unsubstantiated accusations, but in this case, various witnesses mentioned the matter, without having been asked about it, both in 1551 and ca. 1560.

15. Diego de Ordás a Francisco Verdugo, Madrid, 2 June 1530, in Enrique Otte, "Nueve cartas de Diego de Ordás," *Historia mexicana* 14, no. 54 (1964): 328.
16. Numerous witnesses in the residencia, in *AM*, 1:62, 99, 123, 159, 202, 443.
17. Jerónimo de Aguilar and Catalina González in *AM*, 2:196, 309.
18. Catalina has had her own biographer. See Francisco Fernández del Castillo, *Doña Catalina Xuarez Marcayda* (Mexico City: Editorial Cosmos, 1980).
19. In 1529, when Cortés's position in Mexico was vulnerable, due to the residencia, doña Catalina's mother brought suit against her former son-in-law. The witnesses were thus speaking of their memories of events that occurred seven years earlier, and there are variations in their stories. Most of the proceedings were published in *AM*, vol. 2. See especially pages 353, 366, 372.
20. AGI, Patronato 56, N. 3, R. 4, "Méritos y Servicios, Marina," testimony of Pedro de Meneses, fol. 36. Other witnesses mentioned her having had encomienda tribute delivered to her at this time but were unclear about where it was coming from. Meneses is likely to have had his story straight, for he mentioned that the two altepetls were soon turned over to Sebastián Moscoso, which is true. See Himmerich y Valencia, *Encomenderos of New Spain*, 200–201. Don Diego de Atempanecatl called himself her criado (then and afterward) in AGI, Justicia 168, "Auto entre partes," pt. 8. See chapters 7 and 8 for more discussion of this figure.
21. See Restall, *Seven Myths*, 83.
22. "In otztli in ie quimati iiti, in mitoa oacico in imiquizpan." See *FC*, 6:167.
23. *FC*, 6:160. On women's dying in childbirth and becoming *mocihuaquetzque,* see 161–65.
24. Ibid., 6:167. Several scholars have commented on the diving god's association with birth in certain cultures in Mexico. See, for example, Susan Milbrath, "Birth Images in Mixteca-Puebla Art," in *The Role of Gender in Precolumbian Art and Architecture*, ed. Virginia Miller (Boston: University Press of America, 1988). Malintzin was from the isthmus, home of the ancient Olmecs, many of whose giant carvings represent gods diving headfirst out of caves.
25. There is extensive evidence for the envisioning of children this way—and for the praise heaped upon their mothers—among the Nahuas in general, not just among the dominant Mexica. See not only *FC*, 6:179–89, but also Karttunen and Lockhart, *The Art of Nahuatl Speech*, 109–29. Sixteenth-century wills and testaments convey the same sense.
26. *FC*, 6:169.
27. Bernal Díaz tells us what little we know about the boy Orteguilla. Charles Dibble researched the life of Alonso de Molina, creator of the dictionary. See his "Molina and Sahagún," in *Smoke and Mist: Mesoamerican Studies in Memory of Thelma D. Sullivan*, ed. Kathryn Josserand and Karen Daken (Oxford: British Archaeological Reports, 1988), 1:69–76. Himmerich summarizes what is known about Juan Pérez de Arteaga in *Encomenderos*, 215.
28. AGN, Hospital de Jesús, L. 446, E. 4, "Carta de Carlos V a Hernando Cortés, 4 de noviembre de 1525," fol. 620. Of the criticism leveled against him the monarch wrote, "Se debe pensar que los que lo escriben e dicen es con alguna pasión o envidia."

29. "Ordenanzas de Buen Gobierno Dadas Por Hernando Cortés, 20 marzo de 1524," in *DII*, 26:135–45.

30. Much of what scholars know about the earliest Franciscan efforts comes from the enthusiastic writings of fray Toríbio de Benavente or Motolinia, meaning "Poor Suffering One," who was one of the original twelve. His statements must be taken with a grain of salt, as he was anxious to demonstrate that the Spanish had accomplished a great deal. He is probably most useful regarding the first two to three years, as he was not interested in masking how difficult the mission work had been at that time, although he was very invested in covering up problems in later years. See his *Historia de los indios.* Scholars have analyzed his work from the perspective both of the history of education and of the history of religion. On the first subject, see Pilar Gonzalbo Aizpuru, *Historia de la educación en la época colonial: El mundo indígena* (Mexico City: El Colegio de México, 1990). The second subject touches on an extensive literature. In the 1930s, the French scholar Robert Ricard coined the phrase "spiritual conquest of Mexico," and the notion endured for many years. Today, however, scholars have largely abandoned the idea that Motolinia can be taken at face value, and that the Indians changed their worldview almost overnight. See Lockhart, *The Nahuas*, and Burkhart, *Slippery Earth.*

31. Motolinia later wrote extensively about his experiences in Mexico, and he did not mention the summit. Or at least he did not do so directly. One could argue, however, that he referred to the event—or to events of that kind—unwillingly and indirectly. According to the surviving notes, the meeting was a fiasco from the Spanish point of view, as aging political figures and priests essentially told the newcomers to mind their own business and let their people worship as they chose. In one of his books, Motolinia mentioned, almost despite himself, that very early on, elderly leaders who were accustomed to having their own way in everything stubbornly refused to hear the truth. God solved the problem, he added contentedly, by sending diseases to kill them off, leaving more flexible young people to fill their shoes (*Historia de los indios*, 66). The existing notes on the colloquy are so detailed as to make it unlikely that they were entirely the figment of someone's imagination. There was, however, no one in the world in 1524 who could possibly have taken notes in Nahuatl. Yet as scholars have observed, someone could have taken notes in Spanish, based on what a translator said. And the famous fray Bernardino de Sahagún could easily have translated the notes back into Nahuatl as a sort of exercise, the like of which he loved to do. The work seems to bear his imprint. Leading scholars agree that the text that has come to be known as the Coloquios is certainly accurate in spirit, reflective of what generally went on: the Spanish did not encourage dialogue, but simply began to preach, expecting to be listened to, and the Nahuas, for their part, were perfectly willing to add the Christian god to their pantheon, but bridled when they were told they must discard everything they had ever believed in before. Then, too, there was a social and political element in what was purportedly said on both sides that was missing from religious texts produced in the 1540s and onward; thus the text is unlikely to have been a pure fabrication from the later

period. Of course, the notes with which someone worked later in the century were probably taken at more than one event in the early years. See Lockhart, *The Nahuas*, 205–6, and Jorge Klor de Alva, "La historicidad de los coloquios de Sahagún," *Estudios de Cultura Náhuatl* 15 (1982): 147–84. John F. Schwaller has studied the hand of Sahagún at work, noting the extraordinary similarity between the opening lines of the Nahuatl version of the Coloquios, those of another work definitely attributed to him, and the Tenochca creation myth as it was recorded elsewhere. John F. Schwaller, "Conversion and Creation: Two Events and One Model in the Works of fray Bernardino de Sahagún" (paper presented at the American Historical Association, San Francisco, January 2002).

32. See Motolinia, *Historia de los indios*, 276; and "Fray Toribio Motolinia al Emperador Carlos V, Tlaxcala, 2 de enero de 1555," appended to Motolinia's larger work, *Memoriales*, 422. After her death, Motolinia also testified on her behalf at the request of her daughter. See Justicia 168, "Auto entre partes," fol. 995 and following.

33. The Nahuatl and Spanish texts are published in Miguel León-Portilla, ed., *Coloquios y doctrina cristiana* (Mexico City: UNAM, 1986). An excellent English translation of the Spanish text appears in Kenneth Mills, William B. Taylor, and Sandra Lauderdale Graham, eds., *Colonial Latin America: A Documentary History* (Wilmington, DE: Scholarly Resources, 2002), 20–22. I have quoted from that text, rather than including a direct translation from the Nahuatl, because this is one case in which it is likely that the Spanish version more closely represents what was originally said than does the Nahuatl version, almost certainly recreated in the 1550s or later. I have, however, inserted parenthetical asides where the Nahuatl translation probably includes the original metaphors employed. My thanks to Michel Launey for insisting that his seminar translate directly from the Nahuatl at the Yale Summer Language Institute, July 2002.

34. "Ca ixquich ic ticcuepâ ic ticnanquilia in ami'iyotzin in amotlatoltzin, totecuyohuané." Inic chicome cap (seventh chapter) in León-Portilla, ed., *Coloquios*.

35. Contador Rodrigo de Albornoz to Charles V, 25 December 1525, in *DHM*, vol. 1.

Seven

1. Bernal Díaz del Castillo, *Historia verdadera de la conquista de la Nueva España*, ed. Joaquín Ramírez Cabañas (Mexico City: Porrúa, 1960), 62, 460. As we have seen, what Díaz asserts regarding Malintzin cannot be accepted uncritically, but his description of the entourage's itinerary is in keeping with actual geography and entirely consistent in two widely separated places in his text. He said twice that she married near the Spanish town of Orizaba. At the second mention of it, he added that it was "in a little village belonging to the one-eyed Ojeda" (en un poblezuelo de un Ojeda, el Tuerto). He said he learned this within days of the event from a friend named Aranda and other witnesses of the ceremony when he and some companions who had been living in Coatzacoalcos left the town to go out and meet the arriving travelers. The details, and the unselfconscious way

of referring to the events, ring true. Moreover, there did in fact exist one Alonso de Ojeda, who had lost an eye in the siege of Tenochtitlan, and who had received as his encomienda the altepetl of Tiltepec, not far past Orizaba. It was in Zapotec territory, near the border of Coatzacoalcos. See Himmerich, *Encomenderos*, 205, and Peter Gerhard, *A Guide to the Historical Geography of New Spain* (Norman: University of Oklahoma Press, 1993), 367–68. In addition, a number of witnesses also later swore that they had observed the marriage ceremony—and they did so in legal documents Díaz could not possibly have seen and probably did not know existed. AGI, Patronato 56, N. 3, R. 4, "Méritos y Servicios: Marina." Later, in another set of testimony, a witness who was asked only if Jaramillo and Malintzin were legally married gratuitously mentioned that it was near a place called "Totutla." This was almost certainly how he heard (or remembered) "Olutla." AGI, Justicia 168, "Auto entre partes," statement of Juan de Morales.

2. Díaz, *Historia verdadera,* 460; HC, "Fifth Letter," 339.
3. FLG, 346. Díaz, *Historia verdadera*, 62. "Y la doña Marina tenía mucha ser y mandaba absolutamente entre los indios en toda la Nueva España."
4. Cortés refers to these events, but Díaz, as a participant, describes them in painful detail in *Historia verdadera*, 390–95, 417–29.
5. Himmerich y Valencia, *The Encomenderos*, 127, 138, 150–51, 159, 162.
6. "Escritura de mayorazgo e mejoría, vínculo y mayoría, otorgado por don Hernando Cortés Marqués del Valle, en favor de sus descendientes, Colima, 9 de enero de 1535," in *DHC,* 151–70. On ancient traditions regarding the barraganas see Heath Dillard, *Daughters of the Reconquest: Women in Castilian Town Society, 1100–1300* (Cambridge: Cambridge University Press, 1984). Frances Karttunen was the first to point out that Cortés probably thought of the boy as a potential heir in "Rethinking Malinche," in *IWEM*, 308.
7. Herren, *Doña Marina*, 141.
8. HC, "Fifth Letter," 376, 407; AGI, Patronato 56, N. 3, R. 4, "Méritos y Servicios: Marina."
9. James Lockhart assessed the situation this way in the Peruvian case in *Spanish Peru, 1532–1560: A Colonial Society* (Madison: University of Wisconsin Press, 1968), 210–12. For Mexican examples, see Carrasco, "Indian-Spanish Marriages," in *IWEM*, 96–100.
10. The term "hidalgo" has been used before in this volume but requires some additional commentary here. It stemmed from the words *hijo de alguien*, literally "the son of someone" but implying "the son of someone with status." A short definition would be a member of the untitled nobility, but that definition does not convey the sense of the word. It included a variety of social positions, ranging from men who in England would have been called squires, in that they were from locally prominent families who had at least a bit of land, to men who had married into lords' families, to the cousins and younger sons of counts and dukes. The best discussion of the fluidity of the term is Lockhart, *Spanish Peru*, 34–39.
11. The men's situations were as follows: Alvarado, in Guatemala; Sandoval, ahead in Coatzacoalcos; Olid, leading rebellion in Honduras; Velázquez, dead (noche

triste); Olea, dead (siege of Tenochtitlan); Escalante, dead; Ordás, never married; Montejo, possibly unmarried, but in his mid-fifties; Ircio, courting or already married to Leonel Cervantes's daughter (also spoken of disparagingly by Díaz); Avila, in Spain; Luga, dead; Tapia, available to marry; Jaramillo, available to marry; Marín, ahead in Coatzacoalcos. It is interesting to note that there would not be many more choices even if we broadened the list of eligible suitors beyond those who held the rank of captain and included those who had no pretensions of gentility: only 21 of the 135 surviving "first conquerors" acquired wives during the second quarter of the sixteenth century. See Himmerich y Valencia, *The Encomenderos*, 74.

12. AGI, Patronato 54, N. 8, R. 6, "Méritos y servicios: Juan Jaramillo, 1532," fols. 1–2. "Actas de cabildo," 10–18 June 1524, in *Primer libro de las actas de cabildo de la ciudad de México* (Mexico City: Ignacio Bejarano, 1889), 14–15. Juan's name could of course be an error, but that seems unlikely, given that Alonso's name appears regularly, then is replaced by Juan's for two weeks in a row, then reappears. On Andrés de Tapia's marriage, see Himmerich, *Encomenderos,* 247.

13. Himmerich, *Encomenderos*, 27.

14. AGI, Patronato 56, N. 3, R. 4, "Méritos y Servicios: Marina." Despite the file's name and archival categorization, the documents actually comprise a legal case spanning a decade. In 1542, apparently having learned that Juan Jaramillo's will left the bulk of the encomienda to his wife—or perhaps fearing that it would do so—the newly married sixteen-year-old María and her ambitious husband gathered witnesses together to speak in support of Malintzin's character and contributions. In 1547 they gathered more testimony concerning the legitimacy of their own marriage. (See chapter 8 on their need to do so.) The case became active again in the early 1550s, probably because Jaramillo died. Leonel de Cervantes acknowledges his position on fol. 40. "Dixo: ques dedad de mas de sesenta años, e ques suegro del dicho Xoan Xaramillo, e que por eso no a de dexar de deszir la verdad de lo que supiere en este caso."

15. "Marina, 1542," fol. 51. Juan de Limpias said this. Limpias called himself an hidalgo and was part of the original *entrada* of 1519 as well as several other ventures, so he could have been in a position to know. Cuéllar seems to have lived until about 1545; it is unlikely that others would have lied about his affairs in 1542, while he was still present to contradict them, though of course it is possible. See Himmerich, *Encomenderos*, 148.

16. "Marina, 1542," fol. 49.

17. There is a classic study of this culture, highly recommended for everyone from advanced scholars to undergraduates: Scholes and Roys, *Maya Chontal Indians*.

18. The best treatment of these events is in Restall, *Seven Myths*, 147–57. Restall analyzes a variety of sources. Participants who left accounts include Cortés (HC, "Fifth Letter," 365–68), Díaz (*Historia verdadera*, 468–71), and the Mactun Maya, though several generations removed ("Relación que presentó Francisco Maldonado en lengua Chontal," in Scholes and Roys, *Maya Chontal Indians*, 391–92). Other accounts were written by descendants of some of the Nahua participants, and by Malintzin's grandson. (See chapter 9.) The first segment of

the set of documents known as the Annals of Tlatelolco contains a very interesting account of the events. See Mengin, *Unos anales históricos*, 53–56.

19. Díaz, *Historia verdadera*, 470. The Maya also asserted that there was some sort of Christian ceremony, though they interpreted it as a baptism.

20. HC, "Fifth Letter," 380.

21. Ibid., 386.

22. Ibid., 417–22. "Item 4, Instrucciones dadas a Hernando de Saavedra, lugar teniente en las villas de Trujillo y Natividad de nuestra Señora en Honduras (1525)," Yale University Library, Manuscripts Division, MS 307, Series I, Box 1. This is a copy, probably made in the nineteenth century, of a document concerning labor drafts that I have not been able to locate in Seville. However, in Cortés's general orders to Saavedra, which are preserved in Seville, he directs him to follow the set of instructions he has left regarding indigenous labor drafts.

23. "Probanza hecha en la villa de Trujillo, Cabo de Honduras, a petición de Hernando Cortés, sobre el Bachiller Moreno," 23 October 1525, in *DII*, 10:541–43.

24. "Instrucciones y Ordenanzas dadas por Hernán Cortés para las Villas de Trugillo y Natividad de Nra. Señora (1525)," in *DII*, 26:185–94 (where there is an important line missing) and in Polavieja, *Hernán Cortés*, 338. These instructions are distinct from those in note 22, chapter 7.

25. "Carta de Hernán Cortés, dando cuenta de los Alzamientos que habian ocurrido en México," Havana, 13 May 1526, in *DII*, 12:367–76. "Carta de Hernando Cortés al Ayuntamiento de México," San Juan Chalchicuecan, 24 May 1526, in Actas de cabildo, 31 May 1526.

26. It is possible that in addition the child was a namesake of someone in Jaramillo's family. However, this does not seem likely, as his mother would have been the most likely candidate, and his mother was named Mencía de Matos. See AGI, Patronato 56, N. 8, R. 6, "Méritos y Servicios de Juan Jaramillo, 1532," fol. 2. Juan de Limpias later made an ambiguous statement that may be interpreted either as "the child was born in Honduras at the shore" or "the child was born [during the expedition to] Honduras at sea." He said: "durante su matrimono, estando en las Higueras en la Mar parió la dicha Doña María una hixa." AGI, Patronato 56, N. 3, R. 4, fol. 51. In either case, it seems that the child was conceived around the time the party reached the coast and experienced the great relief described by Cortés in his letter to the king.

27. "Memoria de lo acaecido en esta ciudad despues que el gobernador Hernando Cortés salió della," 1525, in *DHM*, 1:514. This account seems to have been written by the treasurer Alonso de Estrada or by someone in his employ. A variety of contradictory accounts were produced by the various actors involved, but the basic facts remain the same. See, for example, AGI, Justicia 1017, N. 1, "El Fiscal vs. Alonso de Estrada y Rodrigo de Albornoz sobre haber intendado sublevar el pueblo contra Hernando Cortés," 1525.

28. "Carta de Hernán Cortés a su padre Martín Cortés," Mexico City, 26 September 1526, in *DHC*, 29.

29. The clearest treatment of these events is Chipman, "Isabel Moctezuma," in

Sweet and Nash, *Struggle and Survival*, but see also Amada López de Meneses, "Tecuichpotzin, hija de Moteczuma," in *Estudios cortesianos, recopilados con-motivo del IV centenario de la muerte de Hernán Cortés (1547–1947)* (Madrid: Consejo Superior de Investigaciones Científicas, 1948). The concession to Isabel Moctezuma is in the AGI and has been printed as an appendix to several articles. As an example of the Crown's increasing preoccupation with cruelty to the indigenous in this period, see AGI, Patronato 180, R. 21, "Prohibición de la esclavitud de los indios," November 1528. Some historians have doubted that the child Leonor was really Cortés's daughter, but the archival evidence cited by Donald Chipman seems to me to be clear enough. See also his new book *Moctezuma's Children: Aztec Royalty under Spanish Rule, 1520–1700* (Austin: University of Texas Press, 2005).

30. "Relación de las demandas que se han puesto en residencia e fuera della, a don Hernando Cortés," in *DII*, 27:152–67. Records of many of the cases are still extant in the AGI and AGN. The case pursued by Martín López, housed in the Manuscripts Division of the Library of Congress, makes particularly interesting reading.

31. Gerhard, *Historical Geography*, 39; Himmerich, *Encomenderos*, 189. Gerhard, *The Southeast Frontier*, 36–38. The settlement did not thrive. The indigenous continued to rebel, and the Spanish colonists were drawn off to other areas, where placer gold had been found, for example. In 1531 the region was dissolved as a political unit and divided up for governing purposes between Veracruz, Tabasco, and the Marquesado del Valle. The region essentially remained a back-water until the twentieth century, when oil deposits were found on the gulf.

32. AGI, Justicia 226, N. 3, "Residencia a Nuño de Guzman. Cargos contra el licen-ciado Delgadillo oydor que fue en esta audiencia, 1530," fol. 3v. AGI, Justicia 109, "Ana de Pedrosa vs. Juan de Soldevilla sobre la muerte de Catalina de Pedroso, 1531."

33. Actas de cabildo, 16 June 1526.

34. Instituto Valencia de Don Juan, Madrid, archivo histórico, caja 35, numero 23, documento 258, "Memorial del pleito entre Gaspar de Santillana, con Juan Jaramillo, difunto, y doña Beatriz de Andrada y don Pedro de Quesada, 1586," containing "Hernando de Santillana pone demanda a Juan Xaramillo, 1538," reproduced as an appendix in Georges Baudot, "Malintzin, imagen y discurso de mujer en el primer México virreinal," *Cuadernos Americanos* 40 (1993): 181–207. The man's words were as follows: "Hernando Santillana simpre muy pobre y el dicho Xaramillo muy poderoso y criado del marques, cassado con una criada suya." He recurs to this theme more than once. Baudot misinterprets the case in several places, but his transcription appears to be good. Santillana had written the king in 1532 begging for help: "Carta al rey, del conquistador Hernando de Santillana, suplicando se le den indios," in *ENE*, 2:141–42, from an original in the AGI. There has been considerable confusion as to Jaramillo's possession— or lack of possession—of the encomienda of Xilotepec because so many people were involved. Cortés first assigned it to Francisco de Quevedo, but he soon died. Then Cortés divided it between Jaramillo and the bereaved shoemaker

Santillana. Himmerich in *Encomenderos*, 79–83, notes that he often divided up encomiendas in just this way.

35. On the Cervantes family tree, see López de Meneses, "Tecuichpotzin," 477. Himmerich in *Encomenderos*, 63–65, details the background of the spouses of each of Leonel's daughters. Beatriz was the youngest of the five girls from Spain; another sister was born in Mexico. She married Francisco de Velasco, brother of the viceroy, in the early 1550s, not long after Jaramillo's death, when she herself was still only in her thirties and very wealthy. See chapter 8.

36. Actas de cabildo, 14 March 1528. "En este día los dichos Señores le hicieron merced a Juan Xaramillo e a Doña Marina su mugger de un sytio para hacer una casa de placer e huerta e tener sus ovejas en la arboleda que está junto a la pared de Chapultepec a la mano derecha que tenga doscientos e cincuenta pasos en cuadro come le fuere señalado por los diputados." Cervantes de Salazar, who arrived in the city in 1533, later described the houses that grew up along the aqueduct. See Benítez, *The Century after Cortés*, 7. On Jaramillo's purchases and debts, see the extracts from the Archivo de Notarías de México, cited in Baudot, "Malintzin," 193. On his *solares* in Mexico City, see Helena Alberú de Villava, *Malintzin y el señor Malinche* (Mexico City: Edamex, 1995), 127. I have not reconfirmed the location of the latter, but Jaramillo would undoubtedly have received just such a grant.

37. AGI, Justicia 168, "Auto entre partes," fols. 1078–83. This exchange was held in 1551 or very early 1552.

38. Ibid., fols. 997, 1028, 1031. Don Diego Atempanecatl testified in 1551 or 1552, by which time he would have been a respected middle-aged man. On the title "atempanecatl," see *FC* 9:34, 47. The term seems to have crossed cultural boundaries, as it is used in the Annals of Cuauhtitlan and the Annals of Tecamachalco, as well as the two sets of Mexica annals known as the Codex Aubin and the Annals of Juan Bautista. In each context, a personage of great authority is indicated.

39. On documentation regarding Cortés's plans while in Spain, see chapter 8. In Spain, two of his travel companions would make a sworn statement regarding Malintzin in the present tense, demonstrating that they had all known her to be alive when they left Mexico. "Expediente de Martín Cortés, niño de siete años, hijo de Hernando Cortés, y de la india Doña Marina," Toledo, 19 July 1529, printed in *Boletín de la Real Academia de Historia* 21 (1892): 199–206. The original is in the Archivo Histórico Nacional, Madrid, Ordenes Militares, 34, E. 2167 (1529). On the testimony of Malintzin's old acquaintances, Indian and Spanish, regarding her dress, see Justicia 168, "Auto entre partes," fol. 1030v. I am taking a minor liberty in this paragraph: there is no documentary proof that mother and son met to say good-bye. To my mind, however, certain elements of the story can be taken for granted. It is certain that Martín was in contact with his mother at this time, as he passed on memories of her to his son. (See chapter 9.)

40. On January 29, 1529, Juan de Burgos, a witness in the residencia against Cortés, referred to her as "*ya difunta*"—literally, "already dead," implying that her death had been recent and premature. See *AM*, 1:160. We do not know what Malintzin died of, but barring the extremely unlikely scenario that she died in

her twenties of an inherited disease such as cancer, she must have succumbed to one of the constant epidemics introduced by Europeans. If she had died of complications of pregnancy or childbirth, that fact undoubtedly would have come out in the lengthy case pursued by her daughter, as it would have strengthened the case that María really was Jaramillo's child, not Cortés's. In older works on Malintzin, it is often assumed that she lived to a ripe old age, as historians often confused her with another doña Marina, wife of the treasurer Alonso de Estrada. The problem was laid to rest years ago by the thorough study of Joanne Chaison, "Mysterious Malinche: A Case of Mistaken Identity," *The Americas* 32, no. 4 (1976): 514–23.

Eight

1. In AGI, Patronato 56, N. 4, R. 3, "Méritos y servicios: Marina," fol. 2, María Jaramillo makes the statement that her father had been remarried for twenty years. This statement has been assumed by some scholars to have been made in 1547, and since Malintzin died in 1528 or 1529, the "twenty years" would therefore be approximate—in reality, about eighteen. However, the statement actually appears in an undated document, which it seems to me is meant to be included with the 1552 material, and was clearly written as Jaramillo lay dying, which occurred in the early 1550s. This would date the marriage to about 1530. Doña Beatriz said, as a widow, that she had been married for twenty-two years, and Jaramillo died in late 1551 or early 1552. See AGI, Justicia 168, "Autos entre partes," fol. 1069. Himmerich y Valencia in *The Encomenderos* has researched the background of the spouses of each of Leonel's daughters. He also had one son. A sixth girl was born in Mexico, and Himmerich assumes that Beatriz, known as the youngest, was that child. However, that is impossible, as she would then have been no more than eight when she married, even if the nuptials occurred as late as 1532. She was undoubtedly the youngest of the five older girls and could have been born no later than 1519, when her father left Spain, and no earlier than about 1515, if she was the youngest of six children and her mother was still of an age to bear another one ten years later in the mid-1520s. Antonio Oliver remembered Beatriz as being "just a little thing" (*muchacha de poca edad*) when she came to Mexico. See again AGI, Justicia 168, "Autos entre partes," fol. 1088v.

2. AGI, Patronato 54, N. 8, R. 6, "Méritos y servicios: Juan Jaramillo, 1532," fol. 9. On the experience of enslaved Africans in the early years of the colony, see Herman Bennett, *Africans in Colonial Mexico: Absolutism, Christianity, and Afro-Creole Consciousness, 1570–1640* (Bloomington: Indiana University Press, 2003). The earliest imports to the colonies are recorded in AGI, Contratación 5756, Licencias de Esclavos, and Contratación 5760, Libros de Asientos. The ledger books reveal that slaves at first were transported to the Indies in very small numbers; individuals were even listed by name, along with the owners with whom they traveled. By 1527 the pattern had changed. At that point, one Spanish individual might be given a license to transport twenty-five, for example. Most of these did not go to Mexico, but to the Caribbean.

3. On the situation in Peru, see Kathryn Burns, *Colonial Habits: Convents and the Spiritual Economy of Cuzco, Peru* (Durham, NC: Duke University Press, 1999), 32–40. That María was seen as a wealthy and therefore desirable bride is proven by statements her husband later made; that Beatriz was always conscious of her stepdaughter's mixed blood is demonstrated by comments she later made. Beatriz had no children by her second husband, either, and was probably infertile. That some people assumed María may have been fathered by Cortés is indicated by statements that the conqueror had "children" by doña Marina. Even Gómara, who worked for Cortés, made that assumption.

4. In "Méritos y servicios: Marina," numerous witnesses insisted that María grew up in Jaramillo's household and was understood by everyone to be his daughter; it is also in that set of documents that a signature of hers survives. Other legal documents reveal that even wealthy young ladies often could not sign their own names. Peter Gerhard tells us that Xilotepec was "by far the most populous private encomienda in New Spain in the late sixteenth century" in *A Guide to the Historical Geography*, 383. It had 18,335 tributaries in the mid-1560s. However, the population fell after that, due to epidemics that hit in 1576–81 and 1604–7. The fascinating 1533 reference to early literate Indians is in "Carta a la emperatriz de la Audiencia de México," 9 February 1533, in *ENE*, 3:31–32. The text is as follows: "El señor e principales de Xilotepeque que esta encomendado a Juan de Jaramillo, nos dieron en acuerdo la petición que con ésta va para vuestra majestad e la joya de oro de que en ella se hace mención: quisimos saber del guardian quien la había ordenado y escrito y dijonos que el que la escribió es un indio que está en esta cibdad en [el barrio de] San Francisco, y que la ordenó otro, el cual falleció habrá diez días y murió como grand cristiano y en presencia de ciertos españoles los cuales se admiraron de ver su fin: hay muchos indios que saben leer y escribir que tienen esta capacidad."

5. "Nueva Petición de Hernando Cortés por procurador a la audiencia de México, explicando por que debe anularse la cédula en favor de doña Marina Gutiérrez," 22 November 1532, printed in *DHC*, 93–99

6. Himmerich, *Encomenderos*, 30, 138, 215, 221. Tomás de Rigioles is referred to as *naguatato del marques del Valle* in AGN, Hospital de Jesús, L. 264, E. 151, "Antonio Serrano de Cardona, encomendero de Cuernavaca, que le restituya el marqués los indios [1531]," in Silvio Zavala, ed., *Tributos y servicios personales de indios para Hernán Cortés y su familia: Extractos de documentos del siglo XVI* (Mexico City: Archivo General de la Nación, 1984), 18. Mention of the new interpreters working for offices of the government—such as Agustín de Rodas, Juan de Ledesma, Alvaro de Zamora, and Pedro García—occur throughout Zavala's volume, beginning in 1529–31.

7. LC, Harkness Collection, num. 2, "Pleito contra el licenciado Juan Ortiz de Matienzo y Diego Delgadillo, para recuperar la renta del pueblo de Toluca que en su calidad de oidores habín dada a García de Pilar durante la ausencia de Cortés en España, 1531," printed in Zavala, *Tributos y servicios*, 67–81. Jorge Cañizares-Esguerra has written about the phenomenon of the sixteenth-century Spaniards' privileging the words of the natives as being revealing of truth. See

his *How to Write the History of the New World: Historiographies, Epistemologies, and Identities in the Eighteenth-Century Atlantic World* (Stanford, CA: Stanford University Press, 2001), especially chapter 2.

8. "Declaración de los Tributos de la provincia de Guanavaquez, en Nueva España, hacían a su señor el Marqués del Valle, 1533," in *DII*, 14:142–47.

9. For Delgadillo's comment, see LC, Harkness Collection, num. 1, "Pleito de Hernando Cortés contra Nuño de Guzmán y los licenciados Matienzo y Delgadillo para recuperar la renta del pueblo y provincia de Guaxucingo, 1531," in Zavala, *Tributos y servicios,* 53. On Pedro García's experience, see "Visita Hecha a Don Antonio de Mendoza, Cargo Segundo, 1546" in *DHM*, 2:73–74.

10. AGN, Libros de Asientos de la Gobernación de la Nueva España, "Caciques, Principales y Comunidades Indígenas," 14 March 1551, fol. 79, and 4 April 1551, fols. 82–83.

11. For an overview of the ways in which women's legal status was eroded under the Spanish, see Susan Kellog, "From Parallel and Equivalent to Separate but Unequal: Tenochca Mexica Women, 1500–1700," in *IWEM*. For a study of a different cast, in which it is clear that despite Spanish strictures, women remained vocal and active, see Lisa Sousa, "Women in Native Societies and Cultures of Colonial Mexico" (PhD diss., University of California–Los Angeles, 1998).

12. On the younger Juan Jaramillo's account of his participation in the New Mexico campaign, see AGI, Patronato 20, N. 5, R. 4, "Relación que dió el Capitán Juan Jaramillo de la jornada que hizo a la tierra nueva de la cual fue general Juan Vasquez de Coronado." The account is undated in the original hand. In another hand, a date has been added that has been interpreted as "1537," but that is impossible, as the events described occurred in 1540–41. I would suggest that the paleography should be interpreted as "1551." This date makes sense, as the text reveals that the author is writing many years after the fact.

13. AGI, Pasajeros L. 2, E. 1293, 26 June 1535, don Luis de Quesada; and Justicia 168, "Auto entre partes," fols. 1065v, 1093v. Don Luis acknowledged very forthrightly that he had married doña María on the understanding that she would be an heiress: AGI, Patronato 56, N. 3, R. 4, "Méritos y servicios: Marina," fol. 2. We should not think too hardly of him: don Francisco de Velasco later said the same about his marriage to doña Beatriz. In their context, this was a perfectly reasonable legal argument.

14. We learn what happened from Hernando Cortés, who was in Spain and had clearly been informed either by letter or by a traveler. He had been trying for months to convince the monarch to investigate Viceroy Mendoza's conduct. Among his other accusations, he said that Mendoza encouraged his followers to wreak havoc among the susceptible wives and daughters of Mexico City, always supporting the young men in their efforts to marry the richest widows and heiresses, no matter what the cost to others. (See, for example, "Petición que dió don Hernando Cortés contra don Antonio de Mendoza, virey, pidiendo residencia," n.d., printed in *DHM*, 2:62–71.) At length in about 1543 Cortés drew together an interrogatory, a list of questions to be put to witnesses he had selected. Among the specific questions appears the following: "XXIV: yten si saben que usando

de la dicha parcialidad e fabores el dicho don Antonio, faboresció a don luys de quesada, que fue con él, que se casase con una hija de juan de xaramillo contra la voluntad della e de su padre, e le consentió e le disimuló que porque pidiendola el dicho don luys, que no se la quería dar el dicho du padre en casamiento, el dicho agustin guerrero su mayodomo del dicho don Antonio, e asi mismo otros sus criados fuesen como fueron con el dicho don luys e tomasen la calle donde bibia el dicho juan de xaramillo de parte e de otra, e les escalaron la casa para sacar por fuerça la dicha donzzella e hija, e como no pudo salir con ello, publicó que estava casado con ella e le hizo tantas molestias asta que el dicho juan de xaramillo, por no se veer tan afrentado se la dió por su muger, digan lo que pasa." Interrogatory printed in its entirety as an appendix in Carlos Pérez Bustamente, *Don Antonio de Mendoza, primer virrey de la Nueva España, 1535–1550* (Santiago: El Eco Franciscano, 1928), 175–81. For his appendix it seems that Pérez Bustamente drew from AGI, Patronato 16, N. 2, R. 52 (1543) and a document in the Archivo Histórico Nacional, Madrid, Diversos 22, documento 46 (1543). Quesada's claim that he and María had already had sexual relations would certainly have been a successful tactic. On old Spanish traditions in this regard, see Dillard, *Daughters of the Reconquest*, especially chapter 5. Cortés, of course, was motivated to claim that the young woman was resistant, but no part of the episode would make any sense if she had not given don Luis any encouragement.

15. There has been little work done on the war in Jalisco, which has come to be known as the Mixton War. Ida Altman is currently engaged in a promising study.

16. AGI, Justicia 168, "Auto entre partes," fol. 1065.

17. AGI, Patronato 56, N. 3, R. 4, "Méritos y servicios: Marina." This document includes only the materials gathered in the 1540s and cuts off without resolution. The full case as it was pursued after Jaramillo's death comprised the *legajo* above, Justicia 168.

18. On only two children having survived out of the numerous ones conceived, see AGI, Justicia 168, "Auto entre partes," fol. 1014. Pedro said he had attained his twenty-fifth birthday as of August 21, 1571, fol. 15. Later, in 1581, he said he was thirty-two, not thirty-five, but as he was asking for a government post, he probably preferred to appear particularly young and hearty. See Patronato 76, N. 2, R. 10, "Méritos y servicios: Luis de Quesada, etc., 1581." (This document is erroneously labeled. Pedro mentions his father Luis in the first paragraph, but it is his own probanza.)

19. On references to the friendly relations near the time of death, see AGI, Justicia 168, "Auto entre partes," fols. 1015, 1050. Don Luis mentioned the unwelcome agreement between his wife and her stepmother in a document written while Jaramillo was still alive, Patronato 56, N. 3, R. 4, "Méritos y servicios: Marina," fol. 2. That particular document is undated but refers to Jaramillo having been married about twenty years, putting it to about 1550. One of doña Beatriz's witnesses later insisted it was not only doña María but also don Luis who seemed amenable to the agreement around the time of the funeral ("Auto entre partes," fol. 1050v) but his turn of phrase is suspicious, and the statement seems unlikely

to be true since Luis began to prepare his case while Jaramillo was still alive and contested the will immediately after his death. By June of 1552, Jaramillo was definitely dead: documents contesting the will were submitted in Spain ("Méritos y servicios," fol. 3), and we know that doña Beatriz was remarried by the middle of 1555, having waited, she said, thirty-four months. (See note 25, chapter 8.)

20. AGI, Justicia 168, "Auto entre partes," fol. 1066v.

21. Ibid., fols. 1078, 1079v, and 1083. This set of testimony is undated, but doña Beatriz refers to having been a widow for six months, thus putting it to 1551 or 1552.

22. Ibid., fols. 1078–80, 1083, 1083v.

23. Ibid., fols. 1011–12.

24. Ibid., fols. 995v, 997, 1031.

25. Ibid., fol. 1048.

26. In this paragraph, I am making an inference without absolute proof. We know that don Luis traveled to Europe in late 1556 or 1557 and then returned home, and that by the early 1560s, don Pedro was living in Spain. It is theoretically possible—but highly unlikely—that the child Pedro did not accompany his father, but traveled alone at a later date.

27. Don Luis refers to his trip to Bologna and Florence in AGI, Justicia 168, "Auto entre partes," fol. 982v. For more on the events in Europe and don Martín's role in them, see chapter 9.

28. It is clear that the two brothers-in-law met in this period, because they refer to their personal friendship in their lawsuits against others in 1557 and the early 1560s. See chapter 9, note 20, and AGI, Justicia 168, "Auto entre partes," fol. 4.

29. In 1556 don Luis has petitioned the Audiencia, claiming that the figures noted in the recent *visita* were inaccurate because the royal officials had used nahuatlatos as translators, and the Indians of his encomienda spoke Otomí. See AGI, México 205, N. 12, "Informaciones de oficio y parte, Luis de Quesada," 1556.

30. AGI, Justicia 168, "Auto entre partes," fols. 1062–63v. This set of testimony is undated, but in-text references show it to have been collected between 1558 and 1562. I therefore refer to it as the material gathered "about 1560."

31. Ibid., fol. 986v.

32. Ibid., fols. 1063–65.

33. On María's death in 1563, see AGI, Justicia 168, "Auto entre partes," fol. 4 and throughout. On January 7, 1570, Jorge de Mendoza, *clérigo presbítero capellan* of the Church of the Santíssima Trinidad swore under oath whence the funds had come for the daily Mass. Six days had been paid for by doña María Jaramillo, who left a *capellanía* when she died, and the Sabbath day had been arranged for years earlier by the *cofradía* of Spanish tailors. I have not been able to find this document myself, but it is transcribed in full in Mariano Somonte, *Doña Marina, "la Malinche"* (Mexico City: Edimex, 1969), 148–49. Somonte's book includes some interpretations that can only be termed modern projections onto an Indian woman; however, he seems to have been very careful only to include genuine documents and casts aspersions on what he views as undocumented claims, so

I trust him in this regard. Mexican historian Ricardo Herren is convinced that there must have been some family connection to the church for doña María to have taken this step.

34. Royal *cédulas* concerning don Pedro's travel plans were twice issued to the Casa de la Contratación (AGI, Indiferente 1966, L. 15, 1566, fol. 243; and Indiferente 1966, L. 15, 1565, fol. 243). He traveled in 1567 (Pasajeros L. 5, E. 624, 20 June 1567). On his involvement in the ongoing case, see AGI, Justicia 168, "Auto entre partes," fol. 15 and onward. On his personal situation as of 1581, see his probanza, Patronato 76, N. 2, R. 10, "Méritos y servicios: Luis de Quesada, etc., 1581."

35. AGI, Escribanía 952, 20 August and 21 October 1573, fols. 761, 762.

36. AGI, Patronato 20, N. 5, R. 20, "Lista de las encomiendas de indios que en esta nueva españa an sucedido de maridos a mugeres por la sucesion general e los que lose posen por haverse casado con las tales viudas," and "Relación de las personas q. tienen yndios encomendados en esta nueva España q. son viejos y no tienen hijas ni hijos." Both lists are undated but are clearly products of the late 1570s or early 1580s, judging by in-text references. Doña Beatriz merited a full entry in each list, fols. 2, 3v.

37. AGI, Justicia 168, "Auto entre partes," ca. 1560, fol. 964. On the inheritance of the encomienda by Pedro's son, Luis, see Gerhard, *A Guide to the Historical*, 383, and AGI, Indiferente 449, L. A2, 30 March 1613. Don Luis, the great-grandson, requested permission to visit Spain even though, as a holder of Indians, he was supposed to remain in New Spain.

Nine

1. Diego de Ordás to Francisco Verdugo, 2 April 1529, in Otte, "Nueve cartas," 102–29. For painstaking research on the Indian visitors to Spain, see Howard F. Cline, "Hernando Cortés and the Aztec Indians in Spain," *Quarterly Journal of the Library of Congress* 26 (1969): 70–90. The departure of the Tlaxcalan noblemen for Spain was perceived in Tlaxcala to be an important event and is marked in Tlaxcalan annals. See, for example, Zapata y Mendoza, *Historia cronológica*, 136–38. Spanish records indicate that the only noblemen in the delegation were the visitors from Mexico City, plus the most important visitor from Tlaxcala, but that merely reflects Spanish misperception about the political hierarchy of central Mexico. In Tlaxcala three of the men were understood to be important nobles, and two others relatively highborn. For more on Moctezuma's sons who went to Spain, and their document trail, see Emma Pérez-Rocha y Rafael Tena, *La nobleza indígena del centro de México después de la conquista* (Mexico City: Instituto Nacional de Antropología e Historia, 2000), 29–39. For a thorough study of don Pedro in particular, see Chipman, *Moctezuma's Children*, 81–95.

2. Hernando Cortés to Francisco de Santa Cruz, 6 March 1528, in *DHC*, 41–47.

3. Surviving correspondence by and about Cortés during such well-documented periods as his visit to Spain has been extensively studied. I have checked published

versions of the sources in reconstructing his itinerary but will not cite them here for they are copious and I would be "reinventing the wheel." Instead I refer readers to the most thorough biography, Miralles, *Hernán Cortés*, 461–67. For all matters beyond the itinerary, however, I will provide full citations. For the letter about the ocelotl, for example, see Hernando Cortés to Martín Cortés, 24 November 1527, in *DHC*, 37–38. I take a minor liberty in this paragraph: there is no actual proof that Cortés visited his mother at this moment, in that it is not mentioned in letters. He had to pass very near the village on his way to the monastery, however, and between docking in Seville and taking his leave in Toledo, he had clearly spoken to her in person, in that they had decided she would come to live with him.

4. Hernando Cortés to the King, 15 July 1528, in *DIE*, 113:485. "Memorial de Luis de Cárdenas contra Hernando Cortés," 15 July 1528, in *DHM*, 2:25–27.

5. "Cédulas del Emperador Carlos V," 6 July and 20 July 1529, in *DIE,* 1:103–8.

6. Diego de Ordás to Francisco Verdugo, 2 April 1529, in Otte, "Nueve cartas."

7. Cline, "Cortés and the Aztec Indians," 82–84.

8. There has been considerable confusion regarding Cortés's itinerary at this point, as his declared plans in the spring of 1529 do not fit with the ensuing paper trail. Ordás, in a letter to Francisco Verdugo, 23 August 1529, provides us with the explanation. See Otte, "Nueve cartas," 112.

9. "Expediente de Martín Cortés, niño de siete años, hijo de Hernando Cortés y de la India doña Marina," Toledo, 19 July 1529, printed in *Boletín de la Real Academia de la Historia* 21 (1892): 199–202. The original is in the Archivo Histórico Nacional, Madrid, Ordenes Militares, 34, E. 2167, 1529. The papal bull from Clemente VII is dated April 16, 1529. For a general sense of how applications to the Order of Santiago were received, see Mark Burkholder, "Honor and Honors in Colonial Spanish America," in *The Faces of Honor: Sex, Shame and Violence in Colonial Latin America,* ed. Lyman L. Johnson and Sonya Lipsett-Rivera (Albuquerque: University of New Mexico Press, 1998), 21–22.

10. Estefania de Zúñiga to Juan de Zúñiga, 1537, cited in Henry Kamen, *Philip of Spain* (New Haven, CT: Yale University Press, 1997), 6. Kamen succeeds in evoking a sense of the lives of the prince and his companions. We no longer need to take the word of Hernando and Martín Cortés themselves that Martín was placed in the royal service. Anna Lanyon has found documentation: receipts for payment signed by Martín's tutor, as well as a mention of his 1539 transfer to Philip's entourage, housed among the papers of Isabel's household in the Archivo General de Simancas, in Valladolid, Casa Real Imperatriz, Legajo 31, N. 55 and Legajo 35, N. 28. See her book, *The New World of Martín Cortés* (Cambridge, MA: Da Capo Press, 2004), 44–46.

11. See Alejandro Galindo's film *El juicio de Martín Cortés* (1974) and Carlos Fuentes's short story, "Sons of the Conquistador," in *The Orange Tree* (New York: Farrar, Straus and Giroux, 1994). There have been numerous studies of the evolving image of Malintzin, but Anna Lanyon (note 10, this chapter) is the only one even to have touched on a study of the image of don Martín. For Cortes's frequent mentions of his son, see his recently published correspondence with Francisco

Nuñez, found in the Archivo de la Real Chancillería de Valladolid: María del Carmen Martínez Martínez, ed., *Hernán Cortés: Cartas y Memoriales* (León: Universidad de León, 2003), 134, 153, 176, 201, 212, 215–16, 229–30, 260.

12. "Hernando Cortés a Francisco Nuñez," 20 June 1533, printed in Mario Hernández Sanchez-Barba, ed., *Hernando Cortés: Cartas y documentos* (Mexico City: Editorial Porrúa, 1963), 514–23.

13. For more on these events see Kamen, *Philip of Spain,* 6–7; Lanyon, *Martín Cortés,* 76–77; and Carlos Eire, *From Madrid to Purgatory: The Art and Craft of Dying in Sixteenth-Century Spain* (Cambridge: Cambridge University Press, 1995), 1–3.

14. Hernando Cortés to the King, Madrid, 18 March 1543, printed in Camilo Polavieja, *Hernán Cortés,* 444–46.

15. Hernando Cortés declared that he went to Algiers with his sons, and Martín himself said that he had been there during the proceedings of 1566 and 1567, to be discussed later. It was at that time, also, that the nature of his relationship with his brother in the long term made its way into the historical record. On the interactions between Charles V and Suleiman II, see Royall Tyler, *The Emperor Charles the Fifth* (Fair Lawn, NJ: Essential Books, 1956) and André Clot, *Suleiman the Magnificent: The Man, His Life, His Epoch* (London: Saqi Books, 1992).

16. Both Martín himself in 1566 and later his son in 1592 referred to the places he had been and to his various wounds. (See notes 24 and 33, this chapter.) Their statements are perfectly congruent with the military histories of Charles V and Philip II. The name "Fernando" should be treated as identical to "Hernando." Indeed, "Hernando Cortés" could equally well be referred to as "Fernando"— and often is, in Spanish—as the name was spelled that way on many occasions. Over the course of the sixteenth century, spelling conventions became firmer, and the grandson's name seems always to have been spelled with an *f.* I find it useful to retain the distinction in that it helps to differentiate between grandfather and grandson for the rest of the chapter.

17. "Testamento de Hernando Cortés," in *DIE,* 4:239–77. Cortés's will has been published in numerous places.

18. AGN, Hospital de Jesús, L. 235, E. 4, "Escriptura de transacción e concierto entre doña Juana de Zúñiga y don Martín Cortés su hijo, 1550." The document reveals that doña Juana really wanted half of what her husband had accrued, trusting that she would husband the wealth more effectively than would her son. However, she bowed to pressure from her male relatives in Spain, spoke directly to Martín of "the love I have for you as my inheriting son," and agreed to accept the stipulated sums. Mother and son had been separated from each other at that point for a decade. See also Hospital de Jesús, Legajo 276.

19. On the marriage and on Spain's relationship with England at this time, see Kamen, *Philip of Spain,* 54–59, as well as works concerning the Tudor monarchs. On the young Elizabeth, for example, see David Starkey, *Elizabeth: The Struggle for the Throne* (New York: Harper Collins, 2001) and Jane Dunn, *Elizabeth and Mary* (New York: Random House, 2003).

20. A description of the tournament and its participants appeared in Sir William

Segar, *Honor Military and Civill* (London: Robert Barker, 1602), 192–93. The material was almost literally hidden between other more salient items, as Segar's book was printed as a tribute to Elizabeth's reign, and mention of any honors to her Catholic sister had to be circumspect.

21. AGN, Hospital de Jesús, L. 300, E. 117. Historians, including myself, had glanced through the many cases brought against the Marqués del Valle, without noting anything of particular interest. Anna Lanyon, however, showed more perseverance and found this case between the two Martíns. See *New World of Martín Cortés*, 137–41. It fits perfectly with another document surviving in Seville, in which Cortés transfers the slaves in certain mines to his three sons' joint ownership just before leaving for Spain. "Carta escritura de donación intervivos de Hernando Cortés a sus hijos," 27 November 1539, in *DHC,* 189–99.

22. AGI, Patronato 284, N. 2, R. 78, "Real provision comissiando a los miembros del consejo de Indias," 17 May 1558, and Patronato 286, R. 107, "Ejecutoria del Pleito de Luis Cortés," 26 October 1561.

23. AGI, Pasajeros, L. 4, E. 3955, "Bernardina de Porres [sic]," 23 May 1565. As was usual, the passenger's place of origin, parents' names, and traveling companions were listed. We know that don Martín's older son was not also her son because she was said to want to travel with her daughter and with "don Hernando Cortés," as if he were no relation. Furthermore, in later events in Mexico, it was noted that she had a daughter by don Martín, but no son was mentioned. It is safe to assume that Fernando was born out of wedlock because when he filed two probanzas later in life, he never once mentioned his mother. It is Anna Lanyon who raises the possibility of Martín and Bernardina having met while he was on a pilgrimage. See *New World of Martín Cortés*, 114.

24. A contemporary witness described these events in his 1589 manuscript. See Giorgio Perissinotto, ed., *Juan Suárez de la Peralta: Tratado del descubrimiento de las Indias y su conquista* (Madrid: Alianza Editorial, 1990). Benítez in *The Century after Cortés* concluded that Juan Suárez was probably a relative of Cortés's first wife, but he was nevertheless a partisan of the famed conquistador. It was Suárez who recorded the popular rhyme: "Por Marina, soy testigo/ ganó esta tierra un buen ombre,/ y por otra deste nombre / la perderá quien yo digo" (195). More on this period and the role of Malintzin's son is revealed in the investigation into the 1566 plot. A number of those documents were transcribed and printed long ago in Manuel Orozco y Berra, *Noticia histórica de la conjuración del Marqués del Valle, años de 1565–1568* (Mexico City: Tipografía de R. Rafael, 1853). Some of the originals are in the LC, but most are in the AGI, Patronato 208, 209, 210, and 211.

25. On don Martín's state of mind, see references in the transcripts printed in Orozco y Berra, *Noticia histórica,* 223 and elsewhere. I infer the reasons for his gloom, which are not specified.

26. AGI, Pasajeros, L. 4, E. 3956, 3957, 3958, 3959, 3960, and 3961, all dated 23 May 1565. For the royal cédulas giving doña Bernardina permission to travel with two dependents, later expanded to two children and six criados, see AGI, Indiferente 1966, L. 15, 20 April 1565, fol. 272, and 6 May 1565, fol. 281v.

27. The indigenous in the city recorded that the funeral procession was led by the dead viceroy's brother and son, mentioning don Francisco by name. See Luis Reyes García, ed., *¿Como te confundes? ¿Acaso no somos conquistados? Anales de Juan Bautista* (Mexico City: Biblioteca Lorenzo Boturini, 2001), 225. Very little work on the plot of 1566 has been done, despite the existence of the documents mentioned in note 23, this chapter. Older books that give summaries of the events include Luis González Obregón, *La semblanza de Martín Cortés* (Mexico City: Fondo de Cultura Económica, [1906] 2005), and Lesley Byrd Simpson, *Many Mexicos* (Berkeley: University of California Press, 1963), as well as Benítez, *The Century after Cortés*. More recent treatments appear in Lanyon, *New World of Martín Cortés*, 148–221, and Chipman, *Moctezuma's Children*, 78–81. There is also a good dissertation by Victoria Anne Vincent, "The Avila-Cortés Conspiracy: Creole Aspirations and Royal Interests" (PhD diss., University of Nebraska–Lincoln, 1993). The consensus is that there really was some sort of conspiracy, albeit an ill-formed one, but that the marqués, despite his role as a figurehead, probably in truth knew little of the specifics. Don Martín does not seem to have been involved at all. At one point in July of 1566, the marqués actually acknowledged having hosted some impolitic discussions, and he mentioned his brother, don Luis, but excluded don Martín. The following paragraphs come from a reading of the *Noticia histórica* in the context of these secondary works.

28. In Spain the king made a great show of stripping the Cortés brothers of their wealth, sequestering the estate of the marqués, confining them for a time, and sending them both off to Oran in North Africa to serve in the military, supposedly for ten years. They later returned to his good graces, however. Luis was able to go back to Mexico in later years, and when the marqués remarried in 1581, his first wife having died, Philip gave the bride a substantial dowry. He restored the right to govern the estate to the marqués's son Fernando upon his marriage in 1589.

29. Orozco y Berra, *Noticia histórica*, 228–33. A scribe was always present to record and "legalize" the torture proceedings, so we have a full record. This was true not only in Spanish dominions but also in England and other European countries.

30. Suárez, *Tratado*, 231.

31. Ibid., 224, on the reaction of the Spanish townsfolk at the time. Ian Miller offers great insight into cultures dependent on the concept of honor in *Humiliation, and Other Essays on Honor, Social Discomfort, and Violence* (Ithaca, NY: Cornell University Press, 1993). I am grateful to Lyman Johnson for an illuminating conversation on this subject and for noting the bitter irony of the parallel between Cuauhtemoc's treatment and don Martín's. Indigenous men who were keeping annals in the native tradition in the 1560s all mentioned these events as well. The most detailed treatment is found in Reyes, *Anales de Juan Bautista*, 149. Briefer treatments are found in the Codex Aubin and the Annals of Tecamachalco. Malintzin's son, don Martín Cortés, is not mentioned by name in any of these. Rather, the marqués is mentioned, as are "the sons of Cortés." There is a certain confusion in evidence which it seems to me is caused by two of the sons being named "don Martín."

32. Don Juan to Ruy Gómez, 5 November 1570, cited in Kamen, *Philip of Spain*, 131. On the war in Granada see Andrew C. Hess, *The Forgotten Frontier: A History of the Sixteenth-Century Ibero-African Frontier* (Chicago: University of Chicago Press, 1978), and Mary Elizabeth Perry, *The Handless Maiden: Moriscos and the Politics of Religion in Early Modern Spain* (Princeton, NJ: Princeton University Press, 2005), 97–118. The latter book contextualizes the rebellion marvelously and gives sensitive treatment to its aftermath. It was Martín's son who reported that his father had served close to don Juan and died under his command in Granada. See note 33, this chapter.

33. Fernando petitioned the Crown the first time from Lima in January of 1592. In recompense for the services of his grandmother, his father, and himself, he asked either for an annual income or for a position in the bureaucracy. AGI, Patronato 17, R. 13. He may have been somewhat successful, for in about 1605, not long after Philip's death, he petitioned the Crown again, acknowledging the help that a letter from the viceroy of Peru had given him in securing a position in Veracruz. (He was at the time of writing the alcalde mayor there.) That document was deposited at Valladolid and was printed in *DHC*, 289–94. It was received by the Council of Indies in 1606. See *DIU*, 18:136. At that time he asked either for a pension (he named a smaller sum than he had before) or for some more lucrative position, so that he could maintain his family in the style to which they had become accustomed. In mentioning the latter, he was only adhering to the classic formula for such petitions. He did not make much of his descent from Cortés. That was apparently for the legitimate scions of the family to do. Rather, he emphasized the story of his grandmother and underscored the same kinds of contributions that indigenous petitioners tended to use—descent from indigenous nobility, early conversion to Christianity, and crucial help rendered to the Spaniards in the earliest stages of colonization . (See Pérez Rocha and Tena, *Nobleza indígena*, 16–17, for a study of the typical formula.) He had several of the elements of Malintzin's life wrong, but nevertheless, it is clear that her story formed a prominent part of his identity. Apparently in response to don Fernando's petition, the king wrote a letter of recommendation on his behalf to the viceroy of Mexico, and later he received a coveted office. See AGI, Indiferente 449, L. A1, "Real cédula al marqués de Montesclaros," 26 March 1606, fol. 18v; and México 179, N. 46, "Confirmación de oficio: Fernando Cortés de Monroy," 1612.

34. The historian Federico Gómez de Orozco claimed descent from her. In his *Doña Marina, la dama de la conquista* (Mexico City: Ediciones Xochitl, 1942) he published a family tree, which he had earlier given to Gustavo Rodriguez for use in his book, *Doña Marina* (Mexico City: Secretaría de Relaciones Exteriores, 1935). He clearly had genealogical evidence of a Cortés family living at the "Recuenco" *obraje* in Tizapan, near Coyoacan, from 1625 onward, but there is no hard evidence that Malintzin's grandson Fernando Cortés sent a son also named Fernando to Coyoacan to found that family line. Gómez de Orozco claimed that the son arrived as *corregidor,* but there is no archival record of a corregidor of that name near the turn of the seventeenth century, though there was one named

don Francisco de Velasco y Cortés from 1636 to 1638. See Horn, *Post-Conquest Coyoacan*, 218, 150. Coyoacan was part of the marquesado, control over which was fully returned to the legitimate Cortés family in 1593. It is therefore conceivable that one of the mestizo don Martín's descendants asked for help from one of the legitimate Martín's descendants in establishing himself at Coyoacan, but there is absolutely no proof of that. The family who ran the "Recuenco" obraje in Tizapan, whoever they were, had the dubious distinction of being part of a tightly knit group of merchant families dominating the textile industry in the area, using a range of labor, including forced labor. See Louisa Schell Hoberman, *Mexico's Merchant Elite, 1590–1660* (Durham, NC: Duke University Press, 1991) and Richard Salvucci, *Textiles and Capitalism in Mexico: An Economic History of the Obrajes, 1539–1840* (Princeton, NJ: Princeton University Press, 1987). In 2001 Anna Lanyon interviewed Gómez de Orozco's son and met his grandson. See her *Martín Cortés*, 242–47.

Appendix

1. I am grateful to Jonathan Amith, Michel Launey, Jennifer Ottman, and most especially, James Lockhart, for their help with this translation. I listened to all that they had to say, but then made my own decisions, so I accept full responsibility for the errors that will undoubtedly become apparent as scholars learn more about the conventions of the Cantares. I have not consulted the original manuscript but have used what I take to be a faithful transcription in Bierhorst, *Cantares Mexicanos*. *For the non-Nahuatl speaker*: It must be emphasized that the prevalence of vocables (or "nonsense" syllables with which the Nahua song tradition is peppered) renders any translation somewhat dubious. Often it is unclear, for example, if certain vowels are included as vocables only, or if the intent was to render the preceding verb in the imperfect tense, or to turn the preceding noun into "a place where" such things may be found. Still, in the case of this song, the general sense remains relatively clear. *For the Nahuatl speaker*: I have placed what I believe to be vocables in brackets. I have added letters that it was customary to exclude (such as word-final *n*) in parentheses, where I believe they should be.

2. Michel Launey and Jonathan Amith believe an equally plausible translation would be: "He had placed them in subjection even though they were women." In that case, the song would speak more directly to the experience of the concubines themselves, rather than to their political symbolism.

3. Probably a sunflower, *Helianthus annuus*, and certainly a symbol of war. See *FC*, 9:34, 45.

4. This word does not appear in dictionaries in this form. *Yecoa* (*nitla*) is to finish a job, or to sample something. *Yecoa* (*nite*) is to copulate with someone. *Teyecolli* should thus be "sexual partner." The word appears here only as *noyecol*; it is an unusual form without the *te-*, but given the meaning of the word, the generic possessor's omission when a personal possessor appears seems perfectly within

keeping. Note also that the word's formation indicates the female vocative. This is the first time that the form appears in the song; it appears frequently henceforth.

5. It is difficult to determine how best to render this verb tense. I take my cue from Carochi. "Se usa tambien del tla, que aun es mas comedido, que el ma, y con el se ruega o anima mas que con el ma. . . . En otras lenguas no suele ayer primera persona de Imperativo, en esta la ay, con la qual muestra uno animarse, o resolverse à hazer la cosa." Horacio Carochi, *Grammar of the Mexican Language*, ed. James Lockhart (Stanford, CA: Stanford University Press, 2001), 104–6.

6. This phrase has puzzled all translators, but it is definitely about making noise. James Lockhart recognized the pairing from Book Twelve of the Florentine Codex, when the Indian allies enter Tenochtitlan with the Spaniards making quite a racket. *FC*, 12:41.

7. Only children (and servants) went to gather firewood.

8. This was apparently a Chalcan expression. In the original there is a marginal gloss: "*chalco tlatolli q.n. xitlatlati*." The phrase is still common in modern Guerrero (Jonathan Amith, personal communication).

9. A mark of a king's status was the richness of his mats. They were made of the furs of ocelots, mountain lions, and bears, as well as cured leather and elaborately painted woven reeds. See *FC*, 8:31.

10. It may say, "You will be happy, he will be happy," indicating a change in who the speaker is addressing, first the man himself, then the audience.

11. This meaning is common in modern Guerrero (Jonathan Amith, personal communication). If we do not accept this construction and seek another meaning, there is a problem here: either the verb is reflexive, in which case the syllable—*mo*—is missing, or it is transitive, and the speaker is asking him not to throw something else down, in which case the object—*c*—is missing. Another possibility is that it means, "Please don't toss yourself in the blanket." Frances Karttunen notes that in present-day Morelos, *ayahuia* has just this meaning, apparently from *ayatl* + *-huia*. See her *Analytical Dictionary of Nahuatl* (Austin: University of Texas Press, 1983), 16.

12. The implication of *ach* in this position is unclear.

13. The original has an editorial insertion: "[ticmitlacalhui]li[z]."

14. On the body painting of noblewomen, see *FC* 8:47.

15. I do not yet have a translation for *tenchalohtli*, but it seems to be part of the man's body and the implication is clear.

16. The verb in Molina is *cochhuia* without the *i* and has a specifically sexual connotation. "Hazerlo a la muger que esta durmiendo." Karttunen points out that in modern Morelos, even without the embedded *ma,* the verb just means to rock in one's arms (*Analytical Dictionary*, 36).

17. Probably *Cordia elaeagnoides* and *Plumeria rubra*.

18. *Anquiço* might be translated very literally as "You make him bleed" (that is, honor him as a god in religious ceremony) but it might also be a cluster of particles whose meaning we do not know.

19. Girls learned to spin before they learned to weave. Often only the mistresses of the household did the weaving, while children and servants did the earlier

processing of the fibers, as weaving was in some ways a sacred act. If this is not after all in the imperfect, then it means, "Maybe I even [now] know how to weave, but all for naught."

20. This might mean time or condition of having a man. It might mean, more literally, the place or household wherein a woman would have a man. In modern-day Guerrero, for example, it is used to refer to the traditional home of one's husband, of the bridegroom's parents (Jonathan Amith, personal communication). The overall effect in terms of this song remains the same.

21. This is another particularly doubtful translation. It might equally plausibly mean: "Am I to spread myself out the way men spread out in the fields of war?" Still, that kind of sexual metaphor does not fit with the style of the sexual repartee of the earlier section, while talk of sacrifice is very much in keeping with the rest of the song.

22. Literally, "Is there obedience?" This is the reciprocal impersonal passive construction of *tlacamati* (to obey).

23. I do not yet have a translation for "neoc" or "meoc," but it seems clearly to be an interjection.

24. "A skirt, a blouse" is frequently used as a metaphor for "woman." The implied opposition is not only to maleness but to youth: young girls wore single-shift dresses; only when they came of age did they exchange them for a separate skirt and blouse. This is still true in parts of modern Mexico (Jonathan Amith, personal communication).

25. Carochi, *Grammar of the Mexican Language*, 419–21. *Quen titlaca'* is translated as "What will become of us?" My thanks to James Lockhart who pointed this out to me.

26. This is yet another sentence of whose meaning we cannot be certain.

27. This is a particularly difficult segment. The first sentence is ambiguous. The middle part contains clauses that I may not be relating to each other correctly. And I have no translation at all for the final clause.

Bibliographic Essay

This book is deeply embedded in three different literatures. At the broadest level, it addresses general questions concerning large patterns in history—especially the pattern of European conquest of indigenous peoples in the Americas and elsewhere. At another level, it participates in discussions of what we do and do not know about the Nahuas of central Mexico in the age of contact. At the narrowest or most specific level of all, the book adds to the literature on "Malinche" herself and on first-contact translators and intermediaries. I would refer readers to different sets of resources depending on their primary interests.

I begin at the broadest level. Questions about the ability of Eurasians to dominate peoples they met elsewhere in the world beginning in the fifteenth century were publicly addressed by Jared Diamond in his Pulitzer prize–winning book, *Guns, Germs and Steel: The Fates of Human Societies* (1997). Anthropologists and archaeologists had long associated technological advances in wide-ranging societies with agriculture and a sedentary lifestyle that allowed for the division of labor. What scholars had not been able to determine was why people in the Old World became full-time farmers long before anyone else did. As a scientist, Diamond was able to help digest and interpret data from recently improved radiocarbon dating techniques, yielding a crucial contribution to the literature. It turns out that protein-rich wild plants that could support human life were far more abundant in the Fertile Crescent than anywhere else. That simple fact would have an extraordinary impact on world history, leaving Middle Easterners and those who borrowed from them—the Europeans and the Chinese—with more power than other people had in the year 1500. Many historians have resisted Diamond's contribution, focusing instead on other parts of his argument concerning more recent history. Not having historians' familiarity with archival evidence, Diamond sometimes oversimplifies in the more recent period, but I believe that we need not let minor parts of his work distract us from the core. No sustained critique has been published by a historian, but students may consult reviews of his book and exchanges on the Internet to gain further insight into the reasons for some historians' opposing views.

If we do not accept the evidence of the plant seeds, we are left wondering why the Europeans were in a position to ultimately overpower all the Native Americans whom they met in the course of their explorations. If we deny that there was a technological differential, then the repeated losses—even before diseases set in, and even after populations had recovered from them—must in some measure be blamed on the Indians themselves. Yet despite this, we have often shied away from admitting that there was a technological differential, for fear that such an acknowledgment would be tantamount to admitting some sort of mental deficiency on the part of the indigenous for having "fallen behind." In this book, I accept the evidence of the plant seeds. I believe the evidence proves that the indigenous were the intellectual match of the Europeans every step of the way, but that their intellectual acuity and impressive strategizing could not possibly make up for the fact that they were essentially in the Stone Age and had less powerful technology. It was hardly their fault that they had been sedentary for far less time than Old World peoples.

The people popularly called "Aztecs" have been the subject of scholarly attention since the eighteenth century. That, in fact, was when such a term for them was popularized. No people called themselves "Aztecs" in the year 1500. The Tenochca people, like their brethren the Tlatelolca, were both part of the Mexica ethnic group. Usually people have used the word "Aztec" when they meant either the Tenochca or the Mexica. That is how I use the word in this book. Some people, however, have applied the word to all Nahuas, or Nahuatl-speaking peoples of Mexico. In that case, Malinche was an Aztec, too, but in 1518, she certainly had nothing in common with the housewives of Tenochtitlan, for example. Readers of any piece of literature on the subject should ask themselves exactly whom the author is talking about.

Traditionally, the Nahuas and other Mesoamerican Indians have been studied via the archaeological record as well as the written record—the codices. All but about twenty preconquest indigenous texts were either burned by the Spanish shortly after the conquest or hidden away so well by indigenous priests that posterity has lost track of them. In general, then, researchers have relied on texts written under Spanish rule, often for a Spanish audience interested in preserving the ways of the ancients. There is a rich scholarly literature in this vein. I would suggest that interested readers turn first to the recent collection of essays entitled *The Aztec Empire* (2004). The volume was produced in tandem with an extraordinary exhibit of material culture at the Guggenheim Museum and includes contributions from many of the most talented scholars in the field. Another key text stemming from similar sources, perceptive and sympathetic, is Inga Clendinnen's book *Aztecs: An Interpretation* (1991).

A different approach has been taken by historians working from archival materials produced by people in colonial Mexico who were matter-of-factly living their lives, without making any conscious effort to preserve their heritage. Texts such as wills, land transfers, lawsuits, or even the words of popular songs may reveal as much or more about the way people think about their past and their present as texts explicitly designed for that purpose. Charles Gibson helped to inspire this trend when he published *The Aztecs under Spanish Rule* (1964) based on archival evidence in Spanish. Later, others began to work with a variety of materials written in Nahuatl. The most important figure in that field is James Lockhart; his fullest work is *The Nahuas after the Conquest: A Social and Cultural History of the Indians of Central Mexico, Sixteenth through Eighteenth Centuries* (1992). Students will see that in working with colonial documents, Lockhart is able to cast some light "backward" as it were onto precolonial thought patterns. Readers will find many other scholars who work with wide-ranging Nahuatl texts as well as other indigenous sources cited in this book. Those who have been most influential on my thinking include Louise Burkhart, Pedro Carrasco, Josefina García-Quintana, Susan Gillespie, Ross Hassig, Rebecca Horn, Frances Krug, Matthew Restall, Luis Reyes, Susan Schroeder, Lisa Sousa, and Stephanie Wood, among others. Between them, they have opened doors to a fascinating world otherwise frozen in stone and on maguey paper and breathed new life into it.

People studying Mesoamerica must of necessity confront the philosophical question I raise in the pages of this book: were the Indians defeated, suffering pain the likes of which most of us will never know, or did they rely on their inner resources to transcend conquest and remain themselves? Both are true. Different scholars emphasize different aspects of the experience; the best historians always acknowledge the other truth. For examples I refer readers to two wonderful and contrasting books: Karen Powers, *Women in the Crucible of Conquest* (2004) and Stephanie Wood, *Transcending Conquest: Nahua Views of Spanish Colonial Mexico* (2003). The latter as well as the former includes treatment of women's mixed experiences. Readers wishing to pursue the vein of women's history should consult Susan Kellogg, *Weaving the Past: A History of Latin America's Indigenous Women from the Prehispanic Period to the Present* (2005) and Susan Socolow, *The Women of Colonial Latin America* (2000). Both include accessible treatments of the conquest period and both blend the two philosophical approaches. They offer rich bibliographies, opening doors to the study of specific topics. Lisa Sousa has a wonderful book on indigenous women's experiences, forthcoming with Stanford University Press, based primarily on native-language sources.

Last but not least, this book is written in response to other work on "Malinche." Literally dozens of novels and novelized biographies have been written about her over the years. I considered including a lengthy list of such works but rejected the idea, on grounds that readers with little experience in the field might perceive me to be leading them to "further information" about this most interesting figure, when in fact I consider such studies to be part of the problem, to be objectifying and even dehumanizing to Malintzin and other indigenous people. A few, however, have been better than the others. Mariano Somonte in *Doña Marina, "La Malinche"* (1969) took steps in the direction of sifting purported evidence and rejecting some of it, but even he was unable to escape his own fantasies and imaginings regarding the young woman's life. Ricardo Herren in *Doña Marina, la Malinche* (1992) moved further toward bringing a study of her life into the realm of serious biographies. I believe that if Herren had had Nahuatl, he would have written the definitive study. Recently, the Mexican novelist Marisol Martín del Campo published a brief book entitled simply *Doña Marina* (2005), in which she collects some of the contrasting statements that have been made about the famous translator over the years.

In the anglophone world, Frances Karttunen has written the most accurate works on Malintzin that we have had up to now: her two superb short pieces appear in her book, *Between Worlds: Interpreters, Guides, and Survivors* (1994) and in *Indian Women of Early Mexico* (1997), edited by Susan Schroeder, Stephanie Wood, and Robert Haskett. Anna Lanyon, an Australian language teacher, followed in the footsteps of Malinche before writing *Malinche's Conquest* (1999). The author is not a trained historian, and the book is not always accurate or transparent as regards sources, but it is a charming travel narrative and a "good read." In her most recent work, *The New World of Martín Cortés* (2003), Lanyon has truly come into her own, producing a fine book on Malinche's son that demonstrates a subtle understanding of how to evaluate sources. I highly recommend it to those who want "more." Alida Metcalf has a new book (unfortunately not yet available at the time of writing this one) that promises to go far toward putting Malinche and others like her in Mexico in comparative context: *Go-Betweens and the Colonization of Brazil, 1500–1600* (2006). Pamela Scully has already begun to theorize on a comparative basis in a recent piece, "Malintzin, Pocahontas, and Krotoa: Indigenous Women and Myth Models of the Atlantic World" (*Journal of Colonialism and Colonial History* 6, no. 3, 2005).

In an article cleverly titled "The Maid of the Myth: La Malinche and the History of Mexico" (*Indiana Journal of Hispanic Literatures* 12, Spring 1998), Ross Hassig has gone far toward proving to those who would like to blame Malinche for the conquest that she was in no way responsible. He shows that the Spaniards lied, for example, in the story of her supposedly having betrayed a Cholulan plot. Unfortunately, in my opinion, in pursuit of his laudable agenda, Hassig goes to the extreme of insisting that we do not even have reason to believe Malinche was a good translator and that Jerónimo de Aguilar was far more important. It is certainly true that far fewer people could function in both Maya and Spanish than in Maya and Nahuatl, and Aguilar clearly played a key role for a brief period. But all the evidence indicates that he gradually dropped out of the picture, while Malintzin's linguistic skills were such that Cortés came to rely on her more and more. I believe it is not necessary to deny that Malinche translated deftly in order to rescue her from infamy; rather, it is important that we adequately understand and convey her reasons for translating. The full story speaks volumes in her defense.

The book that I have written here is based on a wide range of primary sources and inspired by the work of many other scholars, as the notes demonstrate. Many of the primary sources I have used appear in printed collections. (See the list of abbreviations.) Most of these were produced by nineteenth-century Mexican scholars who worked tirelessly to transcribe the exceedingly difficult sixteenth-century paleography and then published the fruits of their efforts, so that the texts would be accessible to all the world. Because of their work, we today can absorb a body of knowledge within a few years that it would otherwise take a lifetime of painstaking labor to acquire. Of course, a significant problem with using printed collections is that they may include errors, either in the transcription or in the printing. Thus I have insisted on consulting the originals when treating the statements of Malintzin's daughter, son-in-law, grandsons, and husband, even where they exist in printed form, as well as in cases where I am relying on a single document to make an important point. I cite each document in the form in which I consulted it, either the archival original or as part of a printed collection. Whenever I particularly disagree with a given translation from the Nahuatl in a printed source that I am using, I note the change that I am making in the notes and include the original words so that Nahuatl speakers can make their own judgment. In all cases, I have been as transparent as possible. There has been far too much mythologizing of Malintzin and obfuscation of her context. I hope this study goes far toward rectifying the past.

Index

Grijalva, Juan de, 31, 40
Guayaquil, Ecuador, 212

Hassig, Ross, 5n8
Herren, Ricardo, 3n5, 153n7
hidalgo, 8, 154n10, 181
history, indigenous. *See* annals
Honduras, 152, 161
honor, 181–83, 210
horses, 35, 42, 60–61, 116
Huamantla Codex, 65–66
Huitzilopochtli, 91, 102
hybridity, 3

Indian, as social category, 3, 170, 177, 196
inheritance: in indigenous tradition, 17,
    21, 23, 95, 130; in European tradition,
    152, 156, 179, 187, 197
interpreters. *See* translators
Isabel of Portugal (wife of Charles V),
    195, 198
Isabel (daughter of Moctezuma), 95,
    109–10, 120–21, 164–65, 181
Isabella of Castile, 11, 37, 95, 192, 198
Ix Chel, 27
Ixtlilxochitl (king of Tetzcoco), 129–32
Iztapalapa, 83, 104

Jalisco, 179
Jaramillo, Alonso (Juan's father), 155
Jaramillo, Juan, 148–50, 155, 167–69,
    178–80
Jaramillo, María: as a young person, 163,
    172–74, 178; in legal battles with
    stepmother, 180–82; 184–85; death
    of, 186
Julian (captive translator), 30–32, 35

Karttunen, Frances, 36n7

la Llorona, 77, 213
law. *See* Council of the Indies, New
    Laws, Siete Partidas
Lienzo de Tlaxcala. *See* Tlaxcala

Long, Haniel, 2
López, Martín, 108, 114, 166, 184
López de Gómara, Francisco, 76, 201
Luisa (daughter of Xicotencatl), 108,
    111–12, 141–42

maize. *See* corn
Malinche: images of, 2–4; significance of,
    6–7. *See also* Malintzin
Malinche (volcano), 77
Malintzin: names of, 12, 36, 55; as a young
    person, 11, 22–23, 36; in the conquest,
    78–79, 82, 120; in Coyaocan, 133–
    34,137–39; in marriage to Jaramillo,
    148–50, 154–57; death of, 171;
    accusations against, 133, 184–85; in
    indigenous sources, 70–72, 76–78,
    122–23, 129–31; as a mother, 139–41,
    163; as negotiator for peace, 62, 105–
    6, 120, 129–31; translating abilities
    of, 41–42, 144, 146, 158–60. *See also*
    Malinche
Marín, Luis, 166
Marina. *See* Malinche, Malintzin
Marqués del Valle. *See* Hernando Cortés
    and Martín Cortés (son of doña
    Juana)
marriage: among the Nahuas, 20–21, 95,
    130; between Indians and Spaniards,
    74, 154–55
Mary. *See* Virgin Mary
Mary of England, 202–3
Mary Magdalene, 78
Maxixcatzin, 74, 111
Maya, 25–34, 158–63
Medellín, Spain, 37, 191
Melchior (captive translator), 35
Mendoza, Antonio de, 176, 178–80, 183,
    199
mestizo, 173, 177
Mexica, 14–15. *See also* Nahuas;
    Tenochtitlan; warfare
Mexico City, 132–33, 163–64, 166, 206
migrations, 14, 16–17, 54

smallpox, 109–11, 114
songs, indigenous, 1, 19, 21–22, 27–28, 56,
    88; examples of, 123–24, 215
Suárez, Catalina, 136–38, 166
Suazo, Alonso, 126–27
Suleiman the Magnificent, 199

Tapia, Andrés de, 94, 155, 181
technological difference, 51–52, 61, 106,
    112–19
tecuhtli, 17
Tecuichpotzin: see Isabel (daughter of
    Moctezuma)
Temples, 91–92
Tenochca, 14. See also Mexica
Tenochtitlan, 15, 85, 91–95, 103–4, 115–21
teotl, 49–50. See also gods
Teticpac. See also Tetiquipaque
Tetiquipaque. See Olutla
Tetzcoco, 15, 94, 129–32
Tizatlan, 68–70, 78
Tlaloc, 91
Tlacopan, 15
tlacotli, 19. See also slaves
Tlatelolco, 14, 92; school of, 46, 49, 115–16
tlatoani, 17, 56, 104–5
Tlaxcala, 59–62, 81, 129; conquest
    pictorials in, 67–76; travelers to Spain
    from, 189, 194
tlaxilacalli, 13
Tlecuiluatzin: see Luisa (daughter of
    Xicotencatl)
Tochtepec, 22, 150
torture, European practice of, 61, 102,
    127, 159–60, 208–10
Totonacs, 43–45, 53. See also Cempoala
Toxcatl, 102–3
trade, long-distance, 15–16, 25, 158–59
translators: importance of, 57–58, 74, 141–

42, 146, 184–85; professionalization
    of, 174–76
Triple Alliance, 15
Trujillo, Honduras, 161–62
Tuxtla mountains, 13, 40

University of Mexico, 175

Valencia, Martín de, 143
Vargas, Diego Pérez de, 197–98
Velasco, Francisco de, 183, 206, 208. See
    also Beatriz de Andrada
Velasco, Luis de, 183, 206
Velásquez, Diego de, 43–44, 53, 96–97,
    136
Veracruz, 44, 53, 212
viceroy, 167, 176, 193
Virgin Mary, 39, 78–79, 141

warfare: in tradition of Europeans, 61,
    86, 94, 127, 179, 211; in tradition of
    indigenous, 13–15, 20–22, 32–33,
    71–72, 90, 103–5, 118–19, 124
Water-Pouring Song, 123–25
weaving, 1, 17, 26–27
women: among the Maya, 26–27; among
    the Nahuas, 17–21, 56, 124–25, 140–
    41; in relation to the Spanish, 121,
    128, 167, 177
writing, indigenous. See annals, codices,
    pictoglyphs

Xicallanco, 25, 29, 40, 147, 158
Xicotencatl, 61, 68–72, 114
Xicoténcatl (novel), 2
Xilotepec, 156, 167–68, 174, 176–77

Zamora, Margarita, 57n7
Zúñiga, Juana de, 165, 196–97, 201